THE BODY, IN THEORY

HISTORIES OF CULTURAL MATERIALISM

# STATELY BODIES

## LITERATURE, PHILOSOPHY, AND THE QUESTION OF GENDER

*Adriana Cavarero*

TRANSLATED BY ROBERT DE LUCCA
AND DEANNA SHEMEK

ANN ARBOR
THE UNIVERSITY OF MICHIGAN PRESS

English translation copyright © by
the University of Michigan 2002
First published by
Giangiacomo Feltrinelli Editore Milano 1995
All rights reserved
Published in the United States of America by
The University of Michigan Press
Manufactured in the United States of America
♾ Printed on acid-free paper

2005    2004    2003    2002        4    3    2    1

A CIP catalog record for this book is available
from the British Library.

Library of Congress Cataloging-in-Publication Data

Cavarero, Adriana.
    [Corpo in figure. English]
    Stately bodies : literature, philosophy, and the question of
gender / Adriana Cavarero ; translated by Robert de Lucca and Deanna
Shemek.
        p.    cm. — (The body, in theory)
    Includes bibliographical references (p.    ).
    ISBN 0-472-09674-5 (cloth) — ISBN 0-472-06674-9) (paper)
B105.B64.C3813    2002
128'.6—dc21

                                                    2002005681

# TRANSLATORS' NOTE

Cavarero's prose is a particular example of the complex, embedded sentence structures and impersonal verbal constructions that mark Italian. They result in maddening obscurities if translated directly into English and so we have often broken up Cavarero's sentences and "activated" her verbs. Among the key terms in Cavarero's work are several that are best translated differently according to context. The original title of this work, *Corpo in figure,* calls attention to a consistent vocabulary of figuration, in which Cavarero recurs to the words *figura, figurazione, metafora, immagine,* and others that we have aimed to convey with consistency of meaning, while at the same time attempting to retain as much as possible the flavor of her elegant and witty prose. Where writers of English may have chosen the adjective *feminine,* in our correspondence Cavarero often opted for more strictly corporeal translations such as *women's* or *female.* Similarly, the term *gender* does not translate directly into Italian with the sexual-political nuances it has acquired in English. Given the focus of her work on the materiality of sexed bodies, Cavarero in most instances uses the word *sesso,* for which she prefers the translation *sex.*

We have submitted our translations to the author's approval at all stages. We thank her warmly for her participation in this dialogue.

Note: Translations of quoted material are those of the translators unless an English edition is listed in the bibliography.

# AUTHOR'S PREFACE

This book grows out of my persistent intellectual curiosity about the strange relationship between the body and politics. Such a curiosity perhaps merits some explanation, especially in an introduction. In short, I am fascinated by the remarkable paradox whereby politics expels the body from its founding categories while for thousands of years the political order has been figured precisely through the metaphor of the body.

Hannah Arendt observes in the dense pages of *The Human Condition* that the body for the Greeks comes to represent that mere requirement of biological life which the political space, founded on speech and action, banishes from its domain. Setting aside the specific categories and different contexts of Arendt's study, we may speak—even in the post-Hellenic world—of an explicit exclusion of the domain of bodies from the "rational"—or at least "logocentric"—ground on which politics claims to be founded. I draw here on Arendt's text merely as authoritative confirmation of a well-known phenomenon: politics professes to base itself upon reason and tends to reject the reality of bodies. Bodily reality comes back into play, especially in modern times, in relation to the generative power of women, but that is another story, with its own, internal coherence.

One hardly need cite authorities to illustrate politics' frequent recourse to the image of the body as it figures its order through organological metaphor. In fact, in the texts examined in this study we find the exact opposite of the body's exclusion. Here, albeit only through metaphor, the body returns to politics, indeed illustrating and sanctioning political organization in images of a "body politic" complete with a head, heart, organs, and members.

Something very strange indeed seems to characterize the history of the West: while politics rejects the body from the specific categories on which it founds itself, it also retrieves the body as the shaping metaphor of political order. On one hand, beginning with the Greeks, politics is ascribed to the sphere of the logos, insofar as the logos constitutes a *specifically* human characteristic. Whether it be the universal means of a common good, or a calculable means at the service of mere power, politics is thus generally defined as the project of a pure, incorporeal reason. On the other hand, this political order, which likes to define itself as essentially rational, as contrary to or perhaps overcoming the murky licentiousness of bodies and their regime of mere biological necessity, often employs the image of the body to illustrate its form in metaphor. A good example is the expression *body politic,* which, although technically relevant to the Middle Ages, still operates today in political language, both as an explicit term and as an allusion to bodily organs and functions carried out in the state by its various parts.

The most interesting aspect of this problem lies not in identifying political theories that claim to expel the body from the principles of lawful community built by the so-called rational animal. Nor does it consist in seeking out those political discourses that frequently draw upon the body as metaphor. The interesting thing is to understand by what odd theoretical routes a body that has been expelled stubbornly returns to regain, even if only figuratively, the prejudicially incorporeal sphere of the political order. Surprisingly, a human body that is by definition unpolitical lends the scheme of its organic nature precisely to politics. In turn politics, which is by definition incorporeal, entrusts the representation of its order to the exemplarity of a naturally ordered body. It is this contradiction that arouses intellectual curiosity, urging us to get to the bottom of the implicit seesaw play that binds politics to the body.

From the logocentrism of the ancient polis on, nothing concerning politics appears to have anything to do with the body. This is because the polis is the site of that discourse concerning the "just" and the "good" that is intrinsic to the specific nature of the so-called rational animal. It is within the political community that man realizes his happy and good, and therefore fully human, life. At most the body, as for Aristotle, resides within the simple and nonpolitical domestic sphere, where mere life manifests its inherent bodily needs and the biological cycle demands a continuous labor of care by women and slaves.

Precisely in Greece, however, the figural analogy between the human body and the community has its auspicious beginning. This analogy will be repeated for thousands of years. In the Middle Ages, it surfaces in the explicit identification of the body politic, and it extends well into modernity—not to mention into contemporary banality—as a frequent, if now faded, metaphor.

The strange story of this body, first banished and then welcomed back, would therefore seem to rely on mere paradox. But its innumerable and extremely coherent plot elements urge us to tell the story otherwise—in a language that has lost its trust in the sexual neutrality of discourse. Well known is the essentially masculine character of the political logocentrism inaugurated by the Greeks and entrusted to a tradition that endures (both in fact and in theory) to this day. The constitutive nonpolitical—or rather antipolitical—nature of the body as the opposite of the logos within this tradition finally comes down to the basic opposition between female and male natures. Beginning with the Greeks, in fact, corporeality as such, in the symbolic representation of the two sexes and as the fleshly component of existence, is assigned overwhelmingly to women. To men falls the more glorious component of the logos: the only characteristic considered to be specifically human.

In thinking of the body as woman and woman as body, the polis founded upon the male synthesizes within a single idea everything it considers to be its dreaded *other*. This other then corresponds to whatever the polis has already liquidated and conquered. Rooted in the female, corporeality is represented as the prelogical stage of a life that is still a blind end in itself. It is thus the precinct of that animal immediacy—naturally unregulated, cannibalistic, and incestuous—from which the civilized community of men takes an unbridgeable distance of polar negation.

Tracing the story from its Greek origins, we easily discover how the body expelled from the polis is, in its full and true substance, a female body. The body here already symptomatically consists in the problem of its sexing. At the same time the body is already *completely resolved* as perturbing, female matter precisely by that sex which has judged itself to be (naturally) "rational and political."

We may thus begin to note the strange fortunes of a body, banished by politics and then welcomed again, within the symbolic design of its first stirrings. The terrifying nature of the banished body is substantially female. It could not be otherwise within a logocentric (or, as it is also aptly called, "phallologocentric") polis. In the polis, free males reserve the power of the logos for themselves, uprooting themselves from a carnal existence perceived only as the disquieting attachment to a life that is prelogical, prehuman, and nearly animal: therefore female.

The second movement of this odd twist by which the body returns as a metaphor of the political order may also easily be inscribed within the horizon of sexual difference. The body that here returns to the city as an analogical image is conceived in a perfectly coherent way to be male. This is not the essentially female body banished from the polis and conceived as the other or the opposite of the political order. Clearly the body that appears in the political usage of the organological metaphor in no way resembles the banished body, since the body of this political metaphor is imagined as already adult, perfect, harmonious, and vigorous. Neither infancy nor old age can weaken its flesh. Its equilibrium is indeed prey to sudden maladies, but these have nothing in common with the irresistible impulses of an animal order of life that overflows into maternal symbiosis and primitive indifferentiation.

At least two bodies seem to be involved here, or rather, at least two accepted meanings of the body appear to mingle within this context. The first, which the polis banishes from its armored walls, is a body with dreadfully female characteristics; it is therefore uncontrolled, symbiotic, and obscure. The second, which politics welcomes in suitable metaphor, is a male body, largely static and bloodless, whose nature has been tamed to the commands of an overbearing reason that determines its functioning and structure. The adventure of a body expelled and then accepted anew thus becomes a double and complex enterprise.

The roots of its apparent contradiction reach deep into the experience of sexual difference, which is transformed by the androcentric symbolic system into precisely divergent roles. The history of the bodily metaphor itself is also elaborate, since its figural structure changes through the ages, adapting to the political forms that employ and reshape its image.

The body of which we speak is obviously an imagined one: the body as represented, belonging wholly to the discursive order. This is true although its mere physical givenness often comes to undermine the order of the design that adopts its figure. Thus, something inherent within the elementary potency of the *given* ultimately exceeds the discourse that has taken it as its object. Precisely via the hermeneutic thread of sexual difference, the story of the strange relationship between the body and politics finally untangles itself from its curious and twisted knots, although the weave grows more complicated in other ways, hinting perhaps at the mystery of its deepest weft.

This book consists of the montage of its own possible narrations. The stories I have thus far summarized function, in fact, only as a frame for the book, or rather as a sort of historical filigree. The book's most technical section lies in its central chapter, a short synopsis of the bodily metaphor used in politics. This background simply serves to sustain a sort of philosophical narrative that delights in rereading the body's political vicissitudes by looking at the complex, seductive features of several widely acclaimed literary figures. The fortunes of the dramatic characters I have chosen are so immense as to seem, perhaps, discouragingly formidable on the hermeneutic plane. It would be hard to come up with works more famous than Sophocles' *Antigone* and Shakespeare's *Hamlet*. Antigone and Creon, Ophelia and Hamlet are nonetheless the masks I have chosen, largely because they are characters in dramas that represent the apex of Greek culture and the strain of impending modernity.

Ancient Greece and the threshold of the modern age are two decisive epochs for a possible philosophical narrative concerning the paradoxical relationship between the body and politics. This book—to anticipate for a moment its plot—is built around the most famous theatrical figures of these two "scenes," while its long intermission (Latin and medieval) is dedicated to a brief synopsis of the organological metaphor. Philosophy, in the strictest disciplinary sense, earns its space in the book through a sort of play between melody and countermelody, which places the literary figures I have chosen alongside two great philosophers. To Sophocles' song we hear Plato's reply, while to Shakespeare's we hear the cold refrain of Thomas Hobbes.

To me—having decided to seek out the female body expelled from the polis—no tragic figure appeared more eloquent than that of Antigone. She is the ancient heroine so often pondered by Western tradition, herself the female body buried alive by the city outside its walls. At the same time, she is the symbol of an incestuous corporeality, both consanguineous and horrific, that alludes to maternal symbiosis and to animal origins. To this intensely bodily figure that the polis, whose horizon is fratricide and war, expels as its terrible *other,* the addition of the countermelody of Platonic philosophy is nearly obligatory for the parsing of my narrative. I speak, obviously, of the Plato who appears as the obsessive and celebrated shaper of a body completely dominated by a logocentric soul; the Plato who inaugurates, precisely around this figural scheme, the analogical play between the body and politics, which will subsequently enjoy such extraordinary success. This Plato also delights in anatomy, notoriously running up against a mother-material that seems to evade the control of the text in his *Timaeus.*

After looking at Greece, with its awkwardly buried female bodies and its male bodies restored to politics under philosophical supervision, I present a brief summary of the political fortunes of the organic metaphor, particularly in the Middle Ages and the Renaissance. In that period, the figure underwent an extraordinary doubling in the image of the king's two bodies. Even tomb sculpture was modified to accommodate this metaphor, in the apparent desire to hide the symptoms of a body politic whose death cannot be postponed.

On the decisive threshold of the early seventeenth century, I was attracted to Shakespeare's Hamlet, who so loves to ponder worm-eaten bodies and the stench of carefully unburied corpses, and who alludes explicitly to a completely rotten body politic on the verge of collapse. It seemed to me significant that on the same stage, the body of the beautiful Ophelia, so alien to the carnal horror of that catastrophe, would float on clear water, covered in flowers. Her immortal, and notably apolitical, icon takes its shape just there. The most apt philosophical counter-melody in this case, on English soil, is the doctrine of Thomas Hobbes. With Hobbes, in fact, the body politic that has already fallen into the same organic catastrophe of its flesh rises up again in mechanical form. Famously, however it also possesses the monstrous characteristics of the biblical Leviathan. Thus a terrifying vision of one horrific body concludes the political tale that—with another horrific body—had so oddly begun.

Not that the story of the strange relationships between the body and politics—with its exclusionary games, its metaphorical recoveries, and its clearly sexed codes—ends here. It would be quite easy to document how the tale continues, renewing its strategies even into the present day. And yet, precisely because Hobbes's *Leviathan* may be considered a perfect introduction to the various fortunes of the modern state, it seemed to me that my curiosity could stop there, momentarily at rest.

My book does not end, however, with Hobbes's monster. In a short appendix, I try to restore another sense to the female bodies of Antigone and Ophelia. The history of the organic metaphor seemed to me to have consumed their figures only in order to make its own story fully narratable. I wanted finally to reread the beautiful pages with which María Zambrano accompanies Antigone into her tomb and at last grants her the time to redeem herself from the gratuitous cruelty of her fate. And then, I wanted the Ophelia whom Shakespeare had sunk into a muddy whirlpool to be rescued in her turn by Ingeborg Bachmann's Undine, so that her flower-strewn body might at least find a home among the laughing nymphs who dwell in the sea.

All things considered, the book's appendix is the only true and heartfelt countermelody I offer to the stories sung in the rest of these pages.

## A NOTE ON THE TEXT

A few pages of the chapter concerning *Antigone* are reworkings of two earlier texts: "Forme della corporeità," in *Filosofia, donne, filosofie,* ed. M. Forcina, A. Prontera, and P. Vergine (Lecce: Milella, 1994), 15–28, and "Figures de la corporeïtat," in *Saviesa i perversitat: Les dones a la Grècia Antiga,* edited by M. Jufresa (Barcelona: Edicions Destino, 1994), 83–116. The chapter entitled "The Body Politic" is a reworking and expansion of the article "Il corpo politico come organismo," *Filosofia politica* 7, no. 3 (1993): 391–414.

# CONTENTS

# INTRODUCTION

## DEANNA SHEMEK

Adriana Cavarero's original Italian title for this work, *Corpo in figure*, would be most directly translated as *The Body in Figures*. This phrase, however, refers not to the digital symbols of the mathematician, to numbers that might sum up the body's net worth based on arithmetical calculations; nor does it address the shapes of individual bodies as such. Instead Cavarero's study examines the frequent presence of bodily metaphors in theories meant to explain the state, law, and politics, all of which are resolutely ideal and hence incorporeal institutions. We have rendered her title in English so as to point to Cavarero's paradoxical theme: *Stately Bodies*. Just how paradoxical the idea of the stately body is will become very evident in the course of the discussions contained here. Extending work first encountered by most readers of English in her study *In Spite of Plato* (1990, trans. 1995), Cavarero as political theorist, philosopher, classicist, and close reader reflects in this book on a remarkable contradiction within Western philosophy from the Greeks to our own day. The polis—the space of justice and political order—is famously founded on reason and intellect alone, which are said to rise above the impulses and weaknesses of the body in order to achieve their highest aims. Yet precisely this incorporeal realm of ordered ideas is described over and over by political theorists in terms of the articulations and functions of the human body. The mind/body dualism so foundational to Western thinking is exposed in Cavarero's discussions as an impure opposition in which the body, like some corpse in a botched murder, keeps turning up precisely where it is emphatically not supposed to be. In chapters dedicated to Sophocles, Plato, Shakespeare, and Hobbes (among others), Cavarero follows the vicissitudes of the bodily metaphor in political discourse from ancient Greece to early modern Europe and in the fictional stagings of politics in masterpieces of Western drama. In an appendix she discusses two texts that "narrate women differently." For Cavarero, a dialogue by the contemporary Spanish philosopher María Zambrano, *The Tomb of Antigone,* restores speech to the tragic heroine whose live burial sealed her fate (and her lips) in Sophocles' play. And in Ingeborg Bachmann's monologue "Undine Goes," Cavarero rediscovers among laughing nymphs of the sea Shakespeare's drowned Ophelia, the object of an earlier discussion in the book.

Opening the volume is a reading of *Antigone,* in which Cavarero fixes our attention first on the dead body lying figuratively center stage or—in the play's fiction—just outside the walls of Thebes. This is of course the body of Antigone's brother, Polynices, a body the young girl insists must be buried but which has been denied that loving rite by the laws of King Creon. The squaring off of Antigone and Creon in defense of two opposed orders—the ancient order of blood kinship and the new order of the polis—is not for Cavarero the oft-cited conflict between "private" and "public" responsibility, or even between individual subject and wicked tyrant. Rather, in *Antigone* the polis, theoretically the locus of reason, law, and order par excellence, is confronted with a body that insists on another order, a prelogical, carnal, and passionate order that returns repeatedly, despite the polis's attempts to banish it from social life. The corpse that triggers the play's conflict belonged to a victim of fratricide; it thus serves as a haunting reminder of the incest and violence reigning in the house of Labdacus. But in this house it was a woman, Jocasta, who initiated the lineage that produced not only Antigone and her siblings but before them their father, Jocasta's son and husband, Oedipus. This incestuous recycling of maternal blood—this "carnal implosion," in Cavarero's intense formulation—marks Antigone's speech throughout the play and throws Sophocles' ultimate emphasis on *her* body. For Cavarero, Antigone's is not the body of an individual but the body of a kinship principle intensified in incest, a body disturbingly connected to the animal origins kept at bay by the polis. For her constitutive female otherness and her insistence on honoring the fleshly origins of humans, Antigone's body must be banished: indeed it must be buried alive *outside* the polis, in a disquieting mirror image of the unburied body of the dead Polynices.

Sophocles makes no special reference to Polynices' soul, or psyche, as Cavarero points out. What concerns both Antigone and Creon is not the divide between this world and the next, but the threshold between the human and the animal, which will be crossed by Polynices if he is left to be eaten by brute scavengers. It is this threshold that the rational polis itself stands to defend, and which women, in their clear connection to carnal reproduction, too easily blur (cf. *In Spite of Plato,* 110–11). Taking us deep into the logic that supports man's self-definition as the rational animal, Cavarero meticulously retraces Plato's doctrine of the soul and his complex analogy between the parts of the soul and those of the polis. Situating the soul *within* the body, Plato's development of the soul/polis analogy has enormous repercussions in the history of the "body politic" metaphor. That metaphor, as this book argues, exerts its own power in relations between politics and gender.

In the *Republic,* the model for the orderly polis is the disciplined soul of the philosopher. The order sought and achieved by the philosopher is, as Foucault teaches, the product of self-domination, in which the philosopher's rational soul remains vigilant over the impulses of the appetitive and passionate souls. Reason must dominate over pleasures, emotions, and bodily instincts; logic must supersede animality; and the body itself must be patrolled as a site of disorder. Plato constructs the soul and the polis *against* the body, which must be subordinated, dominated, and even expelled from the political sphere. Yet the soul has a bodily foundation; and the body inescapably serves as a frequent Platonic metaphor for both the psyche and the polis. As Cavarero observes, corporeality invades the figurative language of the philosopher of the soul and the polis, "as if the corporeal positioning of the psyche had led to a hybridization of its immaterial substance."

The *Timaeus* details how the soul precedes the body in Plato's myth of genesis, where the demiurge delivered man's highest, immortal soul to the gods without supplying its outer form. The

3

demiurge also dictated that this form be gendered, however, thereby firmly inscribing the female in a patriarchal order: women, it seems, will result only from badly formed male souls, which will be condemned to a second birth as females or animals. Moreover, as the gods set about their task of housing the immortal soul in a body, they initially give it the form of a head alone: the body they add later is a mere means of transport over rough terrain. Man's three additional, mortal souls—connected to appetites, passions, and reproduction—will henceforth be ruled by the higher, immortal soul still located in that perfect, round human head. Clearly, a political model takes shape in this vertically arranged bodily hierarchy. The head that was its primary form now perches atop an ambulatory body and reigns over all potentially unruly, mortal, and fleshly parts below.

Woman's lower role as defective latecomer requires that birth from sexed human bodies be possible only after man has generated woman himself, out of his own flaws. The mother who is capable of giving carnal birth, however, belongs to a different, third species; she is a receptacle, a "natural recipient of all impressions" (Cavarero quotes the *Timaeus*) from the cosmic model/logos (father) and a space of gestation for copies (sons) of that model (cf. *In Spite of Plato*, 57–90). As Cavarero notes, "Within this system the rational soul, modeled on the male, so emphatically belongs to the logos that it becomes necessary to represent the male itself as pure intelligible form, possessing no body or matter whatsoever, in perfect antithesis to the female, pure unintelligible matter without any form. Thus both the female and the body are expelled from the male realm of pure thought." Building on her own work and on that of Luce Irigaray and Hannah Arendt, Cavarero returns in her discussion of Plato and Aristotle to the "symbolic matricide" at the core of Western philosophy. Ancient philosophy clearly rejects both the mother and the carnal origins of human beings. It unties the soul from the body and elaborately invents a humanity defined by the capacity of *men* to "generate" ideas. Feminists have exposed and discussed these foundational moves before, though Cavarero brings to them a rare combination of intellectual honesty, interpretive brilliance, expressive skill, and playful wit. She enlarges,

4

moreover, on those previous important discussions by insisting on the gendered body's repeated, uncanny return to politics in metaphor, despite its strenuous exclusion *in theory* from that thoroughly rational space. Indeed, she argues, the body's banishment from the logocentric male realm is futile, for corporeality imposes its presence on Plato's imagination to such a degree that the political order so famously founded on the image of the soul turns out, instead, to be founded precisely on the image of the body. Similarly, Aristotle can find no better illustration of the parts of a well-ordered polis than the example of the human body, however inconsistent his extended analogy may be.

For medieval authors like John of Salisbury this classical tradition inspires a view of the body politic as an interdependent, cooperative whole that must be protected against the sickness and decay that naturally threaten living organisms. But later theorists increasingly ignore the time-bound limitations of real bodies. The early modern body politic is always an adult male body that has no history of birth and is not subject to natural deterioration. This body, whose head is a king and whose limbs and organs are subjects of various rank, can die only by violent attack or the infection of some of its parts. The contradiction between the natural mortality of individual bodies and the need for the collective political body to survive gave prominence in Tudor and Stuart England to the doctrine of the king's two bodies, derived from Christian mystical teachings about the body of Christ (and masterfully explicated in the 1950s by Ernst Kantorowicz). Once again a figural paradox emerges, as Cavarero explores in her second chapter how a "crucial blindness" permits adoption of the corruptible body as image of a political order projected as stable, indeed everlasting.

Cavarero next turns to Shakespeare's *Hamlet,* observing from the outset that "the story of the kingdom of Denmark is one of dead bodies." Taking her cue from the German political theorist Carl Schmitt, she develops her own reading of Hamlet as a dramatic mask for the historical Stuart king of England, James I. Examination of James's most important political writing, *The Trew Law of Free Monarchies* (1598), reveals its reliance on medieval figurations of the body politic, but also its absolutist innovations, which place the head in supreme command over the body (as is the king over his people), and which prescribe the surgical removal of parts "affected with any infirmitie." Thus James figures impending political crisis as bodily affliction, for which the cure may well be amputation of the rebellious members. The problem in Shakespeare's play, of course, is that Hamlet perceives an illness within the body politic that emanates not from remote members in revolt—the "general gender" in Claudius's words to Laertes—but from the head, his usurping fratricidal uncle, Claudius. This intimate decay of the political organism inspires Hamlet's endless musings on ruin and corruption but also on the body as "active or passive protagonist" of homicidal acts against bodies real and political.

Opposed to Hamlet in her apolitical innocence is Ophelia, the beautiful maid whose hopes to marry him are dashed by political realities and who ultimately responds to Hamlet's cruelties to her and violence to her father by taking her own life. Ophelia appears to the puerile and misogynistic Hamlet and to all the men who dictate her behavior as a depthless surface, a body lacking the tormented emotions that plague the young prince. Alien to politics and the rhetoric of the court, Ophelia ultimately speaks in a language of flowers and in the "disconnected syntax of insanity." Yet in Cavarero's reading, Ophelia's death by water, her falling through a mirror of aquatic reflection, also associates her with a mythical tradition that gives her a figurative escape hatch from the control of this male text. In highly suggestive pages, Cavarero offers a reading of Ophelia in the ancient tradition of female water creatures, mythical signs within male culture of women's irreducible and powerful alterity. Looking beyond the stereotypes that have encrusted images of nymphs and mermaids over the centuries, Cavarero suggests not a feminine countermyth, but a recognition of the material bases in birthing, nurturing, and bodily care that gave rise to women's powerful association with water. If politics developed as a sphere of action that disavows carnal birth through the bodies of women, Ophelia's female body plunges into water as a reminder of the weighty process by which individual bodies enter the world.

Whatever posterity may say about Thomas Hobbes, we may not accuse him of suppressing bodily materiality in his political

6

theory. Hobbes's body politic takes form as an image of control over the body's natural inclination toward survival and the competition for physical comforts. But like the other theories examined thus far, Hobbes's formulation posits politics as a way to stave off animality and death. The delicate balance of the social contract stands as an alternative to the state of nature in which, according to Hobbes's famous formulation, men would be at constant war with each other for physical survival and gain. Hobbes's range of metaphor is wide and often appears to lack internal coherence, but he turns repeatedly to the body in his figurations of the state: as a gigantic, artificial body; as a machine; as a person; or as the biblical fishlike monster, Leviathan. The new state Hobbes proposes as alternative to violent, monstrous older models is figured as a mechanical body, and it owes its inspiration to the conceptual innovations about the human body proposed by the seventeenth-century English physician William Harvey. Harvey's description of the cardiovascular system as a hydraulic complex reached well beyond the field of medicine, posing striking new questions about the relations between the natural and the artificial. Harvey himself offered a political analogy between the king and the "heart of the state" and described the circulatory system in language of government, power, and authority. This idea of the human body as a machine (and of the state as a complex organism) lies behind Hobbes's notion of the commonwealth as a gigantic political automaton, an imitation by men of God's mechanical artistry. Yet Hobbes, too, finally turns to abstractions of the material body with whose appetites his theory began, presenting a body politic whose most serious pathology is a disease of the soul.

Hobbes's political thought, Cavarero shows, at times ignores the fact of sexed bodies (for example in the egalitarian sphere of the social pact) and at others recognizes them (for example in the declaration that mothers shall give birth to and nourish natural bodies, while fathers shall give birth to the state). Like theorists before him he is little interested in actual birth, preferring symptomatically that we "consider men as if but even now sprung up out of the earth, and suddenly (like mushrooms) come to full maturity" (*De Cive*, 8.1). But the body, in all its

7

bestial horror, returns with a vengeance to Hobbes's theory in his most famous figure for unbridled political power, the monster Leviathan. Cavarero provides an *ekphrasis* of one image of this giant as it appeared on the frontispiece of *Leviathan*'s first edition and reveals the striking coherence among Hobbes's various figures for this most spectacular body politic.

From these grim, if lucid, studies of pivotal works of Western political literature, Cavarero turns in the appendix to two examples of writing that offers a response to the tradition of anticorporeal, male-centered politics. The Spanish author María Zambrano wrote in 1967 a dramatic philosophical dialogue entitled *La tumba de Antígona,* a colloquy between the entombed tragic heroine and a string of relatives who come to call on her. As Zambrano gives speech back to Antigone, she also figures a turning around of the philosophical tradition that gives primacy to death rather than to birth. In Zambrano's mystical text, Antigone does not die but rather is born into truth through a relinquishment of self and a solitary suffering that allow her to transcend all knowledge. Ingeborg Bachmann's text "Undine Goes," from 1961, presents another female figure who talks back to tradition after centuries of silence. Here in monologue speaks the mythical Undine, a composite figure for the seductive aquatic women of timeless male fantasies. The inhuman Undine employs a slippery language befitting her dwelling, as she disdains both men—whom she also confesses to love—and the submissive women who inhabit the earth alongside them. Undine perhaps represents Cavarero's most succinct example of the deconstruction and recontextualization women must carry out as a partial response to phallocentric culture and history: the water creature refuses to renounce her constitutive status as other, the very basis of her function in tradition, fiction, and fantasy; yet through her own analysis and irony she manages to escape the binary code that created her. Irreducible in her difference, Undine taunts the men and women who live imprisoned by that code. Undine as counterfigure is also a figure of historical memory. She carries within her the remnants of all the secret dreams that created her over the ages, dreams of dangerous, fascinating alterity and of passion on the brink of death;

8

yet she throws these memories back at her creators in her parting from their world. In the end, Undine withdraws defiant and unpossessed, returning to the depths of an aquatic element associated with the female body since before the dawn of patriarchy.

Cavarero leaves us at the end of this book with a beautiful image, but one that inspires questions. Her placement of Zambrano's Antigone and Bachmann's Undine in the position of "countermelody" to the sober political refrains she examines in the rest of her book offers two poetic imaginings of feminine liberation from logocentric culture. But Antigone and Undine are also figures of withdrawal and separation, of entombment, submersion, sacrifice, and loneliness. Throughout *Stately Bodies* Cavarero argues persuasively that women have been cast by male thinkers into the realm of the corporeal as nonpolitical. She argues, first, that the corporeal always and everywhere seeps back into political discourse, revealing itself indeed as that discourse's foundation. And she also argues that the corporeality for which women are made to stand as primary signifier is a *good* thing, powerful and undeniable even by the men who discount it in lofty political theories. Yet finally, and perhaps most provocatively, Cavarero seems to suggest that the nonpolitical, apolitical, antipolitical position of women is also a source of power and knowledge, that politics is by its very nature a male game not to be admired or envied—that there are other and preferable spaces, outside or beyond politics, to be constructed and inhabited.

The question might arise whether women's recourse must be that of Antigone and Undine—to witness and subvert, but through self-sacrifice—or whether for Cavarero alternative modes of resistance are also open to us. In other words, what is the status of these utopian figures of disappearance for those of us who dwell neither in sealed caves nor in the waterworld of Ophelia and Undine? Cavarero's discussion of Penelope in her earlier work yields a partial answer to these questions. There she argues not that women abandon any claim to the polis, but that the polis be reimagined. This new political space must be not a disembodied set of ideals but the "home of the living" where the bodily origins of men and women have meaning and where "the

9

rules of common living are found through the concrete matter that concerns it" (*In Spite of Plato,* 85).

A polis designed to incorporate bodily living rather than to keep corporeality at bay: this will not be easy to construct, given the institutional authority of logocentric power. But Cavarero, as author of this eloquent and pungent analysis, indicates by her own example one of the multiple roads toward such a polis: one that requires not women's withdrawal but rather their rigorous development of a philosophy, a history, and a discourse of sexual difference to counter the disavowal of sexed bodies in the long cultural history of the West. This discourse and practice, developed by Cavarero here and in her earlier work, enables critical distance from that history but also draws sexual difference into fields long kept off-limits to women and to the materiality of the body. These new concerns and emphases do not—as some argue—spoil a rich heritage, muddling its intellectual clarity, but rather breathe new, palpable life into that tradition, which has grown rigid within its own, tired abstractions. Cavarero's marking of the *outside* of politics as a primary factor in the construction of its interior—and as the place from which its interior can be most clearly understood—might even be said to refigure and redeem a logos of the humanities whose own myth of disembodied, rational control has helped consign it to its present marginality.

Cavarero's own practice as feminist philosopher and theorist is certainly contributing to a renewed relevance of ancient philosophy for readers today. Illustrating with precision and depth the resonance of ancient culture in current social questions—the utterly crucial importance of knowledge about the past for confronting with awareness the dilemmas of the present—Cavarero also beckons women to engage with the most formidable and fascinating, the most masculinized, and the most sexually implicating texts of the Western cultural heritage, and to pose critical questions from their perspective of sexual difference. Still more broadly, her work points to other problems regarding intellectual endeavors in our societies. What are the ultimate relations between natural forms (bodies, plants, geological formations) and abstract representations, social constructions, and the built environment? At what price do we ignore the pathways between the concrete, corporeal realm and the realm of intellectual activity? How is the "science envy" of the humanities helping to devalue—even to dismantle—the less "rigorous," less "verifiable," and especially less marketable, but nonetheless crucial kinds of thinking that take place outside science? And further, how has the fear of science within humanistic disciplines contributed to their inability to engage in useful conversation with the powerful discourses of science?

Women and history, women and philosophy, women and politics, women and science, women and classical erudition: these are combinations the logocentric tradition long taught us to regard as inappropriate. They are also combinations that feminist work suggests will be key to redressing the destructive effects of that tradition. Not the tomb or the bottom of the sea, then, but the study, the classroom, the printed page (together with the clinic, the home, the artist's canvas, and countless other spaces) are the arenas to which Cavarero's work ultimately points us all, for building a politics so new that it may have to claim a different name.

# 1

# ON THE BODY
# OF ANTIGONE

ANTIGONE
*A Body against the Polis*

In a city "deprived of two brothers in one day by double fratricide" (*Antigone,* 13–14), the blood of Eteocles and Polynices is mingled after battle by the Theban walls. These two are related by blood, yet enemies; adversaries in the polis, and yet brothers in the *genos*. Creon, lord of Thebes, judges them both according to the political binary, friend/enemy. For the first he has arranged funeral rites; to the body of the second he denies burial. Their sister Antigone, who judges instead according to a principle of kinship, is quick to challenge Creon's decree and to grant burial to Polynices. This transgression triggers the tragic machinery that condemns Antigone to be walled in alive and unleashes a chain of suicides. In the end, dead bodies will heap around a tardily remorseful Creon, who then grants burial to all, Antigone included. This turn, however, comes too late, and nothing of political significance has developed on the deserted stage. Creon stands out at the end as less than nothing (*Antigone,* 1325); the undisputed lord of Thebes is now a "living corpse" (1167) staggering amid other corpses issued of his loins.

Centered on the scandalously forbidden burial of a dead man, Sophocles' *Antigone* recounts the tragic, and therefore hopeless, opposition between love fostered by a blood relationship and the logic of the political order: the ancient law of relation by birth versus the new law of the polis. It is nearly impossible to confront Sophocles' text today without filtering it through one by Hegel, to whom we owe the hermeneutic marking of the female and male principles on opposite sides of *Antigone's* conflict, the linking of the tragedy's antithesis to two precise identities for the sexes.[1] In Hegel's interpretation, we find a faithful mirroring of

13

the ancient symbolic order that inaugurates Western tradition, in both the full realization of male identity in the political arena and the confinement of female identity to the immediacy of the family and the domestic sphere. Thus Hegel's analysis, however distinguished for its shunning of platitudes, reiterates a time-worn figural structure for the two sexes' presumed "primary" destinies. This scheme entrusts the universal substance of the polis to men, assigning them the dialectical realization of the Idea, while leaving to women the more humble, natural, and domestic cares of the body.

At least three levels of symbolic reference are present in the tragic tension between the past of myth and the present of the city (Vernant and Vidal-Naquet 1976–91, 1:59). In the first place we have the ideological perspective of the democratic polis. The polis's principles are understood and shared by the Athenian public, though they are also expounded ambiguously by the tyrant Creon during many speeches and contradicted by his behavior (Lanza 1977, 151–59). In addition, Creon, as tyrannical mask, himself constitutes a second figural level, the polar negation (irrational, violent, and myth-based) of a democratic city upheld by principles incompatible with tyranny. The third figural level is expressed in the mask of Antigone herself; insofar as she is completely antipolitical, she fulfills a double function as a radical *otherness* in relation to both contemporary democratic Athens and the tyrannical polis. Thus although Antigone's feminine, nonpolitical universe is denied on two fronts, at each of these symbolic levels, her universe crucially focuses on the historical exclusion of women common to both the tyrannical city and the democratic polis.

Onstage, Antigone incarnates the body as the emphatic space of appearance for incestuous bonds in the mythical law of the blood. Creon materializes a monstrous tyrannical power that, in the distancing play of theatrical fiction, the Athenian public is able to distinguish from the democratic tones of his speech (Vernant and Vidal-Naquet 1976–91, 2:71). Nevertheless, apart from the typical ambiguity of tragic theater, the dual logic that locates the conflict's motives in the masks of the two sexes is especially asymmetrical. These motives divide, finally, into the perfectly legitimate pretext of a dead body that demands burial by a loving sister ready to sacrifice herself for that purpose, and the anomalous intrusion of a political order that unexpectedly denies her this office. With respect to the burial, at first denied and then conceded, it is thus the body, or rather the corpse, that ultimately wins.

In the meantime, this corpse has pulled many other bodies from the same house into a dark vortex of death.[2] Thus, on the symbolic level of the conflict, a body in its blood relations becomes the enemy of the polis, and it emerges victorious from the struggle, though its victory be that of a corpse: the triumph of the body appears in the radical light of the *uncanny* associated with death. On its side, the polis has not sustained notable damage. Its order and even the tyranny despised by the Athenians are still intact, though the man who rules it (notably still alive in the final scene) is punished with the death of his bride and remains alone amid the blood born of his loins. It appears that a willful imbalance based on an unresolved asymmetry of punishments determines the opposing sides occupied by man and woman. And, at least within the story's spare plot, it is the woman who obtains justice: her brother's body gets the desired burial, while the wicked Creon, the tragic figure of a suffering tyrant (Giorgini 1993, 193), pays for his refusal with the unforeseen deaths of his descendants.

In *Antigone* human corporeality and female identity cohere within a single, terrible and unpolitical, concept. Within the drama's contingency, the body that the city excludes and expels outside its walls is first, the dead body of Polynices, and then the body of Antigone, buried alive. But its symbolic value is that of pure body: the unnerving realm of womanly power inscribed in raw life and in the fundamental code of blood. The conflict involves, on the one hand, the city built by men and, on the other, a body rooted in the female. The plot unwinds in an uncontrollable contest between violent expulsions and terrifying returns.

It is well known that classical Greece saw the ultimate establishment of a political order now recognized by all the specialist literature as both logo- and phallocentric. In its very founding

15

categories, that order clearly excludes a corporeality judged to be mere material support for the human capacity for language and thought, at the same time excluding women, insofar as they are "naturally" rooted in matters of the body. Sophocles' Antigone might then simply fit within the codes and symbolic framework of the age.

Regarding these codes, however, the tragedy seems to evoke a series of ambiguous *contrapassi* and unresolved tensions. A body at the drama's center, expelled from the polis, comes back to invade the palace in large-scale slaughter, raising doubts about where, between the polis itself and the ancient law of blood, the true site of the uncanny *(deinon)* lies. If there is a figure who wavers, bends, and finally comes up against his own nothingness in *Antigone,* it is the lord of Thebes, and not the inflexible girl; it is the androcentric principle of the polis, and not the female who bears witness to the body. It is the story of a body that the play crucially recounts, a body that, both in its exclusion from the city and its return to it, takes on the ghastly guise of a corpse, both victorious and vanquished. This body disorders and disrupts through the foul dissolution of its flesh, which was evoked at the play's outset by the haunting figure of the unburied Polynices.

The clash between the polis and the body is here also a clash between order and disorder. This clash takes place in a tragic framework where the body plays the part of the prelogical and the dreadful, both cadaverous nausea and incestuous sexuality, blurring even into a myth concerning our animal origin. In a dramatic fiction in which the polis exhibits that which it has had to repudiate and fight against in order to arise, the body is vindicated by the figural emphasis it acquires through its own expulsion. Clearly it is the body, here associated with the murky, carnal recesses of female power, that is radically *distinct* from the polis, its tragic antithesis and exact opposite. No macrocosm encompasses the body and the polis in a superior embrace, nor does any image of one or the other weave analogies between them.

The irreconcilability of opposites, the extreme that constitutes opposites as *the* problem, is typical of tragedy. Thus between the polis and the body we find no reconciliation here. Rather, we see the radicalization of a conflict that squares off its two opponents against each other on a field of mutual incompatibility.

And yet, precisely as tragedy and indeed perhaps to a degree greater than in any other tragedy, *Antigone* is wildly eccentric regarding the Greek vision of the "whole" that inscribes the nature of each thing within the cosmic order. This vision often links the body and the polis on the philosophical plane through various figurative correspondences and inaugurates, among other things, the long relationship between the corporeal figure and political metaphor. For these reasons the anomalous details of Sophocles' *Antigone* seem all the more numerous and significant. On the one hand the tragedy represents the polis's mythical expulsion of a body that is uncanny by birth and that returns in the form of a corpse. On the other hand, the polis is denied that reclaiming of the body which would turn the corpus into a tamed, metaphorical figure of its order. This raises the question of whether tradition and *Antigone* are telling us two different versions of the strange story that, over thousands of years, has linked the body with politics. It is an ancient tale, perhaps forgotten by the body-politic metaphor in the progressive fading of myth, but which Sophocles' text continues to illuminate with its significant and unorthodox irregularities.

### An Absent Soul

A body is therefore at the center of *Antigone,* that which is declared from the start as the object of the tragic contest: Polynices' corpse. A dead body, or cadaver *(nekus),* but also a body *(soma)* that once belonged to a living man.[3] Strikingly absent on this threshold that leads to the dwelling of the departed, in this scene conjuring merciful burial, however, is the soul, the psyche. That man by the name of Polynices who was once a living body is now *entirely* there, in his unburied body by the Theban walls.

In this tragic sequence hinged on the theme of burial, the absence of allusion to the psyche of the dead man seems exceedingly strange. So strange, indeed, that we must justify the word *entirely* (an equivocal and allusive term) when we adopt it in connection with Polynices. Our reading has initially focused on the unusual fact of an absent soul. And we must confess that the word *entirely* is merely a verbal expedient to avoid the category of the *individual,* or, in other words, of subjective *identity.* Both the term and the idea are indeed too modern to inhabit the ancient world without difficulty. Nonetheless, they are so alluring that we hazard using them, even at the price of continually tripping over them, as we shall soon see. Certainly, there is no reason why the critic cannot attempt a study of Greek foreshadowings of a theory of individuality, what we might call a dim etiology of the ego, or even the tragic affirmation of the self in its individualization. Indeed a predictable appeal to the celebrated Hegelian reading of the text seems hardly out of place: the figure of Antigone is the emblem of the law of the family, whose sole rationale is the "individual as such." Here, we see the particular individuality of the subject that has not yet "passed" into the political sphere. Precisely this recognition of the individual subject, especially as agent and as responsible source of its actions, constitutes the crux of Greek tragedy. So for the moment, linguistic caution allows us to say provisionally that Polynices' individuality consists entirely of his unburied body.

Indeed, the decisive problem here seems to be the body that each of us *is* more than the body that each of us *has.* For enigmatically in this tragedy, a consanguine body verges on overstepping its own boundaries, on merging with the *genos* in a symbiotic union.

On the hermeneutic plane of evidence, *Antigone* seems to express this problem in a strikingly absent psyche, thus in an unusually central body that, given the psyche's absence, can function onstage as absolute symbol. The radical opposition between Creon's and Antigone's reasoning appears most poignant in the emphasis placed by Sophocles' tragic vision on this absolute corporeality. Their antithetical arguments concern what should be done with Polynices' body, but the word *psyche* is never pronounced by either of them in their dialogic conflict over the dead man. As if the topic were merely a body to be buried, the conflict only over a body; as if the burial of a corpse, denied or permitted, would not irresistibly evoke in the Greek spectator the image of a psyche either departing toward a fated dwelling or lingering by the corpse.

The entire tradition concerning funeral rites in diverse forms from Homer to the Platonic myths and beyond tells of the soul's final voyage. The Sophoclean anomaly stands out all the more surprisingly, then, as a kind of reminder of the centrality of the body, here made forcibly explicit, and of its unrivaled figural power. No unseen psyche ever comes to disturb this seductive effect onstage. Rather, the play continually evokes a body at the walls of Thebes, inviting the imagined gaze to fathom the flesh's mythical destiny and the opacity of its red blood. This red blood is the *same* blood that flows in kindred bodies, precisely the same blood shed by the two brothers near the Theban walls.

## Traditional Figures of the Soul

The term *psyche* appears a few times in *Antigone* to indicate, echoing Homer, the "breath" of the living, or something intermediate between "mind" and "consciousness." It does not refer to an entity that separates from the body in order to migrate to Hades. Precisely in Homer the psyche becomes the conventional protagonist in a narrative of final voyage, the shadowy inhabitant of an underworld abode. The ancient symbolic image is careful to separate the realm of the dead from that of the living, rejecting any frightening mixture. The border over which Dike presides is clear.

Homer's Hades is inhabited by the souls of the passed away, who have reached that dwelling thanks to a funeral rite that dissolved the body in fire and allowed the psyche to separate from it. The funeral is therefore a necessary rite that permits the soul, hovering anxiously nearby so long as the body is exposed, to reach its subterranean destination. In Homer the psyche is, first, respiration, the breath possessed by the living body, which abandons the corpse through the mouth or some mortal wound. But at the same time it is the simulacrum (*eidolon*) or the shade (*skia*) of the body, a kind of aerial phantasm that reaches the underworld when the corpse is destroyed by fire. The psyche may thus be defined as a sort of "weaker duplicate" of the body, which is provided with a feeble material consistency (Rohde

1925, 1:6; cf. Centanni 1992, 73). Most importantly, the psyche is far from being the seat of individual self-consciousness. It is, instead, the impalpable phantasm of the dead, deprived of mind (*nekroi aphrades*) and oblivious of any individual identity possessed in life (*Odyssey,* 11:476; Vermeule 1979, 9, 23).

It must be stressed that the notion of this identity is still at its dawning. The *individual* itself—or at least the idea to which it corresponds—is, in Homer, conceived of not so much as a compact unity, bound around a consciousness, but as a multitude of motor, intellectual, and volitional functions gathered in a center called the diaphragm (Snell 1963, 26; Rohde 1925, 1:11). Only in the rigidity of death does the Homeric body acquire unitary stability. In death and as corpse it earns the epithet *soma.* In Homer, corporeality establishes and restricts the sense of what each person is. This sense is figured in two forms: that of the visible, living body, which has full mobility and consciousness, both of which become petrified in the stasis of the corpse; and that of the body's transparent, figural duplicate, the psyche. The latter wanders weightlessly through the underworld in ghostly form, forgetful of itself, although its form is recognizable by anyone who, like Ulysses, undergoes the frightening experience of visiting the realm of the dead while still alive. This is a hellish intrusion, during which Ulysses significantly must prepare a trench full of the blood from the warm bodies of newly slaughtered animals, so that the souls (including his mother's), having drunk of it, may speak to him and—more important—recognize him.

The cruel rite shows how conscious life, through which each of us has a name and a story (what we now insist on calling identity), consists precisely in the body and dissolves along with that body. A bit of this conscious history returns to the bloodless, ethereal simulacrum only through drinking the eminently corporeal, and therefore vital, matter of warm blood. In short, life, consciousness, and self-identity in the Homeric universe are bound within a corporeality that will come to refer to a single constellation of meaning, one that encompasses, at its margin, also the psyche. The psyche exists, however, as something that breathes in the living body and then survives after death, as the body's devitalized unconscious and deindividualized simulacrum. It is, furthermore, typical of archaic reasoning to maintain that the body is de facto existence and that if existence endures, it must be in some sense corporeal.

This archaic conception of a body located within the dimension of existence, however, does not appear to have been inherited by the classical age. Rather, the body arrives at the culminating point of a perspectival revolution with Plato, a revolution that looses existence from its bodily location and entrusts a decisive role instead to the soul. The ancient wisdom that was capable of acknowledging the naive experience of the body as a basis for existence thus dies away. This formidable act of uprooting from experience itself inaugurates the familiar, obsessive dichotomy between a disincarnate persistence of the self and a contingent flesh tormented by death. The psyche must now become "that natural thing which, by its very nature, cannot die" (Rosenzweig 1985, 83).

In Plato, the psyche has symptomatically lost all bodily figurality and comes to be associated with the immateriality of thought. It is now linked with that noetic activity which renders humankind unique, gifted as it is with logos. That activity is also the key to our otherworldly existence. Thus, the Platonic separation between the body (soma) and the soul (psyche) also represents the split between the transient and the eternal, between flesh and thought. A framework of persistent dichotomies now privileges the soul with liberation from death.

Having become the exclusive, intellectual seat of "true" life, of consciousness and identity, the soul is saved above all from death. Or rather from that never-ending flow of becoming, intrinsic to life, which carries in its sweep only a body, now reduced to mere dead weight. The body is merely a carnal vessel for the sojourn on earth. Thus death is "free of all tragic association" (Benjamin 1980, 108), and the mortal body merely figures as temporary seat of functions and impulses that are somehow depersonalized. These, however, may still be pernicious to the soul itself: capable, in fact, of distracting it from that thought (nous) of the eternal which verifies its substance, and from the capacity for order of the logos, which gives it its form.

It is no accident that in the *Phaedo* the separation of the soul from the body through the intellectual accrual of ideas becomes the philosophical exercise of the best men, producing a kind of death-in-life. This state reaches its perfection in a bodily death by which the soul manages to unbind itself once and for all from a body perceived as the material prison of a crucially immaterial individual identity. Thus Socrates, on the point of drinking the hemlock, complains that he is unable to convince Crito:

> I am the same Socrates who has been talking and conducting the argument; he fancies that I am the other Socrates whom he will soon see, a dead body, and he asks, How shall he bury me? . . . I would not have him sorrow at my hard lot, or say at the burial, "Thus we lay out Socrates." (*Phaedo* 115c)

Contrary to what Crito thinks, Socrates is, in fact, nothing but the soul that reasons and holds forth, or rather the noetic part of the soul; while the body *belongs* to Socrates, but *is* not Socrates. It is merely that from which he is unbound by death. He himself, however, remains in an incorporeal soul: Socrates to all effects and in all of his singularity.

In the *Phaedo*, the separation of the body and soul therefore seems to be between "that which is destined to lose its identity and that which, on the contrary, maintains it forever" (Loraux 1991, 154). It is a rift between the corruptible and the incorruptible, between the mortal and the divine: ultimately between the visible and the invisible. The invisible is not by chance the only entity worthy of reaching Hades (which means precisely the Invisible, in Greek), dwelling in the company of wise and good gods and the souls of exceptional men (*Phaedo*, 63b), and abiding there in full and conscious identity.

As is often the case with Plato's works, there is no shortage of problems. The myth of Er at the end of the *Republic* introduces the theory of metempsychosis, overturning in large measure the theoretical framework of the *Phaedo*. This happens especially to the category of individual identity, which seemed to be so definitively established. The category continues to operate importantly, despite the arguable lack of its presence in antiquity that at the outset boded problems and urged our caution. The myth of Er tells of souls reincarnated after having been able to choose between various forms of life, only then to drink of the fountain of forgetfulness before finally falling "like shooting stars" (*Republic,* 621b) into the bodies that are the repositories of the specific lives chosen. In this story's logic, we possess neither a single body—given the cyclical reincarnation into ever-new bodies—nor a single individual consciousness assigned to the soul, since forgetfulness blocks all memory of the previous cycle. Instead we have a unique and immortal soul that migrates into various bodies, accumulating different experiences and spanning multiple identities, which are stratified around its noetic substance. At this point the soul possesses not one name and one story for all eternity (as the notion of individual identity would dictate, and as seemed to be the case with Socrates' soul), but instead possesses many names and stories, each passing into the others. In this complex belief, the notions of individual identity and of the soul's eternity are not compatible. Yet their bond seems to be an established fact, according to our reading of the *Phaedo,* for the self "in its obstinate claim to boundlessness . . . demands an immortality without mutation or migration, requiring the continuation-of-self" (Rosenzweig 1985, 83).

It is more than probable that this is merely a hermeneutic obstacle rising from our inappropriate reference to the modern category of the individual. Indeed Plato does not worry himself over this issue, though it seems certain that the theoretical history of the individual ego, in passing from the Homeric body to the Platonic soul, has now completed its first, decisive phase (Detienne 1973, 51ff.). Plato confirms the altogether secondary role to be played by the body. Within reincarnation's cycles, the body often turns out to be not even human but animal, through the deliberate choices made by souls that willingly take on the forms of other living species, just as they also assume bodies differently sexed from the one previously possessed (*Republic,* 620a–d). In the casual consumption of every sort of corporeality at this divine emporium of possible lives, the psyche becomes ever more the immaterial protagonist of the Platonic myth, establishing itself as an otherworldly substance tending toward perpetuity and possessed by the desire for the eternal.

In this brief digest of ancient notions concerning the psyche, we cannot fail to include *The Suppliant Women* of Euripides.

Written only twenty years after Sophocles' *Antigone,* the tragedy tells of Theseus, who wins at war the corpses of the enemies of Thebes (Creon leaves these corpses unburied for the same reason he denies burial to Polynices). Theseus mercifully gives them up to purifying fire, proclaiming: "Let the dead be covered by the ground, and let each part regain the element from which it came to light: the spirit *(pneuma)* to the air; the body *(soma)* to the earth. The flesh is only ours to dwell in while life lasts; and afterward the giver of its strength must take it back" (*Suppliant Women,* 531–36). From this compassionate speech we may easily deduce how Euripides' hero, though preferring the heavenly *pneuma* to the more traditional psyche, nonetheless ends up sharing the ideas of the Platonic Socrates and thus grants a ritual funeral rite to the bodily vessel.

Within such a tradition, the anomaly of *Antigone* appears doubly surprising. The sister who wishes to grant burial to Polynices and Creon who forbids it are in fact competing, with equal determination, for the fate of a dead body that seems to possess no psyche at all: neither in the sense of the Homeric duplicate image, nor as seat of that spiritual identity recognized by Plato and Euripides. Thus it appears that the centrality of the body in *Antigone,* precisely because of its surplus of meaning with respect to tradition, is meant to be the fulcrum of Sophocles' text. Indeed it is not hard to see how that central positioning of the body brings the rivals together. The symbolic power of the body, inasmuch as it is the substance of the individual and aside from the fact that it is now the corpse of a dead man, becomes the untranscendable horizon of their struggle.

Perhaps unlike with Euripides' *Suppliant Women,* the tyrant's cruelty regarding funerary *custom* is only of peripheral concern here. In the opposing positions of Antigone and Creon, rather, is a common and nearly obsessive regard for Polynices' body, rendered all the more unusual and set in sharp perspective by the ostentatious silence concerning his soul. Largely as a result of this corporeal centrality, strictly observed by both characters and exalted in the anomaly of an absent psyche, the gaze of the two opponents translates into the irreconcilability of two contrary visions, tragically acted out by Creon and Antigone. If it is true that the matter here is *only* the body, it is equally only over the body that the two gazes contend. Antigone's is a consanguineous way of seeing from an extremely close horizon already corporeally oriented and hinged upon incest. While in contrast, Creon's is a way of seeing from afar, a seeing through the impenetrable walls of the polis that has perhaps severed corporeal ties, or tamed their call.

## The Incestuous Body

Antigone and Creon, the family and the state: these are the categories that (in Hegel's reading) the tragedy proposes, although the modern notion of the state does not well convey the sense of the Theban polis ruled by Creon. The word *family,* which should describe a consanguineous principle of incestuous kinship, is also problematic.

Once we have abandoned the term *state* because of its inappropriateness, however, we must then make sure to distinguish between the ancient Theban polis as represented onstage, and the polis in the fifth century when the play was presented. Sophocles' theater, in fact, arises within the context of the decisive democratic order of the classical city that chose Athens as model. This is the familiar political structure that identifies itself with a limited group of free men and that has definitively expelled women from its androcentric sphere. This exclusion is precisely what is played out on stage, and what constitutes one of the play's most genuinely tragic dimensions (Vernant and Vidal-Naquet 1976–91, 2:94). Another, equally important feature—especially when reading *Antigone* in the light of its perception by its public—is that the body is symbolically expelled from the polis along with the women. In that invaluable ideological manifesto of the city known as the funeral oration, the Athenian citizen in his political guise does not, in fact, have a body: "The *soma* was a gift of the city and the soldier's death clears the debt" (Loraux 1991, 84). This body is, in any case, no longer living flesh, in all its physicality, but pure abstraction.[4] All the more, then, must we attend to the unusual emphasis in *Antigone* linking the theme of the body with the excesses of a feminine mask. That irregularity must be seen in the logic of an already liquidated past (which may be authentic or presumed, but is in any case active in the collective imaginary). The fearful reality of that past is now placed onstage, in order to legitimate its definitive defeat.

Still more complicated is our recourse to the word *family,* a single term we use to translate two Greek nouns (*domos, oikos*) characterized by semantic slippage. At first they denote the social group connected by extended kinship and occupying the same "house." But they soon assume the meaning of "building" or the habitat shared by the master's family and his slaves (Benveniste 1976, 226–46). This semantic shift, in which a genealogical term is absorbed by a nomenclature of territorial division, deals precisely with the emergence of the polis. The polis places itself squarely against the genealogical model of the extended family and upsets its configuration. Antigone finds herself at the beginning of this process, and Creon at the threshold of its end.

It is not enough, however, to say that Antigone represents the initial stage of this movement. In the figure of Antigone, in fact, the family, although it is indicated sometimes with the term *domos,* is rooted in the notions of *genos* or *philia,* or rather in the concept of that consanguineous chain linking those who belong by birth to a common breed, and who therefore share not only the same house, but also the same blood inscribed in *generation.* Even this, however, does not say enough, because the degree of blood kinship upheld by the ancient exogamous model of marriage between cousins is radicalized, in *Antigone,* by the endogamous model of a generation whose sole source is maternal incest. Thus, in the skillful weaving of Sophocles' text, another, more audacious anomaly disrupts the scene. Within the centrality of the body that has already emerged with absolute symbolic power, the play inscribes a consanguineous principle that stakes the extreme limits of the symbol on incest.

Put another way, Antigone and the principle of common blood ties that she (literally) incarnates take the already crucial theme of the body and develop it to its utmost symbolic capacity. This is done through an absolute representation of corporeality that, in the end, is revealed as the appropriate base for a family model centered on the Theban myth's closed and radical endogamy of

26

incest. Nothing in this symbolic framework stays quietly in place, and nothing lets itself be docilely inscribed within the parameters of tradition. On the contrary, the anomalous and the terrible invade a stage on which every element linked to the body seems to be blown out of proportion and highlighted as carnal excess, whether on the plane of birth or that of death.

The dead body of Polynices dominates the scene, but it is blood generated by the mother that polarizes the tragic action and creates its antithesis. The sister wishes to grant burial precisely to the "dead man born of my mother" (*Antigone,* 466–67). It is thus the power of blood that moves Antigone. This maternal identification forces her to self-sacrifice in order to carry out *her mother's desire* incarnated in the dead Polynices (Irigaray 1989, 203).[5]

Ordinarily we point to the father, blinded by his own hand, and we invoke the race of Oedipus.[6] The necessarily masculine name of the family is the one known to the Theban polis. Within the family itself, however, and from Antigone's point of view, it can only be Jocasta, the mother, who initiates the blood lineage: so much a mother, in fact, that she is mother not only of her ill-starred last four children, but also of their father. Thus, from the daughter's point of view as represented by Antigone, the father-brother Oedipus is overpowered by the common mother, Jocasta: for Oedipus, a mother-wife (*Antigone,* 53) who generates his sons-brothers and daughters-sisters. Indeed, the endogamic module complicates kinship down to its very terminology (Avezzù 1991, 128ff.). But the consanguineous principle invoked here still indicates its criterion with incisive efficacy. The incest of the son with the mother allows us to attribute to the same generative woman the sons and daughters, like successive bodily offshoots of one flesh.

With the name of Oedipus, the most memorable case of incest in Western culture presents itself as the decisive archetype for posterity's hermeneutic labor and in particular for that of Freudian analysis. The story discloses an incest that is truly extraordinary for one of its curious features, however: it permits the recounting in various versions of the story of a son who couples with his mother, while in the meantime millennia of history keep

27

silent about the paternal rape of daughters. Oedipus, from his own point of view, is the son who kills his father and sleeps with his mother. From Antigone's point of view, he is rather the man who, through incest, recycles maternal blood, which therefore remains uncontaminated by the outside.

In the tragedies Sophocles dedicates to the house of Labdacus, we see a masculine, mythical principle of paternal identification based on the pair Oedipus/Laius operating in *Oedipus the King* (Vernant and Vidal-Naquet 1976–91, 2:116–19), while a mythical principle of maternal identification based on the pair Antigone/ Jocasta operates in *Antigone*. In both, however, it is Jocasta, the mother-earth sown again by the son in the same furrow from which he was born (*Oedipus the King*, 1947–48), who calls the Labdicans the "ones who share seed" (*homosporoi*).[7] This permits the repetition of the legend that told of the mythical race born of dragon's teeth sown in the ground and confirms a destiny in which the maternal blood tie incorporates the offspring, guaranteeing them a ruinous outcome. The Greek word *physis*, from *phyein,* to be born, is here shaded with incestuous meaning.[8] It is furthermore this *physis* as matriarchal blood heredity that, in tragedy, often takes on the semblance of destiny (Fusini 1990, 68, 143).

The centrality of the body makes in *Antigone* for a scene in which self-generating unions (*koimemata autogenneta*) dominate. These spring from the bed of a sole mother (862–65), confusing and exceeding the individual identities of Jocasta's children. Each of her children feels pulsating in his or her body not a specific individual identity, but the life of blood kin, symbiotically becoming one substance with them.

A carnal implosion marks this symbiosis, and it significantly influences Antigone's language in Sophocles' tragedy. It permeates her syntactical and grammatical forms and couches her speech in an obsessive style in which she appeals again and again to the *same blood,* or in other words to a common birth, from the same father and shared mother. Hence we must return to the celebrated and untranslatable line that opens the tragedy: "o koinon autadelfon Ismenes kara."[9] These words Antigone addresses to her sister's head, twice invoked for its quality of being

28

"common" (*koinon*) and "of the same sisterhood" (*autadelfon*). The impossibility of translating this line is due to the density of meanings woven in the very form of the language, easily observable in the line's odd construction. Here Ismene's individuality lies entirely in her given name, which appears, however, only to designate the possessor of the "head" as privileged part of the body. This precise recourse to the archaic notion of an individuality conceived as body, and of a corporeality conceived as head, inscribes itself easily within the horizon of symbiotic attraction already signified by the line's beginning with the terms *koinon* and *autadelfon*.[10] The meaning of "common" for the word *koinon* also carries the possible shading of "related by blood," while the term *autadelfon*, through its intensifying form, emphasizes that *adelphos* which originally signified a co-uterine sister/brotherhood of explicit maternal origin.

To this whirlpool, which plunges individuality into symbiotic substance (and which could probably be represented onstage by the use of identical masks), we may also add Sophocles' use of the Greek dual, that is, the reflexive verbal form that designates a double agent. This form is used by Antigone in the first lines of the tragedy and then changed to the first-person singular after Ismene's refusal to act along with her sister. Indeed the first-person singular grows to be an ego crying out in uprooted solitude.

The symbolic scheme that links this ego of Antigone, who is forced to act alone, and the horizon of antiegoistic, blood kinship on which the action unfolds, is ambiguous. It is improbable, therefore, that Sophocles' play represents the glorification of the individual against the polis, as has often been claimed in readings that take their cue from the chorus's appellation of Antigone as *autonomos* (821).[11] Rather we encounter here an ego in the final stage of violent separation from its symbiotic niche, and which announces with a painful, nearly sacrificial gesture the birth of a self. That self is concerned with the paradox of an act bound to the antiegocentric law of maternal symbiosis.

The ego of Antigone, in fact, persists in seeking its law within the impersonal roots of the self: bodily, incestuous, and consanguineous roots, which are the sources of the tragic trajectory within which the girl both moves and is moved. As if the play aimed to compare Ismene's ego, which has already abandoned those roots to move within the polis in obedience to the masculine laws of the mightiest, with the ego of Antigone who, in her immovable loyalty to consanguineous kinship, suffers in total solitude. In terms of Irigaray's female ethics, Antigone's solitary destiny clarifies the lack of a vertical dimension between mother and daughter not marked by constraint, as well as the lack of a horizontal dimension between sisters in terms of relationship (Irigaray 1985, 86–87).

At the drama's center, and beyond the differences among the Sophoclean masks, lies a pre-egoistic blood tie. That is, a story of flesh narrated through maternal generation, on which singularity is based and into which it is submerged. Here, the corporeal bloodline is transcendental, but it is also the immanent, blooming again in each of its offspring. The closed circle of the familial *philia,* which Antigone takes as her rule, can only allude to a bare life that has its end in itself and in the conservational incarnation of identical blood.

Brought through endogamic obsession to its extreme expressive limits, this framework reaches its greatest iconic power in a tragic caesura that blocks the generative flow. It is petrified, so to speak, into a perfect plasticity. The family of Jocasta comes to an end with the deaths of her children; above all with the death of Antigone, who dies a virgin, thus precluding any potential offspring.[12] The pitiable weeping of the girl over her thwarted matrimony (and thus over the negated potential of her womb) reconfirms the scene of incest that must play itself out within the closed, perfect figure of self-sacrifice. Insofar as she would be unable to preserve in the family line this radical mark of incest, Antigone is denied generative power altogether. Hers is only a backward gaze, concerned with those already born. As disturbing, inevitably, to modern sensibilities as it must have been irksome to the ancient spectator, a famous declaration by Antigone illustrates her fixation on the past and her neglect of the future. She implies that death is not the real end; the real end is the absence of other births proceeding from the prime blood source.

I refer to the unsettling statement with which Jocasta's inflexible daughter declares that she would have defied the burial ban neither for a husband nor for a son: "Had it been a husband dead I might have taken another, and have borne another child, to take the dead child's place. But now my sire and mother are both dead, no second brother can be born for me" (*Antigone*, 909–12). The horizon of kinship forces Antigone to *conserve* those bodies that are already expressions (extreme expressions, since they are the fruit of an incestuous union) of maternal blood. With the mother's death, and that of the father to whom she has given birth and who conserves and recycles her blood, the mother can no longer *directly* produce another child from her womb. So that the present children, alive or dead, and completely identified in their living or dead bodies, represent those maternal offshoots to whom Antigone must henceforth devote her care.

Constitutive, then, for Antigone, are her roles as daughter and sister and not as wife and mother; though in the end, in the sacrifice of the ego, some regret for her denied marriage comes through. But the law of blood kinship is never defied: it "calls" the girl's gaze irresistibly back toward the maternal root. A symbolic order is thus established that arranges kin in equally dependent relationships on a horizontal plane. The carnal perfection of an endogamic figure comes into relief precisely through the absence of future genealogies, of that blood which, recycled over and over through time, would eventually mix with another and become contaminated. Incest initiates and gives shape to the figure; the daughter's sterility closes it. Family relationships are gauged according to the generative power of the maternal body. They mark an absolutely closed horizon on which Antigone moves. She is a daughter who gets her bearings from the fact of being a daughter, and thus from her status as sister of those born of her mother.

Daughter and sister: these names are not very frequent among tragic heroines of the female principle. This principle is usually embodied, in observance of a very ancient, enduring, and familiar social code, in the figures of brides and mothers who act under the cloud of a steady misogyny.[13] In *Antigone*, maternal blood commands the action: the figure of the mother intrudes on the stage with the enormous power of her attraction. It is she who summons the daughter to recognize herself in the law of procreative blood, and thus to take the side of the body and the fleshly bonds sprung from uterine generation. Thus, the lesson of Sophocles is a symbolic composition in which the body, the woman, and the mother are combined in a single figural knot. Through a therapy of excess and a centripetal endogamy under-scored for the occasion, the fearful bond succeeds completely in evoking the full range of pity and terror that the female figure can inspire (Aristotle, *Poetics,* 1149b). It is no coincidence that this feeling of terror is rooted in the corporeal materiality of existence. Existence, here, is utterly rooted in the fact of a death that ruins the corpse and that no immortal psyche seems able to redeem, but also in the fact of a birth that links each and every body to the carnal, internal, and bloody recesses of the female womb.

One is born of a woman's body, of a maternal blood that generates and encloses: a terrifying and uncanny fact from the perspective of the polis's virile logocentrism. The carnal site of a human origin, its speakability seems to be the standard against which the language of this tragedy measures itself, seeking to give theatrical, cathartic expression to "the intellect of man wandering among the unthinkable" (Hölderlin 1989, 103).[14]

### The Horrible Meal

The story of a body made of flesh and bone is that of blood passing from generation to generation. It is a simple story of raw life sufficient unto itself: of a body born of another body, of its blood pulsing in another body. Bodies are born, live for a time, and die, succumbing to the organic dissolution in which they vanish.

Seen from the perspective of flesh and blood, death does not appear as the sudden instant of separation. It is a threshold in the process of metamorphosis toward the realm of the inorganic. He who was body is still body. He who was born in the body dies in the body: completely present, motionless, and carnal, the op-posite of Socrates, who has gone elsewhere. And yet he is *disfigured:* by the long sojourn in the earth, or by the terrible prospect of being torn by animal fangs that transform human flesh into the food of beasts, shredding that precise configuration which renders it a unique body. A body of a man, articulated into a myriad of limbs and functions, which however possesses *figural unity,* and thus a proper name.

The living possess, in fact, an originary identity that relies on the particular shape of the body, and especially on the facial features, which are undone by death. It is an identity with symbiotic roots, and it is crucial in the common resemblance of Jocasta's children. For this reason death, which destroys recognizable resemblances, is the enemy of maternity, which cannot accept this slow disfiguration. There is perhaps some truth in Hegel's assigning to women the care for the burial of the corpse, of the decomposing body generated in the womb, which now seeks to shield itself from the gaze. In Homer, fire spares the comely bodies of heroes from the shame of decomposition. Whether in slow decay or torn by the swift fangs of wild animals, the flesh makes its final celebration in ugliness. And it is precisely the integral form of the brother's body that Antigone protects from sudden and *visible* disfigurement by wild beasts.

Obsessive protagonists in this tragedy of an unburied body are the dogs and birds who feed on the corpse. The malicious fury of their cries as they partake of their horrible meal is evoked again and again. They crowd hungrily around Polynices, *outside* the Theban walls, outside that polis which has built its order "on essential delimitations between the human and the animal spheres" (Steiner 1984, 227).[15]

It is precisely these essential boundaries that are narrated by the chorus in *Antigone,* in lines whose critical importance for interpreters has come to equal that of the incestuous figure's fate. The chorus's famous first line, "polla ta deina" ("the many terrible things" of which mankind is the most terrible, *deinoteron*) already announces its own crucial weight, telling how the extraordinary creature that is man "taught himself the word and the thought, rapid as wind, and civil customs." Man acquired these specifically human traits, however, and acquired human specificity (the "rational" and the "political") at the cost of separation from the natural order. The separation therefore takes place as a domination and subjection of cosmic forces through intellect and technology. These achievements include the cap-

33

ture of fish, birds, and wild animals, and the domestication of the horse and the bull, the former for food and the latter above all for their strength in farming tasks.

The contents of the Sophoclean chorus, then, seem to refer to the traditional definition of a technological and political specificity of man, founded upon his separation from the immediacy of the natural world, and on his ability to tame it, which had already been amply described by Hesiod. Yet Sophocles extraordinarily defines mankind as *deinoteron* (*Antigone,* 333): an untranslatable term pondered philosophically by such exceptional interpreters as Hölderlin and Heidegger, and roughly meaning "terrible," "monstrous," and "uncanny" (Steiner 1984, 174–77).[16] The latter word perhaps seems particularly apt to suggest that bewilderment linked to the estrangement of mankind—burdened with violence and plagued by the awareness of death—from primitive immersion in the pure order of life. It is a sort of sign and destiny of one whose essence is this tearing *away from* and *against* the natural world, in a boundless will to dominate and in anguish over his own death.

As this lacerating action occurs, the crucial link with bestiality is also forged. The tie is severed, yet it remains as the memory of a dangerous relation for the displaced creature. Thus man cannot renounce the repetitive compulsion to tell the story of that constitutive separation. The relationship between man and animal might, in fact, oscillate between the degree of the *nearest* and that of the *same,* if this extraordinary creature did not persist in representing himself as an irreversible and immeasurable rift from the animal. So that the specific differences attributed to the sphere of the logos, techne, and the polis—insofar as these are specific to mankind—are increasingly exalted within the symbolic game of self-representation, while affinities with the animal are reserved for a more ambiguous end. Just as man begins to detach himself from the animal state and establish what he considers an unbridgeable distance, the resemblances seem to reappear, urged on by the very pulsing of the body. It is as if the ancient story of man's continuity with the animal were conserved within the biological memory of the soma, a history that he either does not recall or is afraid to narrate, except through rites of initiation that confirm and mimic the separation.

34

Between the human and the animal, continuity and separation are the decisive terms of a dilemma that seems to have two solutions for the Greeks (Dierauer 1977; Sassi 1988, 46–53). One, theorized by Aristotle, joins them without excessive uneasiness. It inscribes humans and animals within a proximity of genera and a specific difference guaranteed by the logos and by the political nature of man. The other solution, often present in myths and in tragedy, seems instead to fear human-animal continuity or even mixtures, represented as memories of a disturbing origin not lacking in its own seductive features. In this more ancient context, theriomorphic images and figural combinations—the Sphinx, the centaur, the Sirens—pose the problem of a continuity that is still a hybrid sharing and a separation reluctant to abandon its seductive return routes. In the distancing through which the logos, to the detriment of the soma, signals the immense leap of human difference, the soma shows that it is capable of maintaining myth on its side of the gap. It is as if the juxtaposition between the noetic soul and the animal body were unsatisfying; as if the body, in all its uncompromising bestiality, were still claiming its place of origin (Galimberti 1987, 86).

In the soma pulses the fundamental order of life and the paramount law of survival, narrated thousands of times in myth and rite through images of agriculture and especially of hunting. In the former, the earth's products become food, while within the latter the animal clashes with man in a murderous and reciprocal contest between carnivores. "Flesh devours and is devoured: that is its punishment" (Zambrano 1991, 158). The punishment is reserved especially for the human being "who calls indispensable only that which proceeds from the exaltation with which his flesh consumes flesh that, an instant before, was alive" (Zambrano 1991, 158). In hunting, this link between food and death is indissoluble, and each predator runs the risk of becoming the prey of another. The war with animals, obsessively recounted by myth, is in fact also a war for sustenance. The fact that hunters and prey are both carnivorous food cannot help recalling the concept of sameness; and the human bodily resemblance to slaughtered prey that offers heart, innards, and warm blood to the predator's view cannot escape disturbing associations (Gilli 1988, 511–24; Burkert 1981, 34).

35

The awful contest between man and animal would, however, be unequal if man, who is utterly lacking in the natural gifts of the predator, were not aided by the "fraudulent trick" (*Antigone,* 346–47) of technology *(techne)*. By means of this trick, man makes up for his deficiency as the "not yet fixed" animal,[17] or rather as animal whose specialized survival instincts are by now lacking, and shows his ability to capture wild animals through cunning. This capacity does not, however, automatically cancel the terrible law that makes his own body appetizing prey for dogs, birds, and other beasts. The family or the polis must grant burial to the dead body, thus underlining through the culture of last rites the difference between humans and beasts.

It is precisely this culture, with all its terrifying prehistory, that forms the background of *Antigone*. For contrary emotive reasons, the cadaver arouses similar alimentary anguish in the minds of Antigone and Creon. The sister wishes to pluck the sweet treasure of Polynices' corpse from the "birds who gaze at it, hungry for a meal" (29–30), while the tyrant desires that "the dogs and birds devour the unrecognizable pile of limbs" (205–6). In this specular opposition we find a perfect image of alimentary anxiety, in negative and positive.

The horrible meal as symbolic emblem of the inhuman as extrapolitical applies, however, to Creon alone. It is only for the tyrant that there exists a distance between men and animals based on the anthropological foundation of the polis, while for Antigone, who is by definition *apolis,* the political sphere certainly cannot form that boundary. The horrible feasting on the body of Polynices is inhuman for her, but the intolerableness of this horrible spectacle marks for her neither the coincidence of the animal and the inhuman, nor a coincidence between the human and the political. We could even say that animality is as close to the corporeal universe represented by Antigone as it is far from the political order represented by Creon.

In this tragedy where, we recall, the warrior Polynices was earlier compared by the chorus to an eagle (112ff.), we find further evidence for the human-animal association in the "distinctly feminine tonality" (Steiner 1984, 226) of the names Sophocles gives to the birds cited in the chorus. But we see it most of all in

36

the metaphor used when Antigone, at the sight of her brother's body, "laments with the strident voice of an anguished bird at seeing the empty nest that has been robbed of its young" (423–25). The comparison is crucial in many ways. It evokes the nest with the word *lechos* (bed), thus setting up a paradoxical correspondence between the pain of a mother/bird who sees the nest emptied of its young and the pain of a woman/sister who sees no void, but rather the exposed body of her brother. She gains an *empty* marriage bed, without children, because of her decision to bury that body.

Beyond the traditionally recognized mythical female figures with the heads of birds, there is, therefore, in the relationship of Antigone to the animal world, a complex ambivalence that seems to push the system of bodily imagery to its profoundest depths. Here, indeed, carnivorous diet, incest, and cannibalism pile up in a swift allusive series. A distant, animal origin becomes human prehistory, while a woman's body once again conveys the terror of that past. At the same time, the complex image challenges that limit (so often represented in literature) at which "the possibility of metamorphosis is located" (Lacan 1986, 308).[18] In Greek myth and rite, moreover, the figure of the virgin appears to belong to the sphere of the "uncivilized." One example is the imitation of the she-bear by the Athenian girls in honor of Artemis, or else in honor of that virgin huntress, the "Mistress of the beasts" (Vernant 1981, 18ff.) whose story breaks out of its Greek confines to spread throughout Europe, narrating, in various guises, a fearsome and unpolitical link between women and bestiality. This link raises the specter of incest and cannibalism, often present in revelatory, nocturnal dreams (Vermeule 1979, 46; Ginzburg 1989, 105).

Within Antigone's language the animal is extraordinarily present, especially in the image of birds, which conveys the twin stories of a desperate, maternal cry and the horrible meal of fraternal flesh. The noted ancient custom of burying only the bones of the dead, after having offered the body to the beaks of rapacious birds who tear off the flesh, reinforces the tragedy's obsession with burial (Vermeule 1979, 46).

The dramatic absoluteness of a body that evokes female generative potency thus broadens through the allusion to animal origins implied by that potency. And thus we can perhaps appreciate another reason for the disconcerting exceptionality of Antigone, which has led minds over two millennia to elaborate an infinite number of interpretations. Antigone is an *archaic* tragedy in the literal sense: a tragedy of the *arche*. It is a tragedy that speaks of the origin of man, in his quality of separateness from the other animal species. *Antigone's* narrative depends on two equally frightening hypotheses. The first alludes to the terrible aspects of the female, a naked life, a wild corporeity and carnal profundity that prevents the self from becoming the singular destiny and conscious aim of its own existence. The second, instead, contemplates the terrible aspects of the male and the separation from and command of the animal by means of intelligence and technology; in this hypothesis the individual remains controlled by the consciousness and anticipation of death (*Antigone,* 360–62). Thus if the female, in orienting toward birth, risks entrapping her potential subjectivity within the fetters of a paralyzing maternal figure, the male, in looking toward mortality, founds his sense of self upon death itself.

Between technological pride and the uncertain nostalgia for an absolute elsewhere, the human species in *Antigone* ponders itself on the crucial threshold between the animal and the human: no longer animal, yet no more than animal. Not that Sophocles hesitates in figuring the missing link between man and beast in terms of the feminine and the corporeal. Still, the ancient text is inclined, even from its already logocentric perspective, to question its own political foundation and to recount all its political obsessions.

### Dike

Creon "has ordered that no one should fall onto the tomb, nor weep over Polynices' pitiful body. . . . Whoever does either one will be publicly stoned to death" (360–62). This is the ban (*kerygma*) that the tyrant will alter to punish Antigone, ordering that she be buried alive, sealed inside a rocky cave.

The harshness of the sanction is due to the tragic antithesis between the two laws embodied by Antigone and Creon, both perfectly ready to apply them with equal severity. On one hand, we have the proclamation of the Theban lord, thus a political law, and on the other, we have a much more ancient law dictating that the girl must bury her brother. On the legal horizon of Antigone, who by definition is *apolis,* only divine and infallible *unwritten laws* are valid: those set down by Dike "who lives with the subterranean gods" (451).

This is not the Dike in charge of human tribunals, who is perforce absent from the judgment of this tragically unsolvable dispute, but the primordial Dike who is inscribed in the eternity of all things, before time and the polis. Or perhaps this is the Dike of the underworld, custodian of family relations; but also the mortuary Dike, figured on funerary urns, who ensures the dead their entry into a proper final dwelling. Antigone calls on this latter Dike, trusting in the goddess's role as divine arbiter between the realms of the living and the dead.

The goddess had already symbolized in more ancient philosophical tradition the insurmountable separation between the opposing regions that make up the order of the cosmos, as with the Dike of Parmenides, who stands on the threshold between Night and Day, or that of Heraclitus, who prevents the sun from straying out of orbit. Antigone, in fact, invokes the goddess who separates the light from darkness, in keeping with the decree entrusted to Dike, which prevents their union. But here it is not a question of the division between the sequence of dawns and twilights, but the more radical boundary between what is *above* the earth and that which, instead, lies *underneath,* separating the reign of the dead from that of the living according to a distinct cosmic order, whose laws are trampled upon by Creon.

Tragically, Creon violates precisely this order by denying to the dead the dark womb of the earth, and to the living the light of the sun. His actions throw the cosmic order into an extraordinary reversal that demands, and in the end obtains, justice, *dike.* Stoning, in fact, would not have sufficed to effect that perfect, specular reversal we see in a dead brother who remains unburied among the living, and an Antigone, still alive but buried with the dead. The exchange of darkness and light, of exposed corpses and hidden living bodies, is staged perfectly. Dike, once invoked, cannot but restore balance.

39

The wise Tiresias's accusation of Creon is specific: "You have thrown a living being under the earth, and have undeservedly housed one who breathes *(psychen)* in a tomb. What is more, you keep here a corpse, unburied, separated from the gods and without funeral rites" *(Antigone,* 1068–71). And the punishment that Dike, as protector of the border between the two realms, reserves for him is equally precise: "Not many days will pass before you give up a corpse born of your loins in exchange for other dead" (1064–67). What the blind Tiresias sees and foresees comes fully to pass. For in the end, Antigone, having already been preventively entombed, dies by her own hand, hanging herself, while Polynices gains burial by the tardily repentant Creon. Once they are both interred, the scandal of a living human prematurely buried and a dead man left unburied is finally resolved. And yet their resolution also bears out the prophecy, for Creon's son Haemon commits suicide out of love for Antigone, a deed that drags the mother, Eurydice, along with it. "Your children's murderer" (1305) is her curse on her husband. The tyrant's *hybris* has set in motion the series of the deaths of kin, a fateful chain of actions and reactions whose internal logic becomes clear only at the end of the tragedy.

Dike can only punish those who have forbidden the burial of family members with the deaths of other kin. The body, as the law of blood, once again takes center stage, triggering the inevitable and essentially unpolitical punishments of the tyrant. Creon, who from the beginning declares that he will not hold in regard the "strict blood ties" (486) that link him to Antigone, daughter of his sister Jocasta, ends up stricken by precisely those ever-more-binding blood ties that link him to his son, dead by suicide. And having shut up within the underground dwelling of the dead a still-breathing woman, he wanders about in the end "like a breathing corpse" *(empsykon nekron)* among the dead bodies born of his loins (1167). Meanwhile nothing at all has happened to the polis: Creon is in the end lord of Thebes, as before, the others having made no move to rebel or usurp his role.

What emerges from a drama that requites the arrogance of power not with the overturning of the political order but with the deaths of kin, is therefore something that transcends critical approaches focusing on the democratic challenge to tyranny (although the mask of Haemon lends itself to this interpretation). Nor will readings that accentuate the ritual context of funereal pietas in the customs of the time suffice. From the beginning, it was a body that commanded the drama's attention. A corpse to bury has driven the tragic action, and in the end it is buried. This is the only unequivocal message of the play.

In a way, the entire tragic action has thus revolved around the ineluctability of a proper burial. This burial was first attempted by the dead man's sister, and then granted by the polis in compliance with Dike, who stands at the threshold between the reigns of the living and the dead. In the inevitable cadence between living and dying written into our destiny as fleshly beings, it is Dike who grants us our place. She is inflexible; and having established her order with a typically tragic indifference to human pain, she draws even the innocent—and especially those who have called on her—into her logic of justice. As Antigone goes toward her lonely death, without friends or human pity, she laments the absence of divine intervention, which might deliver her from her suffering. But the ego that here dies in total isolation—that ego which, significantly, is revealed to itself in being severed from the symbiotic body and in the experience of solitary suffering—is a self alien to both the living and the dead (*Antigone*, 853). It lacks the human solidarity of its own kind and is deprived of consoling gods.

Antigone, as a tragic mask of the self, is indeed a stranger (*metoikos*) to every given order. Alien, indeed antithetical, to the political order of men, she is also, in the isolated suffering that reveals her uniqueness, alien to that symbiotic order of the maternal body from which she is now torn. So that her mask, more enigmatic than any other in this tragedy that bears her name, finally oscillates between the maternal demand for self-sacrifice and the retreat of the gods, on a stage where the birth of the self is experienced as an unmourned sacrifice.

### The Enemy Body

Antigone and Creon, the female and male principles. Hegel's decisive footsteps have once again shown the way. Typically for

Hegel, the path is extremely complex, because the two principles are also expressed by means of the sexed binomial of sister and brother. According to Hegel, this is a pure relationship, in which a shared blood has gained its calm and equilibrium (1963, 16). This despite the fact that the sister, as a woman, is destined to remain within the sphere of the family, while the brother, as a man, abandons "that ethical nature of the family which is *immediate and elementary*" (Hegel 1963, 18) and passes into the universality of the political sphere. In short, the woman stays home and the man becomes a citizen, in ontological consistency with the female and male principles.

Creon and Polynices (at least while the latter is alive) are therefore on the same side of that symbolic patriarchal order which assigns a domestic domain to women, and a higher and more humanly progressive, political sphere to men, as Aristotle illustrates with inimitable clarity.

Here we are not yet in the vicinity of the orderly Aristotelian doctrine, but rather inside the multithreaded plot and sovereign ambiguity of tragedy. Here, where the already dead Polynices invades the scene only as a body emblematically kept offstage, it is Creon, above all, who most embodies the union between male identity and political identity *against* the unpolitical nature of the other sex. The misogynist notes in his speeches are frequent and obvious, especially if compared with Antigone's position. Antigone, for her part, does not seem at all concerned with proclaiming her sexual identity, almost as if it were already inscribed naturally within that consanguineous horizon, of maternal origin, which strengthens her resolve. Such is not the case, however, with her sister Ismene, who, from the start, accepts the traditional female condition of inferiority and impotence attributed to women by the patriarchal order. In her own words: "Remember we are women [*gynaich hoti ephymen*], we're not born to contend with men. Then too, we're underlings, ruled by much stronger hands, so we must submit in this, and things still worse. I, for one, I'll beg the dead to forgive me—I'm forced, I have no choice—I must obey the ones who stand in power" (61–67). Antigone restricts her response to this argument to a simple reference to the dead of their blood kin, to whose precept of love her gestures are meant to respond.

42

Antigone is, of course, not unaware that she was *born* a woman, because, aside from her sexing as a female, which is read within the social order as the determination of her subordinate role, her action arises precisely from the fact that she was born of a mother's womb. For her, in fact, the significance of being born a woman, and that of being born *of* a woman, are linked by the symbolic code of the generative female body.[19] These facts also link her, with ties stronger than blood, to that brother she buries precisely because they share the same mother. She acts in spite of the polis and outside the preestablished representation of a womanhood whose foundation she locates elsewhere, and which needs no further public confirmation.

On the other hand, Creon's emphasis on male identity is obsessive and insistent (Lanza 1977, 52). At the attempted burial of Polynices he exclaims: "Who among men *(andron)* has dared do this?" To Creon, transgression of his orders is possible only by a male and must be interpreted as a political act. It is in direct conflict with Antigone, however, that the tyrant's words begin to dwell insistently on the political basis of male identity. He repeats over and over his speech concerning sexual difference, in which the roles are as rigidly opposed as they are prone to frightening reversals. "If she can thus flout authority unpunished, I am woman, she the man. . . . No woman will be master while I live," the Theban lord exclaims (484–85, 525). Creon's speeches are markedly misogynistic as he warns his son, Haemon, of the corrupt pleasure that comes from a woman and from the cold embraces of an evil woman, invoking with monotonous regularity the dishonor of letting oneself be overcome by a woman, of submitting to a woman, and so on. A single refrain runs throughout his diatribes: a man who submits to a woman is ignoble (746), because he abandons the human dignity of his superior, and thus political, male sex. Haemon, however, parries this paternal accusation that he is "fighting for a woman" by saying: "If you are a woman, yes—since my concern is all for you" (741; translation slightly altered). The conflict between father and son—which can also be read politically as a conflict between tyranny and democracy—takes as its rhetorical figure the reciprocal accusation of behaving like a woman. It thus betrays a sort of male fear of becoming female, the anguish of doubtful virility. That virility is hence constrained to affirm itself obsessively against its tendency toward the feminine (Loraux 1991, vii et seq.). The greater the feeling of risk, the more the political citadel upon which masculine identity is founded must be reinvigorated with the vital tonic of misogyny.

In addition, it seems here that none of the classic fundamentals of the conceptual horizon of the polis are lacking. The political distinction between *friend* and *enemy,* crucial to Creon, is especially present. Eteocles is a friend and Polynices is an enemy. This discrimination is something that transcends the time and place of the Theban battle, concretizing itself in the two corpses and consigning them to opposite destinies.

With the binomial friend/enemy, we are, in fact, as Carl Schmitt points out, in the presence of the political sphere par excellence. In this sphere, however, the opposition between friend and enemy is only apparent, because the binomial is completely weighted toward the enemy and, in great part, toward the real possibility of war that the opposition presupposes (Schmitt 1972, 101–65). Nothing makes the foundational role of war more apparent than the centrality of the idea of the enemy. This is all the more the case in Greece, where citizen and warrior coexist in one, homogeneous concept (Vernant 1981, 32ff.). The notion of the friend plays a wholly secondary, if indispensable, role.

The history of the political may also be told through the history of the notion of the enemy, a notion that every age elaborates and expresses according to its own particular perspectives. If epistemologically framing the term *politics* around war is characteristic of the ancient world, the term *enemy* and the semantic field surrounding it may also be shown to be equally representative. As Carl Schmitt explains, in Greece we find in fact a distinction between the term *echthros* and *polemios,* conserved in Latin in the words *inimicus* and *hostis,* which modern languages have lost. Those ancient tongues entrusted to two separate words the distinction between internal and external enemy, on which Plato expounds in detail in a celebrated passage of the *Republic* (469d–471a). The argumentative context within the dialogue is importantly the burial reserved for soldiers fallen in battle. This becomes an excellent occasion for Socrates to ponder the notion of "enemy" through an examination of the terminology for denoting hostility. He does this after advising that the city bury its dead with honors and also allow the burial of the enemy without any plunder of their corpses. The Socratic discourse distinguishes between two types of conflict, to which correspond the two meanings of the word *enemy*. There is the internal fight or civil war *(stasis)*, in which the enemy takes the name of *echthros*, and the external conflict *(polemos)*, in which the enemy is instead called *polemios*. The lexical pair *stasis/ echthros*, therefore, points to the meaning of an internal conflict between men of the same community, while the pair *polemos/ polemios* indicates war against strangers and foreigners (*Republic*, 470b).[20]

Socrates' philological precision functions above all as a condemnation of the internal struggles and hostilities between fellow citizens. The distinction between *echthros* and *polemios* does not, however, translate into different attitudes toward the corpses left on the battlefield. It would thus appear that Socrates takes Antigone's side against Creon. This is a bit more than simple literary fancy: Socrates' speech concerning the burial of the bodies of the enemy, in fact, fits so perfectly with our reading of *Antigone*, that it seems to be a specific commentary. This hypothesis—or rather this possible use of the text by the interpreter—is supported by the fact that certain parts of Plato's analysis seem to be implicit allusions to *Antigone*.

It is curious, to say the least, that when Socrates refers to the "plunder of the corpses and the placing of obstacles to the burial of the enemy" (*Republic*, 469e), he declares, "To consider the corpse of the enemy *polemios* is worthy only of a woman or those with wretched natures, because the *echthros* has by now left it. That with which the *echthros* fought is all that remains." It bears noting that in this statement Plato plays with the term *polemios*. To a Greek ear the meaning of the term is something like "belligerent" or "warlike": that which wages war. It is precisely against this meaning of *polemios* that Plato, by distinguishing *polemios* from *echthros*, elaborates his theoretical position (Centanni 1992). The point, however, is that in this page of the *Republic* the possible allusions to *Antigone* are recognizable in two strange turns of argument.

The first has to do with the fact that Socrates calls defining the body (instead of the soul) as enemy an attitude "worthy of a woman." From this it would logically follow that to deny burial to the enemy's corpse would be a piece of female obstinacy, when tradition has it that this atrocious custom is typically male. In fact women are not infrequently represented as *supplicants* for the honor of burial to the dead. So that, leaving aside the plausible hypothesis that "worthy of a woman" has value simply as a generic term denoting stupidity, the reversal of traditionally masculine and feminine attributes may allude here to the accusation of "behaving like a woman" that Creon and Haemon make to each other in *Antigone*. The indictment seems to upset especially Creon, the man who denies the enemy burial.

The second oddity in Socrates' analysis is even more intriguing. He suggests that, contrary to what women think, it is not the body that is inimical *(echthros)* but the enemy *(polemios)*, whose hostility is totally substantiated in his soul and whose body is only an instrument for fighting. Once again, an implicit allusion to *Antigone* is plausible. In fact, Creon reserves for Polynices the term *echthros*, even when Polynices is already a stinking corpse. The term fits perfectly with Plato's philology, since the *echthros* is nothing other than a friend, of one's same group *(sungenes)* and familiar *(oikeion)* by nature, who subsequently transforms into an enemy. This is just what happens to Polynices. He is indeed *oikeion* and *sungenes* to Creon, being of the same blood, since he is the son of Creon's sister Jocasta. All the more reason for the name of *echthros:* an internal enemy, extreme symbol of an internecine struggle played out in the fratricide of a common, incestuous blood.

Even if all these possible allusions were unintentional, Plato's text would remain a sort of perfect and synthetic definition of the criterion guiding Creon's actions. This criterion judges the dead *body* to be the *enemy*, considering it not as a mere envelope of muscle and flesh by means of which the enemy fought while alive, but as possessing an untranscendable corporeal individuality to which the definition of "enemy" clings utterly, whether the body is dead or alive. "An enemy can never be a friend, not even when he is dead" (*Antigone,* 522; translation altered), the tyrant exclaims. For Creon, being an enemy to the polis has little to do with the one who fought by means of the body and who by now has gone elsewhere, leaving on the battlefield only his lifeless and unpolitical corpse, as Socrates would have it. The body itself *is* the enemy, insofar as it substantiates all the enemy's reality.

Our recourse to Platonic philology has been valuable. We can now see how a body that already commands the stage also comes to contaminate Creon's political language, forcing onto it a carnal theme. This is rendered possible by the absence of a psyche separate from the body, or rather of a psyche that, according to a tradition already established in Sophocles' time, laid claim to being the true seat of a subjectivity that could be labeled enemy. Within that tradition, the body figured as a mere material envelope, devoid of any political quality whatsoever: neither friend, nor enemy. The Platonic distinction between the psyche and the soma means, for all intents and purposes, just this: that only the soul may be the principle of action. Of that which may properly be defined as political action for or against someone, the body is a mere instrument. The Sophoclean horizon, in contrast, remarkably lacks this distinction and impels Creon to regard the body itself as the active protagonist, thus to attribute to it those political qualities that even the corpse, as individual body, preserves. Both in theory and in fact, the enemy appears as pure body: a body that takes sides against the bodies of co-citizens, a warring body, a body that kills and is killed: *body politic* in a direct, rather than metaphorical, sense. No distance separates the immaterial soul, where the mind and therefore the political function resides, from the carnality of existence. In fact, this existence is so carnal that it is narrated in consanguineous events that render the enemy even more internal, construing politics to linger this side of its decisive foundation upon the concept of the external enemy, this side of the politics Plato had already illustrated and that legitimated itself in the rightness of war against the *polemios,* the external enemy.

If it is true that political history as traditionally represented is founded on the binomial *philos/polemios,* the more painful and thus more tragic conflict is inscribed in the binomial *philos/echthros*. Sophocles places this opposition on stage, stressing its meaning within a sphere of incestuous blood. This sphere endows the concept of *echthros* with all the radically corporeal elements woven into the concept of *philos*, thus making the enemy consanguineous in the same way that the friend is supposed to be. Hence the play confirms the unbalanced system it owes to the centrality of the body: the corporeal universe of Antigone overwhelms Creon's law and shows that the conflict between the two protagonists is not at all balanced by a symmetry that the tyrant claims exists (*Antigone*, 387). It forces politics, or at least the lexical foundation of politics, to compete on a field not its own.

If in Antigone's case the ambiguity of the tragic depends on an affirmation of the self whose action is necessitated by symbiotic flesh, in Creon's instance ambiguities multiply around a body that carries a double connotation. It is unpolitical, even antipolitical in its mythical, symbolic suction into a prelogical abyss of animal and female potencies. It is political, however, insofar as it is the sole, true locus of the notion of the enemy. Thus the body not only throws the scene out of kilter when it reappears before Creon in the form of a consanguineous corpse; it also saturates the political lexicon, including its founding category of enemy, with its bloody substance. The politics that banishes the body from within its walls speaks indeed, from beginning to end, only in the grammar of the body.

The *philia* of incestuous kinships, represented by the mask of Antigone, predetermines the symbolic terrain of battle between the tyrant and the maiden. The terms *friendship* and *love* are inadequate translations of this *philia*, since they are too weak to recall the symbiotic tie transmitted by maternal blood, which roots the incestuous closure of family relation in the original meaning of *philos* as "one's own" and "his/hers" (Vernant and Vidal-Naquet 1976–91, 1:77; Lanza 1977, 243–47). If, in fact, Eteocles is *philos* for Creon, because Eteocles comes to the defense of Thebes, Eteocles is *philos* for Antigone also, whatever side he takes (and despite his being the champion of an arrogant misogyny in another drama of Aeschylus's).[21] Eteocles is *philos* for An-

tigone in a different and openly carnal sense, however, in which
he is on the same level as Polynices, "brother, by the same
mother, the same father" (*Antigone,* 513). They belong to the
same *philia* that political events may perturb in earthly life, but
that death re-equilibrates in Hades (519). The contrast between
polis and *genos* also implies incommunicability between, on the
one hand, the changing seasons of one who was "first" friend and
"then" becomes an enemy, and on the other, the atemporality of
the uterus as the time of the "always" preserved by death.[22]

Antigone pits the *philos* against the *echthros,* rendering only
the former term absolute. In so doing, she severs the political
binomial *philos/echthros:* "My nature is for mutual love *(sun-
philein),* not hate *(sunechthein)*" (523). This celebrated statement
splits the single, bipolar concept friend/enemy (which had been,
moreover, weighted on the side of the enemy), and at the same
time it affirms *philia* as a symbiotic union that knows no opposite. Friendship "according to nature" and based on ties of
kinship is for Plato unnaturally disrupted by the emergence of
the internal enemy. It is radicalized in *Antigone* by means of an
incestuous consanguinity whose cohesive power is so strong
that it allows no reversal. Precisely this is the female principle of
Sophocles' play: an unpolitical *philia,* inscribed within maternal
generation, which neither contemplates nor recognizes its contrary. It is the principle of an absolute and unconditional bond in
which brothers, because they are loved by the sister out of love
for the mother, exist only as objects and not subjects of the
*philein:* of the same blood, the same mother and father, brothers
who kill each other as enemies by the Theban walls. This death
observes the political criterion of *philos/echthros,* for which there
is no better figuration than simultaneous and mutual fratricide.

### Blood

As George Steiner has written, "Antigone speaks, literally as it
were, 'out of the womb,' out of a timeless centrality of carnal
impulse" (1984, 185). It is a voice that certainly comes from the
inside, from a bodily depth within whose incestuous abyss the
blood pulses as an elementary trace of life. It is a blood that, as
the last, absolute cipher of the already absolute horizon of the

body, obviously links men and women, but that Sophocles assigns differently to the one and the other.

Male blood reddens the sword: blood spilled, life in exit, death by cutting. Although they are both born incestuously of the same mother, Eteocles and Polynices are on this violent side of the horizon, brothers who kill each other in battle. They fall together in a puddle of their "same blood," in a sort of reciprocal suicide that frames the masculine political principle in red death. Antigone stands, instead, on the other side: on the feminine side in which the horizon of blood is a symbiotic substance of maternal origin. For this reason its direct offspring are lovingly preserved and cared for by her, even if they are now corpses. The antinomy is clear: blood spilled and scattered in the name of a masculine principle; blood saved and transmitted in the name of a feminine principle. Or a blood that, when spilled, dries into arabesques of death but that, when inside the body, pulsates and flows with life, almost suggesting a game of contrasts between the deadly symbolic system of the phallus and the natal code of the *omphalos* (Bronfen 1992a, 145–58). Or between bloody male violence and the maternal sign of the navel, even if here the mask of Haemon seems to be a tragic mediatory figure.

The name of Creon's son, in fact, recalls the etymology of the word *blood* (*haima*). Haemon virilely kills himself by sword and embraces for the last time the corpse of Antigone, whose feminine suicide was a bloodless hanging (Loraux 1988): "breathing hard, [Haemon] released a quick rush of blood, bright red on her cheek glistening white" (*Antigone,* 1238–39). Haemon has thus "brought this marriage to completion in the house of Hades" (1240–41), and with his blood has symbolically marked a deflowering that never took place. At the culmination of this tragic scene, male blood spilled by the sword substitutes for the trickle of female blood spilled during deflowering, as well as for the rhythmic spills that during the lunar cycle mark time in a generative body.

Furthermore, in a line once again notoriously difficult for translators, Ismene had presaged the tragedy's bloody code when she said that Antigone, in deciding to bury her brother, spoke "a word red and dark as purple" (20).[23] The difficulty of the translation lies in the adjective *kalchainousa,* modifying Antigone's term *(epos)*. *Kalchainousa* derives from *kalche,* a seashell from which a rich purple-red dye is extracted. The translation is problematic, but the sense seems clear: Antigone's very words are as dense and red as blood; and Ismene, in *hearing* them, *sees* the color. It is as if Antigone's words were reddening, in a sort of linguistic interpenetration of form and content. The unbridgeable distance between speech as expressive medium and its object is annulled, at the same time canceling the difference between hearing and seeing. The excess that characterizes the figure of Antigone is truly presented here as an extraordinary overabundance, within Sophocles' writing, of a corporeal substance that pervades language.

Tragedy's typical excess, like the insolubility of the problem it presents on the stage, seems in *Antigone* to be based upon a corporeal polysemy played out in the infinite modes of its possible figurations. The principal figure is surely the one accredited by myth: a body evoking unheard-of feminine and animal powers that come out of the past to arouse fear. Sophocles' text weaves a dense cloth of mythical legend, setting squarely in the present a series of problems that increase the weight of the undecidable and awaken distress about it.

One of these problems occurs in identifying the mask of Antigone with a free, responsible agent. This same mask must also announce the birth of a self still held back within a symbiotic, maternal body, a self that suffers its very formation as a sort of unbearable rending. It is, in fact, remarkable that such a painful declaration of individuality should choose to speak with the voice of a young woman. In this way, it alludes to the relation between mother and daughter, in which the latter ambiguously wavers between an all-encompassing maternal bond and a detachment that results in complete solitude. It also points, however, to a link between the generative body and the generation of a self: the riddle of all life that proceeds from woman.

The body as life, as pure existence of living beings, prior even to the soul's claim to reign therein, is in fact evoked by the tragedy in two different ways. The first way points to the body in its role of closest origin, for which each of us is a body of flesh and blood born of a mother, and soon to die in the horrible feast of the corpse. The second points to the body as the distant origin of the human species in its superindividual substance. And here the body is a chasm, opening onto prelogical bestiality and onto the uncanny that provokes fear in the long night of the mothers, persisting in both the nostalgia for a vital immediacy that has been irrecoverably lost and a fear that the animal will again take control. Finally, an analogous story seems to narrate the body as death in two versions. There is the death of someone with a specific name who ceases to dwell among the living and disappears into the darkness of the elsewhere; and the anguish of the corpse, which reminds the meat-eater of his "natural" role in the food chain common to beasts and men.

The figural weave is intricate; it makes the most of the ambiguity characteristic of tragedy, while at the same time it lends a dramatic order to this polysemy. The polysemy of the body is heaped onto the mask of Antigone, which is contrasted by the political mask of Creon. Creon's very name significantly contains the word for power *(kratos),* which here represents not the polis of those who, in the Athenian theater are the drama's spectators. *Kratos* here refers to a mythical prehistory that draws the polis as still involved in the struggle against the constitutive *otherness* of the body and of the female sex.

We have already seen how the political order in Greece is founded on a series of exclusions that are as drastic as they are destined to endure in history. In this context, *Antigone* tells a story whose reassuring outcome the public already knows and whose symbolism is already familiar. Yet the expulsion of the body and of the women from the city, so emphatically heightened by the monstrous aspect of what is banished, does not constitute the only feature of the narrative. The expulsion also points to all the problems inherent in a seductive alterity that the excluded themselves seem still capable of evoking. Nor is the narrative silent about an androcentric guilt that the polis, or at least its mythical tyrant, calls upon himself. The fact remains that, because Antigone stands on the side of a deeply flowing blood and the incestuous maternal body, she is the near equal of that formidable feminine nightmare of the Greeks represented by the Amazons. Even if here it is a question of a blood that, unlike the Amazon's fury, returns to the city and annihilates the tyrant's progeny, forcing his very words to follow the corporeal syntax of a language by now alien to politics. Creon, arrogant, misogynist, and vulgar, "monarch of the desert and slayer of sons," is in fact nothing in the end. His crime, punished by Dike, consists in having wished to keep the enemy body of a man outside the city and turn it into food for wild beasts. But it also consists of having banished the live body of a woman, so that the guilt of her atrocious and wicked burial would not fall upon the polis.

We, on the other hand, know that despite the tragedy and the iconic play of the drama's fictions, man's body will return very soon to politics, even if only as an image and by way of metaphor. It will return to illustrate with its figure—now inhabited, governed, and reshaped by a rational psyche—the political order itself. But the female body will never return to politics, not even as a figure, so deeply is it estranged from the city that chose to bury it alive. Perhaps, in utter coherence, this exclusion aims to shut out the historical destiny lying beyond the mythic threshold of the uncanny.

PLATO

## Psyche and Soma

In an etymological game in Plato's *Cratylus,* Socrates risks being "wiser than [he] ought to be" (399a), and attempts an analysis of the terms *psyche* and *soma.*

The tone of his discussion is willfully jocular. With some amusement, the analysis of the term *psyche* begins with a dutiful allusion to that Homeric "breath" which would indicate the soul as the source of the body's life, that which revives it (*anapsychon*). Pulmonary ventilation is also discussed in the *Timaeus,* in no less playful tones; but Socrates immediately if somewhat regretfully abandons this first, Homeric definition, which he judges too crude. The second attempt at the etymology of *psyche* is made in a more refined and speculative manner, and here Socrates enlists the aid of the philosopher Anaxagoras. His doctrine concerning the intelligence (nous) and the soul, "which contain and order nature," provides a precarious etymology,

53

which in the end produces an acceptable definition of *psyche* as that which maintains and orders the entire nature of the body (399d–400b).

Playful and frisky as it is, the quotation from Anaxagoras is not gratuitous, for a close link, if not the identity, between psyche and nous is at the heart of Plato's work. To this is added the directing function of the soul, significantly given the term *diakosmein.* This is a function inscribed not only in the nature of the body, but in the nature of everything, going so far as to permeate the entire cosmos. In short, the allusion to the doctrine of Anaxagoras is crucial, since it permits Socrates to indicate *soul, intelligence,* and *order* as terms that stand together and always refer to each other within a sphere of "natural" correspondences.

The etymological play is no less interesting when it comes to the term *soma.* Here, Socrates pays homage to the Orphic tradition. And here again, Plato delineates a horizon important to him and his work. The body is referred to throughout as *sema,* the tomb of the soul; while as *soma* it is its custodian, a natural carnal sheath that imprisons and safeguards the soul "until the penalty is paid" (400c; Goldschmidt 1982, 115–19): that is, until it has played out its time on earth. It is clear that the doctrine of metempsychosis serves here as background.

The etymological play in the *Cratylus* is, in fact, a game and is not meant to be taken too seriously. It is difficult to say, however, whether these games are ever casual in Plato. Especially here, where the running joke repeats themes that Plato elsewhere argues forcefully and presents solemnly. The notion of the soul as an ordering intelligence and the definition of the body as painful ballast are indeed inscribed within the great Athenian's philosophy. The merit of the *Cratylus,* with its light irony, lies in setting in relief the play concerning psyche and soma, the two perspectival facets of their problematic relationship. This relationship is characterized by a constitutive separateness, which diametrically opposes them in terms of substance and destination. But it also signifies a necessary, albeit temporary, connection: the dwelling of the soul within the *physis* of the body, its function as the giver of life and order.

At issue is the connection between an immortal soul and a mortal body that is, of course, temporary, and thus in many ways inessential and precarious. The discussion traces, however, a topography of corporeal location for that living human soul which dwells, precisely, *within* its body, at least for the duration of its sojourn on earth.

The doctrine of the soul, or of what we may call Platonic psychology, is notoriously complex. In the first place, Plato speaks of a psyche divided into parts and functions, which are then given names as different kinds of soul. To say that the soul has three parts, or else that each man has three different souls, means nearly the same thing for Plato. In the second place, from the *Republic* to the *Timaeus,* the number of souls corresponding to that multipartite unity varies from three to four. The displacement of each part or species of soul into corresponding parts of the body is, in any case, suggested in the *Republic* and illustrated in the *Timaeus.*

Leaving aside the question of Plato's different versions of this psychology, which are interesting but secondary to our inquiry, the model is delineated with extreme clarity. It envisions a rational soul in a dominant and completely privileged position, situated in the head and capable of language and thought. Next comes an impulsive soul, the root of courage, anger, and like passions, which is located, instead, in the breast. Farther down, in the belly to be precise, is found an appetitive soul presiding over the elementary instincts. Thus the faculties of mind, the passions of the heart, and, in the lower belly, the sexual and nutritional instincts, each with a psyche, find precise bodily locations. In the *Timaeus,* a fourth soul is added, which is the result of the splitting of the third into nutritional and reproductive parts. This does not, however, invalidate the basic order of the tripartite model found in the *Republic,* which suggests precise correspondences between anatomical and psychological topography and thus figures the order of the soul through the image of the body.

In addition, it is well known that this model aims in the *Republic* to set up a far-reaching analogy between the parts of the soul and those of the polis, each type of soul corresponding to a precise class of citizens with specific functions within the whole order. Thus we see an extraordinary intersection among different analogical registers, all contributing to a single design in which the parts of the body, those of the soul, and those of the polis correspond with each other in more and less explicit figurations. The analogy between the soul and the polis is completely explicit, indeed constitutive. Much more problematic, on the other hand, is a bodily topography that seems to function only as a simple image for speaking of the soul, and which suggests, almost to the point of constituting a rhetoric, a material placement of the psyche into different parts of the body. Thus a significant problem emerges, which will be no small matter in future studies of political metaphor. It does appear that the analogy between the organization of the human organism and that of the state, which has been so important for political language in the Western world, may be attributed to the Greeks. But this analogy originates within a centralized discourse on the soul that greatly complicates its figural dynamics.

In short, within the history of the metaphor of the body politic and its Greek precedents, the question is whether one can already speak, in Plato, if not of an organological metaphor of the state, then at least of a comparison between the image of the body and the structure of the polis. The crucial aspect of the question regards the undoubtedly central role that the tripartite soul comes to play throughout the *Republic*. In that work, the placement of the soul within the body throws into relief a problematic image in which the body also functions with reference to the political order. The metaphorical framework is quite perplexing, because it already includes all the ingredients for an organological metaphor. But these ingredients are organized around the centrality of the soul, which seems to reduce the role of the body to that of an inessential, though rhetorically suggestive, space.

Thus we must linger a little longer to reflect on the relationship between the soul and the body, knowing that the problem does not lie with their different natures, nor with their temporary connection during a fleeting earthly sojourn. The problem is more subtle, and it turns on the ambiguous folds of a metaphorical discourse. That discourse resorts to bodily images in order to speak of the soul, all the while committing itself to precise topographical correspondences between psychology and anatomy. Indeed, given that in the *Republic* these correspondences remain secondary to the explicit analogical theorem serving to construct the order of the polis upon that of the soul, the analysis becomes still more complex.

In any case, the elements called into play are the following: the psyche, the soma, and the polis. The body's role, however, seems to oscillate notably between internal metaphorical inscription and external and upsetting threat. In other words, the body is the image upon which the psychological and political apparatus seeks confirmation. At the same time, it is that disquieting and nocturnal matter *against* which the apparatus builds its solar order.

### The Soul within the Body

In the *Republic* we read that the soul lives justly when the three parts of which it is composed—defined as the rational element (*logistikon*), the impulsive element (*epithymetikon*), and the appetitive element (*thymoeides*)—all perform their proper functions (*Republic*, 443c). Similarly, the polis lives according to justice when the three classes of which it is composed (the philosophers, the warriors, and the producers) each fulfills the duty proper to it. It is the duty of the rational part to govern (*archein*) the other two parts of the soul, as it is the duty of the philosophers to govern the other two classes in the city.

We know well that in the *Republic* Plato conceives of a perfect analogy between the order of the soul and the order of the polis. The analogy is so close and so explicit that it allows us to think of man as a polis in miniature and of the polis as a man on a grander scale, as reflected in the widespread image of the macroanthropos (*Republic*, 368e). Connected to that image is the justly celebrated image of the macrocosmos as the "beautiful order" that encompasses all correspondences. The interpreter's challenge is to find the starting point, that is, to decide whether it is the organization of the soul that serves as model for the polis, or the other way around, while for the time being allowing the cosmos to function merely as a framework.

The problem is easy to resolve, however (Cavarero 1988, 289–321). Plato hints at how we may do so when he has Socrates say that the correspondence of traits between the polis and "each of us" cannot avoid transmitting itself back from us to the polis (*Republic,* 435e). This is a necessary note, given the particular narrative sequence of the *Republic,* in which the buildup of the dialogue stages, as it were, an inversion. Socrates' query concerning justice revolves first around the polis, insofar as it is a larger and thus more visible phenomenon, and the analysis continues to delineate the model of the three classes (that model which places philosophers at the head of government), only then to recognize an analogous splitting of the just soul into three parts. At the end of this passage, however, Socrates decides to point to the soul itself as the true source of this model (as those characteristics present in "each of us" that are transmitted to the polis). Thus Plato undertakes a sort of reversal of the narrative logic that had begun by delineating the features of the polis.

This reversal is not at all surprising, for it is already inscribed in the historical and literary reality of the narrating subject. It was the philosopher Socrates, celebrated for his virtuous soul and capable of the most perfect justice, who constituted in discourse a model city that finally not only entrusts the functions of government to philosophers, but also names them "painters of constitutions" who aim to design a just polis (*Republic,* 500d). Such a polis is none other than the political model already sketched by Socrates, the design of a good and just philosopher.

In Plato's *Republic* we thus find a sort of narrative game, or a dramatic montage in which the final result is revealed to be the necessary premise. In other words, there is a sort of virtuous circle of argument that serves to confirm a single, basic concept: it is the philosopher who designs the just polis, at the same time installing himself at the head of its government. He can do this because he, alone among men, has put his own soul in good order, which can now serve as model for the political picture. That "each of us" was therefore a specific reference to Socrates and his wise interlocutors (who in the text are Plato's brothers).

So, in the end, the mechanics of this analogical construction are revealed: first comes the ordering of the soul, or rather the philosopher who has always tenaciously sought this order. He is the one who stubbornly bases the sense of his human existence upon the logos. None other than Plato, at bottom, lies under the usual Socratic garb.

Indeed, the *Republic* can be defined as the representation of an existential inquiry concerning the ordering of the soul (Voegelin 1986; Cavarero 1986). Plato stages this inquiry through the exemplum of the life of Socrates and narrates it in a language in which order itself and the philosopher's activity largely coincide. At the very least, these two dimensions establish a network of meanings that tend to order themselves within the same constellation of sense. This order—and thus the model, the hierarchies and the correspondences—becomes a sort of obsession. The more its foundations are threatened by an alarming disorder, the more stubbornly it is sought. Besides, this order, guaranteed by the control of the rational element over the other two, more disturbing, elements, is not found in all men, and not even in man in general, but only in the philosopher. Since the philosopher is the enterprise's only protagonist, he is thus the only one worthy to narrate it. This enterprise, woven from the double thread of the virtuous circle's narration, is essentially twofold: the philosopher who has identified himself with rationality not only has the task of governing this order, but also must govern this precise model of order that he himself has designed.

Beyond its particular narrative structure, the enterprise appears a pivotal moment in the history of ideas in the West. For the first time, the philosopher attempts to define human nature, causing it to spring from his own experience. This exercise of logocentric self-representation models the sense and the paradigm of the human species on the philosopher himself. That definition, which has been handed down to posterity in the Aristotelian formula of man as rational animal (*zoon logon hechon*) famously owes its origins to the central place of the philosopher in Greek classical culture and to Plato's "anthropology." There was, of course, a philosophical tradition before and after Plato concerned with glorifying the logos—suffice it to name Heraclitus, Parmenides, and Aristotle himself—but it is in Plato that this tradition finds its decisive moment. If this is not a turning point, it is at least an occasion for analysis and identification of the terms of the problem, terms entirely formulated *around* the unitary figure of the philosopher (and thus, ultimately, by Plato about himself) (Voegelin 1986, 155).

But what is the problem? The hardly insignificant one of defining the nature of man. This is the problem of uniting the manifold aspects of human experience into a precise order, or a coherent form, allowing them to be labeled and above all arranged into a unitary grouping that may define the peculiarity of *anthropos* as a species. The term *experience* must here be understood generically as life, sensation, desire, suffering, volition, thought, speech, memory, and a thousand other things that Homer had left as a free collection of features not to be consolidated into the unity of the self. Philosophy prevents us from listing these diverse experiences haphazardly; it places them within us at sites where they may be classified and ordered within a self represented as unitary. In the *Republic*, Plato calls those places parts or genera of the soul, and he decides that there are three, describing them in detail. Within his system of representation, the number of parts is not so important as their disciplinary hierarchy within a soul that is *one*, internally articulated into precise repositories of experience. These parts do not detract from, but rather confirm, the soul's unity.

Starting at the bottom, we find the part of the soul that is dominated by the appetitive principle. This part is associated with the pleasures and "makes the soul love, hunger, thirst, and feel the flutter and titillation of other desires" (*Republic,* 439d); it is by its very nature insatiable and deprived of reason (*alogon*). A little higher we find the part of the soul that has to do with the impulsive and passionate principle, the location of courage, of anger, and of all the movements of the heart. This faculty is, however, capable of forming an alliance with reason in order to counter the insatiable elementary appetites of the lower soul (*Republic,* 440c–441b). The third and highest position belongs to the rational part of the soul, called *logistikon*, because it is the principle of everything that has to do with discourse (logos).

This highest soul is also the site of thought, intelligence, memory, and the capacity to learn. And it is precisely this soul that exerts a centripetal, ordering force on the nature of *anthropos* and constructs a doctrine of "autonomous personality" out of the hierarchical arrangement of the human faculties (Havelock 1963, 203–4). Not by chance, this doctrine finds fulfillment in the *sophia*, the wisdom of the philo-soph (*Republic*, 485b–487a).

For Plato this model is crucial because it performs an ordering function, making "one from the many" parts of the articulated psychological figure (*Republic*, 443e). Just as it gathers together a multiplicity of potentially unrelated experiences in three parts of the soul—thus carrying out a preliminary simplification—it also disposes these same three parts into a single, structured order ruled by the rational part. The rational part "possesses within itself the knowledge of that which is suitable to each of the three parts and to the whole common to them" (*Republic*, 442c). *Rational* is a modern term that hinders our understanding here, because the Greek *logistikon* is the only term that can evoke the untranslatable multiple meanings of logos. Logos has the primary role, in its meaning as "discourse," in the narration-delineation of order, and, in its meaning as "reason," of control over that very order. *Logistikon,* moreover, is born to order (*Republic*, 444b), again in the untranslatable double meaning of the term "to order" *(archein),* which means both "to give order to," or put into ordered form, and "to give orders," that is, command or govern (Cavarero 1988, 290–93). These are meanings that effectively coincide in the operations of the *logistikon,* since it is this rational faculty that both determines and governs the order of the soul. Precisely in this way philosophers, in looking at the model present within their well-ordered souls, design and then govern the order of the polis.

This order, communicated from the soul to the city and found even in the shining vault of heaven, is established upon the prejudicial centrality of a logos that has proclaimed itself to be the system's author and lord, following from the philosopher's decision to base the definition of man upon himself. Not by chance, this logos is crucial to Platonic speculation and is cultivated there as a principle of self-discipline. In other words, to echo Foucault, the logos functions as a cardinal element of that "taking care of oneself" which constitutes the specifically Platonic form of technology for individual domination (Foucault 1988, 19–30). Looking at the order of ideas, and thus at the truth of discourse, the philosopher must "dispose well over what in the true sense of the word is properly his own," and having first "attained to self-mastery and beautiful order within himself," he harmonizes these three parts of his own soul, "as if to tune the three harmonics of a fundamental note" (*Republic,* 443d, translation slightly altered).

This splendid situation of balance, this technique for construction and domination of the self, however, dwells only within the philosopher. For only in the philosopher's soul does the rational part govern the other two, which tend to move independently and to disrupt the unity of the whole by establishing disorder. Indeed, the order of the soul is so strictly bound to that constant task of ordering and controlling the other two, for which the rational part is responsible, that an instant of neglect leads to total disorder. As Plato states, "the production of justice in the soul is to establish its principles in the natural relation of controlling and being controlled by one another, while injustice is to cause the one to rule or be ruled by the other contrary to nature" (*Republic,* 444d). Since justice had been defined as the carrying out of the task assigned to each, and since order in the soul projects one part whose task it is to govern and two others whose role will be to obey, everything falls into place. The interesting thing is that in order to illustrate his proposition, Plato makes an analogy between the body and the soul, equating justice with health and injustice with illness. Staying healthy is a matter of establishing "the elements in a body in the natural relation of dominating and being dominated by one another, while to cause disease is to bring it about that one rules or is ruled by the other contrary to nature" (*Republic,* 444d).

This analogy is valuable for a number of reasons. It points out that the body's disorder or illness is whatever ruins health and renders life impossible even when the body enjoys "all the food and drink and wealth and power in the world" (*Republic,* 445a); thus in the end the things of the body and those of the soul coincide (for instance eating to excess and giving vent to the appetitive soul that yearns for food). This placement of the soul at various bodily locations, which blurs into a kind of hybridization, leaves certain details in play, however, since the ordering function of the rational part does not correspond to any bodily location. In other words, the body itself lacks a vigilant and active internal principle of self-organization with which to regulate its own parts. This principle comes from the outside, from the medical doctor, who—in another set of analogies dear to Plato—orders the body, as the philosophers govern the city (*Republic,* 489b–c). The body and its good health, therefore, often serve in figural comparisons between the soul and the polis, but always with a certain degree of imprecision that interpreters cannot fail to notice.

The decisive fact, however, is that the soul's order is pictured as a hierarchical arrangement of parts that guarantees self-discipline. This applies both to the design itself, insofar as it defines human *nature,* and to the ordering role assigned to the rational part.

Self-discipline not only is possible, but also is part of the experience of whoever cultivates true philosophy. Yet it is anything but guaranteed, imperturbable, and definitive. The governance of the rational part over the others is not without problems, even for the philosopher who has constructed the definition of the tripartite soul that now defines man in general. The construction of the self, which here appears one and the same with the description of its own genesis, has as its goal self-domination. But a definitive domination of the self is by no means assured. The constitutive agonistic relations that characterize the three parts of the soul make it a space of conflicts. At stake are power and a strategy of domination that may be obtained only by continuously training the ruling part (Foucault 1991, 70–71). For this reason, the philosopher must always work to make the soul's *projected* order coincide with its order as *enacted.* The rational part governs only by constantly exercising itself: that is, by doing philosophy, contemplating the order of ideas through dialectic. It cannot relax the tension of permanent speculation, because impulses and desires press in, and if left

63

uncontrolled, they tend to establish disorder and injustice in the soul. Here injustice and disorder are synonymous, just as justice and order are. Over this very order a fearful disorder hovers as a constant threat, just as a nearly ineluctable fate of ruin hangs over the just polis.

Indeed, if order was sought in, and founded upon, a sort of self-examination inspired by the Socratic paideia, and if its maintenance involves continual exercise of the logos that sought and established it, then it is also the product of a never-definitive victory over disorder. This is so, even though order sets itself up as the judge of disorder and declares disorderly whatever goes against or escapes it. In the final analysis it is alogical things that are disorderly: the movements of those parts of the soul that tend by their nature to be involved in satisfying drives and appetites. They do this, however, *unnaturally* insofar as the *natural* is now defined as an order both structured and ruled by the logos.

## The Flesh's Nocturnal Memories

When examined close up, disorder has more than one face. It is not only the overturning of or the opposite of hard-won order. It is also that *against* which and *upon* which that order was won, a kind of frightening unnaturalness that man retains, however he may model himself philosophically. "There exists in each one of us, even in some reputed most respectable, a terrible *(deinon)*, fierce and lawless brood of desire" that reveals itself in sleep *(Republic,* 572b), when the rational faculty lets down its guard and the passions and instincts freely unleash themselves. Controllable, yet always latent, the appetites and pleasures "are awakened in sleep when the rest of the soul, the rational, gentle and dominant part, slumbers, but the beastly and savage part, replete with food and wine, gambols and, repelling sleep, endeavors to sally forth and satisfy its own instincts" *(Republic,* 571c). Then, Plato assures us, within dreams everyone lies with his own mother or anyone else, man, god, or beast, or kills in cold blood or stuffs himself with food and "in a word, falls short of no extreme of folly and shamelessness" *(Republic,* 571d).

In Plato also, therefore, the ancient, pre-Socratic categories of sleep and wakefulness signal once again the threshold between the rational and the arational. Thus the succession of sunsets marks a continuous risk of falling again into a realm of human experience preserved by the night. As myth and tragedy have recounted a thousand times, this is a realm that recognizes incest, unrestrained sexuality, the bloody act of murder, or reckless hunger as basic elements of living. It is also the realm of a prelogical animality preserved by the body and belonging, structurally, to the night. This coheres with the celebrated Platonic analogy between intelligence and sight, between the idea of goodness and the sun, which consigns the unintelligible to darkness. It also reflects the wakefulness of human life, which takes place in the light of day, interrupted by sleep in a frightening collapse of watchful, conscious thought. The body itself becomes protagonist at night: as hunger, sex, and impulses that by definition unbalance and tend toward excess. The body takes the name of the two lower souls on loan only, since it is the carnal site of the involuntary and the prelogical. We can call it the impulsive or appetitive soul, or whatever we like.

Since we are dealing here with a crucially early phase of the history of the unconscious, a phase that obviously predates any attempts to categorize it, it would be very easy to do a retroactive Freudian reading of Plato. We are looking at a moment when the philosopher's self-discipline, which is based on the centrality of the logos, chooses to cast itself as the result of a victory over the prelogical and as a continuous exercise of vigilance over the stubborn persistence of that realm. In this scenario, the prelogical is such because the logos cast itself as the end product of a process of humanization (thus as a victory over what preceded it). At the same time, the logos decided to draw the prelogical (as alogical and antilogical) into an order of the soul planned and upheld by its logical faculty, which remains perpetually on guard.

Importantly, the nightly unleashing of the passions and instincts takes place in everyone: even in the philosopher. In a way, more is at stake with the philosopher, because he is the designer and upholder of the order inevitably disturbed by the reign of sleep. The philosopher himself becomes the one who can least of all afford to be surprised at dusk, and thus "he goes to sleep after arousing his rational part and entertaining it with fair words and thoughts, and attaining to clear self-consciousness" (*Republic,* 571d).

In Plato, the philosopher and the tyrant are opposed, like order and disorder, like the government of the soul and the realm of the body. They correspond exactly to the excellent polis and its extreme degeneration. The *Republic* can thus also be read as the founding of philosophical order upon and against tyrannical disorder. This is a founding of philosophy against that disorder of the soul and the polis. Here a main role is played by the Sophists: those able charlatans who guide the appetites of the mob with false speeches, those wicked proponents of Socrates' death sentence.

Both the painful episode of the teacher forced by the Athenians to drink hemlock and the image of an Athens where supposed philosophers become accomplices to popular unreason are presented by Plato in terms of order and disorder. Order and disorder are assigned the technical terms *taxis* and *akosmia* or are sometimes contrasted as *logos* and *alogos*. They are also evoked in oppositions such as justice and injustice, the natural and unnatural, sight and blindness, night and day, sleep and wakefulness. These and a thousand other contrasting pairs in Plato all come to rest upon the basic opposition between the soul and the body, whatever multiple and ambiguous figurations this opposition may take.

The tripartite soul, formed and governed by the rational element, is not simply *found* within the body during earthly life. It is itself fundamentally corporeal, at least in its two arational parts. The soul is corporeal in the sense that Plato cannot help adopting a vocabulary of animality when he speaks of it. It is wild and feral, irresistibly prey to reproductive and alimentary impulses and obedient to a vital principle that by now appears prehuman. Dreams bear witness to this character, allowing the return of an animal-like corporeality (in phantasmatic images poignantly recalled during waking life, which can then predict and control them). This is a corporeality that craves food and sex in the frightful unruliness of boundless hunger and sexuality. Hence incest, which myth and tragedy have both narrated through

66

countless metaphors and figures, returns to populate the imagination of the rational and political animal constructed by Plato on the model of the philosopher. And along with incest, figures and metaphors crop up concerning a proximity of the animal to man. The logos is clearly the only faculty that can judge these figures to be transgressions of *its* law, having attributed to them a human bestiality that may have little to do with real and proper beasts. The issue, in fact, is not one of judging the bestiality of animals, but rather of reiterating the distance between the bestial, as immanently corporeal and thus prehuman, and that which is specific to man, who is defined by his exercise of the logos and his resultant political practice.

The order of the soul is thus an order of thought about the body, an order regarding the human capacity of the logos to guide our animal and bodily legacy. That legacy is confined to the night of the terrestrial day and the night of all time. In the darkness from whence it comes and within which it is preserved, it rises up when we lower our eyes in sleep. The soul's order claims to be proper to man and thus semidivine only in its rational part, however. The rational part represents itself as a kind of ordering superimposition on the two other parts that restlessly shift between bodily identity and animal figuration, populating dreams with monstrous forms. And yet symptomatically, dreams turn out to be neither unique nor sufficient for keeping within that shadowy region whatever escapes the daytime work of the intellect. We can thus easily see how Platonic discourse, in its celebrated ability to weave and reweave imagery, inevitably encounters its own obsessions at every turn. In the end it gives over even philosophy to trial by those corporeally originated monsters that still crowd its *internal* prehistory.

This happens, for instance, in a famous passage in the *Republic* where Socrates attempts to "fashion in our discourse a symbolic image of the soul" (588b). This image will enjoy considerable fortune in the development of political metaphor. An extraordinary fashioning of a hybrid figure, the image begins with common surface resemblances among humans and proceeds by internal transparencies, finally plunging itself into the animal and the monstrous. The soul described here by means of images in fact appears on the outside, in the form of a human body, but this is only a kind of envelope encasing a crazed lion and a terrible (*deinon*), multiheaded beast (*Republic*, 590a). Clearly the three creatures shaped here—man, lion, and monster—correspond to the rational, the impulsive, and the appetitive parts of the soul. But the interesting thing about the image, strictly as image (*eikon*), is its suggestion of a stratification that goes from the monstrous and bestial to the feral and animal, only to be encased in the human form. Though this last form is presented as capable of taming the beast it contains, it is also clear that it carries the beasts *inside itself*, since it serves as their body-shaped envelope. The human form then functions in the last analysis as the corporeal figure for a Platonic discourse on the soul that allows such beasts symptomatically to show through.

Also revealed in this transparency is the same secret that a certain lexical ambiguity had entrusted to the discourse on the psyche from the beginning. In that discourse, Plato not only locates the three souls inside the body, perhaps seduced by the body's natural potential to evoke images. He also gives the name *soul* to instincts, impulses, and appetites that are substantially corporeal in their material origins. These are able to survive in the flesh's opaque durability and to reawaken every night during the sleep of reason.

### The Figural Legacy of the Republic

If it is true that after Plato the tradition of political metaphor builds on the corporeal images he elaborated, it is also true that such images are neither simple nor univocal. They range from a minimal level, at which they seem to be used as a sort of rhetorical supplement to the efficacy of discourse, to a maximal level, where they appear to invade the design, throwing into relief its ambiguities and its forced elements.

In the *Republic* we find the corporeally localized, psychological framework that will later inspire the organological figure of the body politic, whose head dominates over its other parts. And we also find reference to the lionlike strength of what dwells in the breast, or the insatiability of what lives in the belly, which will be translated into the many positive and negative variants in this metaphorical system. What is certain is that the richness of metaphor in Plato and the extraordinary imaginativeness of his composition function as a copious reservoir of images, within which the soul, the body, and the polis appear to permit free play among many analogical variants. Excluded from this range of registers is neither the theriomorphic nor the monstrous.

Add to this a correspondence between medical and political knowledge, which Plato extends to the point of perfect specularity. Plato theorizes an internal and hierarchical arrangement of the body, thus innovating on the doctrines of the Hippocratic corpus (Vegetti 1983, 41–58). The discourse on the corporeal order called health and its designated opposite, disease, lends its language to the order of the soul and the political order. The organological metaphor will likewise draw from it, stealing from the doctors both the criterion of diagnosis and the wisdom of treatment.

Yet within Plato's legacy to the doctrines regarding the body politic there seems to be some error or perhaps a sort of paradox, especially if we consider that the organological metaphor violates Plato's declared intention to design the political order via the image of the soul and not that of the body. For Plato, in fact, the body is that against which the soul constructs its order. In the paradox of an inheritance utilized only for the corporeal features of its model, we find a kind of reversal game regarding the original figure. But this works, curiously, to unveil the mechanisms implicit in Plato's design. It is almost as if, looking beyond the letter of his discourse, the inheritors of Plato's political message recognized its bodily foundation, a foundation he sought to deny and remove, even as he betrayed its obsessive presence. It is in fact this obsessive presence that Platonic language makes visible in its ambiguous exchange between corporeal and spiritual imagery. As if the corporeal positioning of the psyche had led to a hybridization of its immaterial substance, and as if the body had invaded the representation of the soul. It thus seems to win out over the "logical" powers so keen on removing it.

From whichever side we look at it, Plato's representation of the *Republic* appears as a philosopher's self-disciplinary exercise that models the order of the polis upon his own logocentric psyche. But he is plagued by a corporeality that invades his figurative language. The invasion is so successful that subsequent political doctrines will base the metaphor of the state on the image of the body, in large measure twisting Plato's sense, yet at the same time revealing his underlying design in the symptoms of its unresolved ambiguities.

The problems in Plato may therefore now be formulated more precisely in terms that are more attentive to later uses of its figural legacy and already aware of that future. In short, given the return to the political sphere, through successive metaphorical development, of a body that politics itself seemed to wish to expel from its logocentric order, what other clues can be found in Platonic psychology (which formed that order) of an indisputable presence of the body? Or again, putting the question in its most basic terms: With the placement of the soul in the body (only alluded to in the *Republic,* but detailed in the *Timaeus*), does the soul itself stand in some more explicit relation of figural osmosis with the form of that body it vivifies and orders?

### The Timaeus: *Divine Shapers of Bodies*

Form, figure, structure, or whatever we wish to call it. No lexical precision is sought at this point in our investigation. We seek, rather, to approach the question with an open mind. Our only intent is to stress that the human body has a precise form, a given and observable figure that is, so to speak, objective. We speak of a head, a torso and limbs, which appear from the outside as a unitary image. Likewise, inside, there are the intestines, the liver, the heart, lungs, brain, and many other organs, as well as tendons, muscles, bones, and nerves: an articulated organism that Plato describes in an incomparable and delighted excursus in the *Timaeus.*

Indeed the *Timaeus* is another extraordinarily amusing dialogue, in addition to being a clear philosophical statement. It attempts to tell a "a probable tale" (29c–d)—almost a myth, narrated by the astronomer Timaeus—about the building of a living cosmos by a divine demiurge, who appears as a sort of supreme artisan manipulating an ideal model. Plato assumes it is obvious that the world here below, in the infinite varieties of its living forms and its starry sky, is a material, created copy of an immaterial and uncreated world that serves as model, just as he takes for granted that the model is structured upon ideas, that is, on the intelligible forms that may be contemplated by the true logos. But any obviousness ends here, because the epistemological coordinates within the design of the *Timaeus*—in the precise relation between ideal model and its generated copy and the material from which it is formed—are extremely complicated, difficult to decode, and indeed sometimes contradictory. The general system, however, is clear: a divine demiurge, who predates even the family of the heavenly gods, builds the visible cosmos, shaping its material according to the order of an intelligible, ungenerated, and eternal model to which he looks. Consistent with the Platonic principle of techne, the demiurge does not act freely but follows a model, a model already presupposed in the eternal perfection of its order and in the rules of its material translation, which operate through the demiurge (Cacciari 1990, 388).

The cosmos thus generated is, then, a unique, great, and perfect living being *(zoon)*, most importantly endowed with a soul *(psyche)*, intelligence *(nous)*, and then even a body *(soma)*. The soul is prior to and more ancient than the body, by generation and virtue, since it must govern the body. The body, mere subordinate material, owes obedience to it *(Timaeus,* 34c). Conceived as a whole that is then divided into parts, the living cosmos gathers in a unitary order all other living beings (30d). These are in turn divided into four groups: "one of them is the heavenly race of the gods; another, the race of the birds whose way is the air; the third, the watery species; and the fourth, the pedestrian and land creatures" (40a). The first is immortal and divine; the other three are mortal. Apart from the divine and immortal race dwelling in the heavens, the work of the demiurge corresponds, of course, to the world we inhabit, in all its many living species, which are, however, the final result of a constructive logic that begins with the whole and then forges internal articulations. All initiates from the soul, which is the invisible, vivifying, and ordering principle. The living species are given a visible bodily shape, to which the soul gives life. This logic is based in the analogy between the great living being and each single living copy contained by it, a logic guaranteed by the indubitable quality of the ideal cosmos that is taken as model.

Looking to this model and forging the world's soul first, the demiurge sets to work. But once he has created the immortal race of the gods, he does not completely finish his task. He decides to hand over to the gods the immortal soul of man, as well as the task of shaping the bodies in which the intelligent soul is "implanted by necessity" (*Timaeus,* 42a), but not without first pronouncing the "fatal laws" of the entire operation. The laws dictate that man, who clearly belongs to a terrestrial and pedestrian race, be generated as the most religious of living beings and as a double being through sexual difference. At the same time, "the superior gender has the name of male" (*aner;* translation slightly altered). These are fatal prescripts that unhesitatingly lay out the details of a future, patriarchal rule. They put the gods on guard against the violent sensations and passions that inevitably follow the birth of an immortal soul within a mortal body, or rather the original birth of the human prototype issuing directly from the hands of the gods.

Such passions take shape, however, not as irremediable disorder, but as passions that can be tamed by the soul, through its prescribed and just command over the body. Of course, the soul must show its aptitude for this domination and thus demonstrate its particular sort of excellence. If it were to fail at this, the soul would be shown to be incurably wicked and thus destined "at the second birth to pass into a woman, and if, when in that state of being, he did not desist from evil, he would be changed into some brute" (*Timaeus,* 42c). The condemnation of the *aner,* foreseen by law, to a diminished humanity in the inferior forms of woman or beast thus translates into a mysterious "second birth." For the moment let us put off the explanation of this mystery. It is already clear, however, that Plato is not referring to birth *by* woman, but the birth *of* woman. So far we have an initial birth of the human prototype, shaped by divine artistry, and a second birth of women (or beasts) that results from a malformation of the soul of the prototype. We must still wait patiently before hearing of the third birth, that *by* a mother.

Apart from its misogynistic tone, this discussion is interesting for the primeval situation that influences the divine shapers. They receive, on the one hand, a human, immortal, and rational soul, and on the other hand, a body that, although it is still not fixed in terms of organic shape, is inscribed with rules. One is the rule, rather curious in this early phase, of gender. Another is the unleashing of passion, which is the necessary result of the conjoining of the body with the soul, the mortal with the immortal. This unleashed passion comes to have an origin deeply immersed in the mixture of body and soul, an origin that prefigures the hybrid nature of a second (passionate) soul soon to take shape. The *Timaeus* does not offer a substantially different design of the soul from that of the *Republic,* at least in terms of what interests us here. In the end we still have a rational soul located in the head, a passionate soul located in the breast, and a nutritive soul located in the belly. To these a fourth soul is joined near the sexual organs, which controls reproduction.

Compared to the model of the *Republic,* the most important difference is not the increased number of souls, but the fact that four interconnected souls are preferred in the *Timaeus,* instead of the figure of an internal, articulated partition. The four souls in the *Timaeus* are not simply "described," which is basically what happens, at least on the narrative level, in the *Republic,* but are observed in the gods' process of shaping the human species. Their work is guided by rules, and they must heed the inescapable laws of the demiurge as well as the principle of analogy between the entire living cosmos and its parts. The starting point of their labor is especially significant: they begin with the rational soul forged by the demiurge himself, which is given already complete to his divine assistants.

In its basic terms, the operation thus consists of shaping a body that is capable, first of all, of joining with the given and unchangeable nature of the rational soul. The task is not simple, and it involves implicit, ineluctable consequences. The initial implanting of the immortal psyche in fleshly material indeed provokes disturbances that require the creation of an additional soul for the passions, to which yet another nutritive soul is joined, and lastly a fourth soul is added for reproduction. Both the anatomical and the psychological design are shaped during a sort of assembly process that advances by stages. The placement of the soul's parts within those of the body thus becomes a cogeneration of each, according to a clear figural osmosis that ultimately seems to be completely based on the body and determined by bodily functions. Souls thus become mortal precisely because they have been shaped along with the human fleshly forms. For in contrast to the first soul forged by the demiurge and endowed with intelligence and constitutive immortality, the other three souls in the *Timaeus* are mortal. The rational soul is in fact the only one that deserves the name of psyche (46d).

The gods' work follows clear laws. Since the generative logic begins from an immortal soul wrapped within a mortal body (*Timaeus*, 69c), the shaping of the human body obviously begins with the head (*kephale*). The gods must imitate the work of the demiurge, who built the world and "put the intelligence in the soul and the soul in the body" (30b). The carnal site of the intelligent soul is therefore the point of departure. In shape it is round, like the world, because only the form of the sphere, with its perfect proportions, could adequately envelop the intelligent soul. Thus the living human being, a terrestrial and pedestrian species nonetheless endowed with intelligence, receives his nice round head. And thus in Plato's account the "rational animal" earns the most comic role in his logocentric story, as an animal who is—at least for the moment—all brain.

This head, which is the first part to be shaped, brings about a curious paradox. It encases the intelligent soul and therefore commands (*Timaeus*, 45a) its servant, the whole body (44d). But in the first phase of creation it lacks a body to govern, for the rest of the body has not yet been created. The hypothesis of a self-sufficient head thus allows Plato to indulge in high comedy, ironically illustrating the reasons that urge the gods to continue their building. In fact he notes that the head's spherical form was an impediment to movement in that first era, since it was forced to roll over a surface full of holes and pitfalls. The gods then decided to provide it with the "vehicle" of the body, with legs and hands, so that it could get about more easily (44c).

At this point in the story, the body is merely a means of transport for the animated and intelligent head. The head already possesses a perfect human semblance, beginning with the eyes for sight. Plato's frequent analogy of the intelligible and the visible also plays a role in the genetic account of the *Timaeus*. Early on, the gods furnish this fleshly sphere housing the intelligent soul with eyes. These eyes are, in fact, its bodily instruments, since they endow it with a sense more suitable to its nature than any other. Because they can contemplate the cosmic intelligence in the starry heavens, they can help human intelligence imitate the divine order (47b–c) and thus observe the law of that unique and great living world to which man belongs. The *Timaeus* dwells on the well-known locus in Plato's philosophical vocabulary concerning the terminology of sight. In sum— and beyond the familiar inscriptions of Plato's terminology of vision—the *Timaeus* forges a truly strong connection between the rational soul and the head equipped with eyes. The connection is all the more interesting because the head and the eyes are here not a well-worn analogy, but rather the explicit, material, and corporeal seat of the intelligent soul. They are indeed still mortal flesh, but a flesh that the soul inhabits and shapes for its intellectual ends.

In addition to the spherical form as a sign of perfection and to the faculty of sight as a constituent metaphor for philosophizing, we find here the spatial coordinates of a decisive symbolic order founded on the body. The head is, indeed, the highest point of the body: it is located upon a vertical axis that stretches from high to low, from heaven to earth. The axis stretches upward in the direction of the divine, and downward toward bestiality and, as we shall see, femininity. The vertical axis then crosses a horizontal one that points forward and back, so that the face, and especially the eyes, are in "the front part of man . . . more honorable and more fit to command than the hinder part" (*Timaeus,* 45a–b). Clearly, an animal who walks erect, advancing forward, has a scale of values inscribed within the spatial coordinates of his corporeality.

So far we have a head that depends on the vehicle of the body: an intelligent soul, already provided with instruments of sense adapted to its task of *intelligere*, which uses the body underneath it only for movement. Man is a terrestrial and ambulating living being, so an apparatus for walking is needed; the figure of a walking head doesn't seem to suffice. A second soul is on its way from the divine artisans, this time mortal, placed in the breast, and surrounded by appropriate organs.

This is the passionate soul, whose formation has already been foreseen and which does not depend on a free decision of the industrious gods, but on their need to give form to the flow of disturbing passions that result from joining the immortal soul to the mortal body. These passions are called pleasure, pain, courage, fear, anger, and hope (*Timaeus,* 69d); they are characterized as being *suffered* by the living human being. Insofar as it is the cause and receptive vehicle of these disturbances, the corporeal element is thus decisive. It causes the nature of the second soul to be hybrid in two ways. First is that of its situation within the breast, near organs (from the heart to the lungs) created precisely to function as receptors and steadiers of the flow of passions (69e–70d) through a rhythmic ventilation. Even more important, however, is its internal substance: the passionate soul is, in fact, made of corporeal material; of spinal marrow, to be precise. It dwells in a specific location, reaching from the top of the neck to below the diaphragm and communicates with the superior soul by means of the very spinal marrow of which it is made. Such marrow is a genuine medium of transmission and as such is protected and channeled within the bony conduit of the spine. It lets the lower soul communicate with the overall system, from the outset centered on the first, immortal psyche. The marrow will push into the fourth reproductive soul as seminal fluid, thus becoming a sort of connection between the individual and the species (Foucault 1991, 135): that is, between the individual as mortal body and his ability to make himself immortal by reproducing himself in the species.

The gods' work is thus indeed complex. They must put together different sorts of souls in successive stages and build organs capable of housing them within the flesh, taking care to provide a means of communication among the combined parts. But beyond the complex work procedure and amused style in which its details are couched, it becomes clear in the course of the *Timaeus* that psychology and anatomy have a common basis, whose criterion is a figural osmosis between the psyche and the soma, and hence also the hybridizing of their substance. This criterion cannot help but be skewed toward the attractive powers of what has already been figured, a body organized into parts, organs, and functions, the observable and necessary result of the gods' labor. It is visible to every human being with eyes to see and tangible to anyone with a body.

The placing of the soul in the body and the process of shaping the body's flesh to serve the soul's needs are thus perfectly reversed. The absorptive process becomes ever more evident as the three inferior souls are drawn into the body's organic design. It reveals a logic that, more than incorporating, embodies and makes bodiful, transforming the psychologization of the body into an authentic somaticization of the soul (Vegetti 1992, 213).

This process is evident in the case of the passionate soul, but it becomes even clearer during the shaping of the third, nutritive soul to meet the entirely corporeal need for nutrition. We should not forget that the divinely directed birth described here is that of a "terrestrial and pedestrian" being. The element of life *(zen)*, inscribed within this living being *(zoon)*, should be of far greater importance than its capacity for terrestrial movement; but the latter has been granted a privileged place within the logical sequence of construction. Clearly the body, which at first extended below the head for purely vehicular ends, must now be shaped in relation to vital functions residing *within* it. These functions are identified primarily with nutrition and entrusted to the third soul, which is located in the "manger of the body" *(Timaeus,* 70e) between the diaphragm and the navel, near the liver. At this point, the only thing missing is a reproductive faculty to complete the design.

Curiously, the ability to reproduce comes last. It materializes in the last and lowest soul, which is almost a superfluous addition to the three types of soul thus far shaped. Timaeus in fact remarks several times *(Timaeus,* 89e) that the souls are three in number, according to the familiar tripartite model that entrusts both reproduction and nutrition to the third part. Plato's writing in the passage in question merits closer analysis, not only because of the differences with respect to the *Republic* and Timaeus's odd loss of memory regarding the number of souls, but especially because the bodily shaping of sexual differences at this point becomes necessary.

## The Gods Shape Sex

From the moment the fateful laws were pronounced by the demiurge, we knew that human beings would be differentiated as men and women. We also knew that, according to the same laws, the bodies of men incapable of living justly and controlling their passions by means of the rational soul would decay into those of women during a second birth. What we now discover at the technical moment of the two sexes' formation, however, adds considerable ambiguity to the primitive model. Now it is said that the gods work on the two different sex organs at the same time, making them compatible with each other. But it is also repeated that at the first birth, human beings are all men, who are fated to become women in a second birth if they turn out to be "cowards or lead unrighteous lives" (*Timaeus*, 90e). The origin of sexing into male and female thus takes place at two points in the narrative, within two different contexts. One version tells that it is simultaneous, another that it takes place over time, from first to second birth, as a feminizing degeneration of the male. The latter version appears much more significant if we take into account that the other mortal species, the animals, are also born of defective men. When men are "innocent and light-minded" they are changed into birds; when they are guided by animal passions they become mammals and reptiles; and the "most entirely senseless and ignorant of all" become fish (91d–92b). The criterion of degeneration from human to animal evolution is thus clear. It is equally clear that women occupy the first step of this descending series in which the perfection of the original male prototype is progressively destroyed (Sissa 1990, 75).

The ambiguous discussion of sexing in the *Timaeus* gives rise to the theory Aristotle brings to its logical conclusion: the passage from a body seen as substantially female in its prelogical and disorderly material, to a body disciplined by rational order, which takes the male as an original, universal prototype. This passage is crucial, because here the male form of corporeality fully regains the sphere of intelligibility, while the female body, which was previously seen as the source of uncanny and irreducible *otherness*, now becomes a specification by lack or insufficiency of a body conceptualized as male.

Already in Plato's *Timaeus*, sexual difference was acknowledged as a constitutive feature of the human species and necessitated a male-female synchrony on the logical plane of the creation story. But sexual difference is also located in an order of temporal succession, on a symbolic plane of degeneration. The latter is a plane we might well call ontological. In any case it assumes the male as a prototype for the human species modeled by the gods and casts the female as a decadent form designed for reproductive purposes.

The ambiguity of this discussion thus translates as the problem of a first birth of the male human prototype (at the hands of the gods) to which is added a second birth (the mysterious metamorphosis of men lacking virtue into women or animals). These make possible a third birth, that is, a true one, by means of the sexual generation of individuals of each living species by the species itself. The fact remains that this third birth also requires the gods' creation of reproductive organs and of a soul implanted within them, which is obviously situated below the navel.

This last type of soul is so identified with the sexual organs' physiology as to be completely coterminous with them in a somatization that requires no metaphorical figures for its representation. In the male this soul is an animated marrow *(myelon empsychon)*, elsewhere called *sperma* (*Timaeus*, 91a–b), which is moved by a vital, furious, and uncontrollable desire to issue from the apparatus that constrains it. In the woman this soul seems either to lose its usual marrowlike substance or to be totally lacking. It is probable that Plato sees in the female uterus not so much the site of the fourth soul, as the bodily location in which the fourth soul of the male finds an outlet and where the generation of sperm comes to fulfillment. Under the navel, the gods form within the woman's body a womb or uterus that is like "an animal desirous of procreating children" (91b). It is therefore a sort of autonomous beast that, when not bearing children, "wanders in every direction through the body, closing up the passages of breath" (91c).

This uterus with its erratic temper is defined as an autonomous being that wanders about unappeased, or an animal within a female body, swallowing up sperm—"animals unseen by reason of their smallness and without form" (91d). It therefore figures a female sex that is the necessary completion of a sexual generation modeled on the male. This sex is also revealed, however, as the punitive mutation of man, who, though born of the gods, may be condemned to rebirth as female. (Sissa 1992, 194). The reproductive soul and the fleshly apparatus in which it dwells come last, regardless of whether or not women possess them. The formative sequence moves from top to bottom not only spatially but, more importantly, in metaphorical terms as well, moving ever further away from the divine, the intelligence, and immortality. Man is thus finally born of a mother only in his third birth, having generated her remarkably through his own mutation into woman by divine punishment.

## Mother Material

A mother, or at least something that goes by this name, is present from the beginning in the *Timaeus*. She is the element that Aristotle, in his *Physics*, unhesitatingly identifies with matter *(hyle)* (*Physics* 209b11–12). Taking her place beside the model and the generated world, she appears third on the scene during the work of the demiurge (Diano 1970, 321–35). In a representation founded on techne and narrating the translation of an intellectual order into its material copy at the hands of a divine artisan, the problem of a material that intervenes in the shaping of the body is unavoidable. This is the problem of the origin of that soma embodying the various forms of the living being. The dilemma consists, then, of that something which necessarily *is also* (like wood for the carpenter or leather for the shoemaker). It is a third species, which must be posited as different from both the immortal, cosmic model and the world generated in its image. It seems, however, not to possess a single name, but rather many names, all with metaphorical valence. Names like *mother, receptacle, wet nurse,* and above all *chora:* a term whose Greek meaning shifts between "space," "abundance," and "place" (Irigaray 1985, 31–47; 1989, 160–69). These are pointedly multiple and quasi-interchangeable names, which furthermore appear within a type of enunciation that reinforces their metaphysical function.

The third species is defined as "an invisible and formless being which receives all things" (*Timaeus*, 50a), or "a receptacle, in the manner of a nurse, of all generation" (49a), or as "like the mother and the receptacle of generated things which are visible and fully perceivable" (50a), or again, as "the natural recipient of all impressions" (50c). Two notions are, however, constant. The first is that all bodily forms of living beings are generated by/in this species. The second is that it is ductile and formless, since it must receive and materialize the stamp (or the copy, the image, or mould) of the intelligible forms present in the cosmic model.

The term *material*, in the technical sense used by Aristotle, does not appear in the *Timaeus*. Plato does not even use a proper name to indicate in a univocal manner what is being described. It is not, however, the customary Platonic taste for metaphor that makes a precise nomenclature impossible, but an explicit prohibition, illustrated by Plato himself: this third species must not in any way claim a name. It is a formless *(amorphe)* thing, ineffable by nature and consequently invisible. This is because the form is a unity whose perfection lies precisely in the intelligible idea. Its imperfect image is the visible copy of the idea itself. But the formless, as such, eludes both intelligence and sight. Forced—if only by the paradigm of the techne—to postulate the existence of a third species and to define it as formless since the forms have been reserved for the intelligible model and its living copy, Plato can only give "a kind of spurious reason" (*Timaeus*, 52b) concerning that species. Or rather a discourse that runs through numerous and inadequate names in an attempt to speak a thing without form, oscillating between the evanescence of a shadow and the credibility of a dream (52b–c).

Dream and fantasy: night's realm again appears at the limit of the logos. Here it is a realm of fleeting semblances, neither fully intelligible, as is the form, nor constitutively invisible, unintelligible and ineffable, as the strictly formless ought to be. For the ineffable is somehow spoken, even if by means of metaphor or allusive names, given that a discourse develops that permits a glimpse of its elusive shadow. The paradox, or better the eternal problem, lies precisely in a discourse, be it spurious or not, that declares that the formless exists and at the same time that it is ineffable. It thus runs the risk of separating being, or at least part of it, from the category of the utterable. This problem, which was raised by Parmenides and then wholly adopted by Plato, is inscribed in the prejudicial autarchy of a logos destined to come up against the undeniable existence of what it has expelled from its confines. It must therefore pronounce the expelled element formless to the degree that it has reserved the realm of form for itself. And here the trap springs on the logocentric dilemma: either one denies that something other than the logos exists, or one admits that something *else* exists and must therefore be utterable, in whatever fashion, legitimate or bastard, at hand.

Plato chooses the second alternative, the bastard way, which cannot help giving some form to the formless, changeable, and fleeting as a ghost on the plane of the visible. On the intelligible plane, he gives the formless many names in a metaphorical system that remains, however, fundamentally monotone, multiplying as it does the facets of a single, cogent figure: that of the mother.

Three species are listed: "that which is the process of generation, that in which the generation takes place, and that of which the thing generated is a resemblance naturally produced" (50d). That is, the visible world that is generated, the *chora* in which it is generated, and the intelligible world of which it is a copy. Plato does not hesitate to compare these three species to the figures of the son, the mother, and the father. The son, insofar as he is generated by the father as his copy and imprint, is the final result. The father is invariably the perfect intelligible form, divine and eternal: the pure, ordered logos of male substance that the visible son resembles. The mother, instead, is "the receiving principle," the space of generation without influence. The mother, in fact, "never, in any way or at any time, assumes a form like that of any of the things which enter into her" (50b) and which leave her. She is like malleable gold in the hands of the goldsmith or the necessarily scentless liquid that receives aromas essential for making a perfume. This is true even if this "nurse of generation" is neither gold, nor liquid, nor any other determining substance, except by way of a metaphorical comparison.

Everything that has a body or a name, including gold and liquid, is already a visible form, a specific substance coming from the nurse herself after a long generative process that materializes the imprints of the father. This is the gradual process by which all things are formed, starting with the traditional, pre-Socratic elements: fire, water, earth, and air. All the rest proceeds from their well-ordered and geometrically harmonious composition, including flesh, which is the material given by the demiurge to the gods who form men. Thus specified into various types of material, the *chora* too is the work of the intelligible father, who in this way inscribes within the mother not only the forms of generated things, but also the order and mechanism of generation from the primary elements to their final mixture.

Through the undeniable complicity of all its metaphors, the scene of the *Timaeus* thus makes evident its workings. It evokes a male logos made of perfect and immaterial forms, the model of both the entire world and of its intelligible transparency. Alongside this logos is a formless passive female material, which is forged by the logos according to its forms. This is essentially an imitation of coitus on a cosmic scale, which is curiously inserted into an imitation of the work of the artisan. In any case, it is a misogynistic scenario, whose symbolic key is not so much the traditional juncture of active and passive or of thought and material stereotypically attributed to man and woman respectively, but rather the extreme radicalization of that bipolar system. Within this system the rational soul, modeled on the male, so emphatically belongs to the logos that it becomes necessary to represent the male itself as pure intelligible form, possessing no body or matter whatsoever, in perfect antithesis to the female, pure unintelligible matter without any form. Thus both the female and the body are expelled from the male realm of pure thought. They remain, however, as an *alterity* that, the more it has been reduced to nothing within the phantasmatic realm of the unspeakable, the more it elicits from the discourse its true name: nurse, mother.

However much he dreams of separating himself from the mother in order to synchronize with pure mental forms and be free of cumbersome ballast, the *zoon logon echon* has a body born of a mother. The maternally generated body encumbers Plato's discourse throughout the *Timaeus,* especially since its entire account, metaphorically or directly, concerns birth: whether this is the birth of the generated world, or the first, second, and third births of human beings; whether it is a mother/material that crowds the primeval scene and exposes the inadequacy of the narrative's language, or a uterus that finally appears, even if in animalistic form, so that the last birth takes place by a human mother.

Luce Irigaray has accurately pointed out that the autogenetic fantasy of a substantially male logos also contains a sort of duplication of the female figure.[24] Here in fact woman, as the female sex shaped by the gods according to a necessarily binary logic, is in a way the mirror image of man. On the other hand, she is the *chora,* something that, as an unspeakable presence lacking all form or figure, goes beyond the very sphere of the logos, although it is indispensable material for the production of copies imprinted with the forms of the father. In an ambiguous way, therefore, the *chora* is both a radical *alterity* with respect to the sphere of the logos (and indeed unspeakable and inconceivable by it) and that which phallocentric discourse produces as its residue and as a necessary precondition for its production of material copies.

The *Timaeus* may therefore be defined as an example of that phallologocentric foundation of Western discourse that is built simultaneously *against* and *upon* a corporeal material identified with the female. A true blind spot of male self-representation concerning the luminosity of forms, the mother-material thus comes to occupy the place of the formless that, though it results from an act of exclusion, retains an implicit, subversive power. It is thus rightly feared by the guardians of the fortress of discourse. The risk, foiled for two thousand years, is that the female might decide to make itself a sign, breaking in on the scene with the thought of an incarnate subject content to exist in its sexed materiality.[25] This is a risk that historically Plato was unable to take, but it nonetheless left its disturbing traces in the logical framework of his text.

84

It seems, indeed, that the theme of the body entangles the argument of the *Timaeus* in symptomatic contradictions. Corporeality, as the amorphic site of the mother, is something irreducible that the logos excludes from its domain but whose existence it is forced to postulate. At the same time, it is something in which the logos itself generates its copies and hence also those (ultimately) sexed bodies that inhabit the world. A phallocentric delirium thus plays itself out, in which the logos seems to fight against a material body that simply "appears" before it. This is done through a game of forced exclusion and of spurious discursive reappropriation. In this metaphorical battle, however, it is the male who takes possession of generative power at every turn, from the first scene to the last.

From the beginning, in fact, we witness a sort of cosmic mimesis of coitus, in which the father is a figure of pure forms who generates *within* the mother. He becomes father in flesh and blood in the more realistic final sex act, where, once again, he is the generative subject of the carnal son who leaves his body in the form of a little spermatic animal, ready to ferment inside a restlessly wandering uterus. The anomalous father has also in the meantime, through generative degeneration, fathered women and animals: for everything that has living form must proceed exclusively from him, just as everything that has intelligible form dwells in him and is transmitted through copies.

## Logospermatic Loins

If it is true that the historically fortunate metaphor of the body politic owes something to Plato's *Republic,* it seems that the *Timaeus* can also help us to understand its development. At this point we see at least how deeply rooted lie the reasons for what we were calling a paradox, an equivocation regarding the legacy of the *Republic,* whereby a political order Platonically founded on the image of the soul comes instead to be founded on the image of the body. In fact the *Timaeus* shows that the encroachment of the bodily metaphor upon the paradigmatic structure of the psyche is neither secondary nor casual, but instead the irreducible figural rebounding of a material that is futilely expelled from the logocentric male realm. Whether in symptomatic transparencies ill-controlled by discourse or through explicit theories about anatomical construction, the body continually imposes its figural order on Plato's imagination. It forces the soul's design to correspond to its fleshly form, already given and visible, and drags the logos-deprived souls into its mortal destiny.

Despite everything, however, the rational soul persists in declaring its separateness, pronouncing at the same time its usual obsession with an eternal and immaterial existence that might conquer death. It rejects a life anchored to the brief splendor of the flesh born of a woman's body. The body that returns figuratively to shake the eternal logos *is* an assuredly female body, the fleshly substance of life, a threat to the vigilant control of bodiless thought. Even when this body belongs to a male (and it is indeed he who poses the problem and resolves it in his fashion), it roots its disturbing material in a prelogical sphere that is considered essentially female, at the uncertain limits of bestiality and terror. It is there that the involuntary laws of the flesh align with the seductive excesses of nocturnal dreams.

The overall framework is thus clear, its basic coordinates well known. On one side, in the strictly human sphere, stands man, or rather the philosopher: in this realm of the rational soul the male body, shaped according to the forms of an eternal logos and disciplined by it, finds a figure that can function as image for the political order. On the other side, within a sphere dangerously entangled with the prelogical, is the woman, in the realm of the body as unspeakable mother/material, the realm of the fourth soul, autonomous bestiality, the uterus, and impolitic disorder.

We should not give too much credit to the famous page in the fifth book of the *Republic* that airs the notion of the equality between men and women and admits the latter into the class of philosophers.[26] This passage is refuted elsewhere in Plato, and its sentiments are repeatedly buried beneath an emblematic and stereotypical misogyny.

The problem consists, rather, in a corporeality perceived as essentially female. As such it is expelled from the logocentric domain of politics, yet it remains capable of ensnaring in its ambiguous metaphors that very discourse of male self-representation which would confine and control it.

86

The *chora,* the mother, is a clear example. Here, in fact, the cosmic image of sexual intercourse, either by implicit mimesis or through explicit metaphor, depicts a corporeal act in the fullest sense of the word. For the performance of the penis, it substitutes an immaterial logos, dispenser of forms, at the same time removing the generative power from a female body, seen as unspeakable material. Not by chance is this material residual, inert, and opaque, yet able to stand up to discourse, forcing it into paradoxes regarding the speakable nature of the unspeakable. The most obsessive representation of a logos eternal and divine, immortal and ungenerated—confirmed by a thrice-repeated paternity and claiming to be the source of all things—finds its figure in precisely that crucial sexual experience of the body in copulation which marks the origin of many living species, in particular the human.

The Platonic mimesis of birth is well known. There, Socrates takes on the role of midwife who helps pregnant male souls to generate the most worthy sons, which are philosophical discourses (DuBois 1990, 229–57; Cavarero 1995, 97–107; Sissa 1990, 59–63). The *Timaeus* also presents this mimesis, though it concentrates on the scene of fecundation. Here the entire world is generated out of the logospermatic loins of the Father-Model, whose Generated Son is a copy of a form that the male generator alone is able to transmit to the Mother-Material. Hence the *Timaeus* represents a primitive act of copulation that permits the replaying of the body theme in many figural variations. From the beginning, a phallic body functions within the metaphor of the eternal model as inseminating father, and this occurs even though no body yet exists in the narrative. In the correspondence of each generated copy with each form contained in the model, a body follows, shaped by the artisan gods, in the creation of the human prototype. This prototype is necessarily a copy of its precise, immortal form. In the end there is a body, or rather many singular bodies, born through sexed generation and thus from maternal bodies.

What emerges from this complex narrative montage is therefore the depiction of a logocentric foundation that, so to speak, wrestles bodily with the body. Indeed, if we can assert on one hand that the body, in its elementary structure and its natural functions, guides the metaphor of a generative male logos, on the other hand we must affirm that the body—despite the exact structuring of its anatomy and physiological framework—is totally dependent on the logos itself for this structure. The question is of no little importance for the future of the image of the body politic. The use of the corporeal image to express the state through metaphor is motivated precisely by that *natural* order possessed by the human body. This is the exact order of an articulated unity that is not merely the sum of its parts, but an organic totality of internal articulations, differentiated and convergent in a whole.

We are speaking of an image, and thus of an operation pertaining to the discursive register. There is no doubt, however, that the given organization of the body is the principle that guides the image's contents. The image is thus wholly free within the creative play of discourse, yet is anchored to an empirically binding datum (what we might call its specific object), necessarily preceding it and constraining it within a specific, objective, and preexisting grid of figural inventions.

In Plato it indeed seems that the relationship between image and what is given, or between the discursive register and bodily material, risks a sort of total inversion, since for the philosopher the logos possesses in advance the order of the body. The logos determines its fleshly conversion into matter. The body itself would thus be not so much the object of representation as its faithful result, were it not for an unresolved primordial matter that contradicts the self-sufficiency of the entire operation.

In other words, it is clear from Plato's account that the idea of the body—the ordered, logical form used to weave its image—comes first. The body itself (our body, such as it is) comes *after,* having been generated in conformity with the idea, through the idea, and by an act of fecundation of the idea itself. For that reason it is not important whether the order of the soul or the order of the body has served as the model for the order of the polis: from the start the only order is that founded on the centrality of the rational soul, and all the rest follows. As familiar Platonic doctrine—or at least the widely shared view of Plato's

88

interpreters—has it, ideas always and in every case come first, and their material copies later.

The interesting aspect of the *Timaeus,* then, is not its clear faithfulness to the doctrine of ideas, but the evidence that corporeality turns the tables on the logos by invading its language and upsetting its self-sufficiency in operation. "Conceiving of the nullification of the body by means of a body-dominated language" (Loraux 1991, 175) is a constant in Plato. The effects are not difficult to discern: the order of the soul ends up crossbreeding with what are essentially bodily metaphors, the philosopher constantly battles his nocturnal demons with obsessive self-discipline, and symbolic matricide haunts narratives of pure thought with images of gestative mimesis. The fact is that the body, which the logos claims to have begotten, never exhibits even a suggestion of tranquil order. The maleness of the creator appears surrounded by logical aporias. We confront the contradiction of a corporeality that is felt to be disquietingly and essentially female, but which then figures itself in the male. Or better, it virilizes itself in the image of a maximally disciplined body corresponding to its paternal and intellectual conception. In its deep and bewildering recesses, the body is that of a woman, deformed insofar as alogical; thrown back upon unconquered animal impulses, permanently unpolitical. But it is also a justly ordered male body, endowed with the vigilant power of a mind, hence the hegemonic role of the head, corresponding to a design valid for the polis as well.

In the images of the body politic to come, this rational head will be linked in truly peculiar ways with the masculinity of the person embodying it. For the most part, at least for several centuries, he will be a king: a monarch who takes on the role of the head and governs the collective body of his subjects, without, however, shrinking from the generative duties of his loins to bear a male heir according to patriarchal laws.

### The Body in The Politics *of Aristotle*
From the thirteenth century on, Aristotle's *Politics* joins Plato in inspiring medieval metaphors for the body politic. One of the many passages cited is the famous paragraph in which Aristotle

seeks to classify the various types of constitution and illustrates his criteria with references to the classification of different animal species (*Politics,* 1209b25).

Aristotle indicates the bodily functions that are needed for the *zoon* to live and lists the parts of the body (the organs) that carry them out. The different combinations of these parts in each living thing will correspond to the various animal species. By analogy, different combinations of parts of the polis will refer to different types of constitution; or at least Aristotle assures us that this will be the case. But it doesn't happen that way. The explanation grows ever more complex, and the analogy with the bodies of animals, only partially developed, is lost along the way. Its biological substance appears insufficient on its own to serve as an example of the forms of the polis. Aristotle names the various forms of the polis (with numerous variants) democracy, oligarchy, and monarchy: government by the many, by the few, and by an individual, describing also their relative degeneration and offering some examples of positive mixtures.

Beyond the variations of types of government and the complex theoretical structure that gives them shape, the outline of Aristotle's investigation is clear: it contemplates a plurality of constitutions and ponders the best criteria for classifying their models. We should not forget that the term *constitution* is a translation of the Greek *politeia,* a name that technically alludes to the political order of the polis and that is identical to the Greek title of Plato's *Republic* (McIlwain 1956, 35; Cavarero 1989, 41–50). We are therefore within the usual context of a political order that is articulated into correlated parts or functions, although the plurality of its types shows that it may be shaped into more than a single form, and not, as occurred in Plato, into a unique model of a just polis, with every other form being merely a degenerate offshoot. Aristotle's typological organization, then, is structurally necessary and may be traced back to the specific criteria of a general valid method.

These criteria are anything but unequivocal concerning the use of the word *part,* at least in the passage in question. Aristotle, in fact, juxtaposes two different points of view: one that looks at the functions needed for the mere natural survival of the polis, and another that looks instead to the higher and more important political functions of its governors (Accattino 1986, 77–84). In the first case, the parts of the city are identified with those who ply trades considered indispensable to the general welfare (such as farmers or merchants). In the second case, the parts coincide with the citizens proper, who are politically active. These citizens cannot be defined as necessary parts since they do not act for the purely material life of the community, but they rightly provide its beautiful and happy elements. In addition to the usual distinction between the beautiful *(kalon)* and the merely necessary *(anagkaion)*—or between the true life of a political community and the mere life of organized cohabitation—the interesting aspect of Aristotle's discussion is the range of analogies he adopts to describe his classifications. Aristotle refers to bodily organs (parts of animal bodies) when discussing the "necessary parts" of the polis. But he alludes, instead, to the control of the soul over the body (insofar as body and soul are the two fundamental parts of man) when his theme is the role of the "political parts." Still more interesting is his change of course when he abandons the typological criterion of animal classification and turns instead to discuss different types of "political part." The political part determines the different forms of the *politeia* based on the different number of those who govern (the many, the few, or the one).

The bodily analogy is initially precise in its aptness for this classificatory illustration. The organs that every animal must necessarily possess are briefly listed (the mouth for feeding, the stomach for digestion, etc.). "The number of ways of combining these will necessarily make a number of different kinds of animals" *(Politics,* 1209b33–34). The operation is then repeated regarding the polis, in which the various trades are singled out as useful and necessary parts for the life of the community. It is symptomatic, however, that the comparison stops here. Aristotle does not proceed to classify the various kinds of *politeia* according to the many combinations of its elements; and the category of the soul must be added at this point to allow a truer comparison.

Within the composite polis the soul corresponds to the governing part. The typology of this part varies according to the number of those who govern and the extension of citizenship within the various governing combinations. The incongruous aspect of Aristotle's analogical structure is thus the gap between the initial recourse to an image apparently based on the body and its physical makeup, and the image of the soul that functions at first as addition to, and then as a refutation of, the initial bodily analogy. The soul supplements the bodily analogy, because it reveals that the body under discussion is a human body, since only the human body possesses that rational soul corresponding to the governing part. Thus it can only be "added" when we are speaking of a *human* body. It also refutes the analogy, because it makes clear that the comparison of the polis to a merely physiological corporeality may allow the ranks supporting the polis to be described; but it does not apply at all in relation to the *politeia*. This is because the bodily organs guiding the criteria of classification correspond to useful and necessary parts. But these parts are secondary for the life of a polis that is not at all *mere* life, but the true, perfect, and happy life of the community of men (Arendt 1989, 23–27).

A kind of error, or perhaps a logical omission, thus occurs in Aristotle's writing. Opening with the analogy of the classification of animal species, the typology of the various political forms is instead brought back to the soul; that is, to the different number of those who play an ordering role in the polis. At the same time, having been anticipated with the animals divided into various species, the comparison shifts to the human species only, the only species possessing a rational soul. The result is that the analogy between the body and the polis features a number of revealing inconsistencies, not unlike those already seen in Plato's mature works.

If in Plato a bodily presence constantly disturbs the text and seems capable of breaking down the very terms of its textual manageability, something similar happens with Aristotle. Although his language is famous for its precision and logical rigor, when the theme of the body interferes in the discussion, this order gives way to logical confusion. This occurs often on the faint boundary between the explicit and the implicit: that is, within a chain of analogies whose links are not always clear when the image of the body appears.

Let another crucial passage of *The Politics* serve as a final example. Here Aristotle uses precise analogies to illustrate the structure of domestic and political order. He argues that the order of the master of the house is different from that of the governor of the polis: the former may be compared to the rule of the soul over the body, and the latter to that of the rational soul over the impulsive soul (*Politics,* 1254b4).

For the former, Aristotle compares the authority of the master over the slave to that which the soul exercises over the body. He thus brings to the fore the conventional difference between superior and inferior things that implies a precise relation of command and obedience. He then points out that, since the soul and the body are one whole, and since the part and the whole have the same interests, it is to the body's advantage to obey the soul. Hence, by analogy, since the slave is also part of his master, "a living but separate part of his body" (*Politics,* 1255b11–12), it is in the slave's interest to obey his master. Aristotle's argument, which was at first based on the analogy of the slave as body in a relationship with the master as soul, has now slipped into the figure of the slave as part of the master's body. This results in an odd logical inconsistency.

The curious thing is that this inconsistency is almost nullified if viewed within the logic of Aristotle's reasoning concerning slaves as the property of masters. Just a few pages earlier in his text, Aristotle discusses the slave as a part of his master, since he is a tool used by the master to live (*Politics,* 1253b30). He thus is a necessary part. What is missing to connect the two arguments is therefore a definition of the body as a tool, which is divided into the many parts and functions needed for the necessities of mere biological life. If we posit this tacit definition, everything works: the master is to the slave what the soul is to the body, since the body, of which the slave is a part, is an instrument needed to live.

The omissions in Aristotle's argument toward a definition of political man's authority are no less interesting. These omissions become clear in the analogy concerning the hierarchical arrangement of the soul. Just as the intelligence *(nous)* commands the appetites *(orexis),* he argues, so the politician commands his

93

fellow citizens, his equals in a democratic regime, though visibly different from him in their conventionally lesser "outward dignity, in the style of address, and in honors paid" (*Politics,* 1259b5–9). The body, it thus seems, is irrelevant; nonetheless it appears. This occurs when Aristotle, adding another comparison to his chain of analogies, compares this type of political authority to the authority of the husband over the wife. With this reference to the female sex, the unstated presence of the body disrupts his argument with such involuntary fury that the whole comparative structure is in danger of collapsing.

Since the wife is female and not male, "unless conditions are quite contrary to nature" (*Politics,* 1259b3–4), she is fit only to obey, never to command. But if that is the case, the wife does not correspond at all to those citizens who, in a democratic regime, are only temporarily willing to obey, since by nature they are the equals of whoever commands them and equally capable of commanding in their turn. The government of reason over the impulses has found its most suitable analogy in the image of the husband's power. Now, in fact, the natural hierarchy of *nous* and *orexis* corresponds to that of man and woman. Before, the natural equality between governor and governed implied a merely conventional hierarchy. Against this conventionality (which, of course, does not compare suitably with the natural reign of the mind over the passions) a judgment of sexual difference clearly inscribed in the human body comes into play with the figure of the wife. Thus Aristotle famously translates sexual difference into the reassuring and irrefutable superiority of the male over the female.

It is curious, however, that an unthematized but ever-present corporeality has again been inserted into the chain of analogies, upsetting its coherence, or at least privileging one of the two terms of a comparison. Given primary emphasis is the husband's marital authority and the natural command of his reason over the impulses, which is difficult to reconcile with the conventional political hierarchy between fellow citizens. At least one thing is clear, if not stated in so many words: master, husband, and politician, Aristotle's free, adult male is compared to the rational soul. But the philosopher struggles to tame within his text the bodily material that defines this paradigmatic masculinity.

94

I seek less to underline Aristotle's familiar misogyny and slaveholding ideology than to point out how this conceptual system, which allows discourse to trip up on unwieldy corporeality, is the same system that defines the logocentric and masculine substance of politics by separating the political from a domestic sphere where women and slaves are naturally destined to toil for the life of bodies. A basic paradox thus emerges in the analogy between the body and *politeia* sometimes used by Aristotle (*Politics*, 1320b35). The paradox lies in the fact that the polis, as a sphere by definition reserved for the male rationality of the soul, finds its figure precisely in that body which is confined to a location elsewhere. If left to itself, this body is merely a dead thing; it requires a soul to uphold it and give it life. The body indeed no longer functions when the discussion turns to government or the governing political part. In this sense, it is perhaps more useless than the body evoked in the *Republic,* at least for future metaphorical illustrations. In Plato, the order of the soul at least involved a bodily designation implicitly usable by the political order, with the head positioned solidly at the apex.

Critics often trace the source of the organic image of the state to another famous passage of *The Politics,* a passage that appears to involve less discrepancy than the ones already discussed. In this section, Aristotle compares the body to the polis to show how the latter is a "whole" that logically precedes the parts of which it is made. He argues that, having eliminated the body as a unitary whole, there will no longer be hand or foot, except by verbal analogy, since these organs may only be defined in reference to the whole body (*Politics*, 1253a18–25). The same may be said of the city, which is an absolute whole in which the parts find meanings that would otherwise be lost. The bodily metaphor is played out in these few lines, but it is based on a material and physiological definition of the body in reference to the polis, with no direct mention of the soul we have seen appear in other instances.

Moreover, the term *part* activates a number of different perspectives. The parts of the city do not correspond, here, to either the productive ranks or to the governing groups, but to the progressive forms of union that human beings naturally assume in view of a final political community. These forms are the union between man and woman to institute the family, followed by the union between a number of families to make a village, and finally the union of villages to obtain a perfect and self-sufficient political community: the polis (*Politics,* 1252a24–1253a9). Aristotle defines the polis, however, not as the result of the various genetic phases that produce it, but as that whole of which individuals and the family are intrinsic components.

The birth of the polis is set within a context completely shaped to underscore the logical and ontological precedence of the polis itself. It appears as a whole *(holon)* in contrast with those parts from which it is generated, parts that have their reality precisely in being components of the whole.

Moreover, on the level of the simple narrative of its genesis, the comparison with the body cannot work at all, since it is hard to speak of a hand or foot or any other bodily member that unites with others toward a final result. As everyone knows—and it doesn't take an astronomer like Timaeus to tell us so—the body is born whole, already equipped with limbs. It can thus be used to form analogies for the shaping of the polis divided into parts, but of course it cannot be used for the genetic account of such parts being assembled by some logical progression. If one wished to base a genetic account of the polis on the body, one would have to speak of birth from something like a mother, and in any case the birth would be followed by growth, maturity, aging, and finally death.

This aspect of the body appears to be of little interest to the metaphor's proponents, be they ancient, medieval, or modern. The doctrine seems to draw its metaphorical inspiration from elsewhere: in general from an image of the body as a thing "already given, determined, fully mature and purified in some way of every trace of birth and development" (Bakhtin 1979, 35). This figure of the body comes closer to the codifications of medical science than to the living flesh of the species. In many ways, it is more like the corpse lying on the dissecting table than a living thing that passes through the cycles of aging. It is a body that must primarily signify order and is thus generally imagined and described as order that can last forever. This is a hierarchical order locked in its static form, whose iconic structure cannot be shaken by infancy or old age.

The inconsistencies that crop up regarding the theme of the body in Aristotle's political doctrine can probably be traced to the definitive hierarchical ordering of the two sexes in regard to the bodily image. In its paradigmatic universality, this image is of a perfect, static, and adult male body (in short, of the Greek, if not Athenian, male). This image accepts the other sex as one of its own internal specifications that is lacking, inferior, or incomplete. So there are two sexes, but the body is still one (Laqueur 1990). It is a male body (and will be employed as such in future political metaphor), on occasion incomplete and impaired because of the defective growth of the embryo within a womb that is too cold. In this case the result is a lower, degenerated version, a female.[27]

In tragedy, a corporeality felt as substantially female represents an unyielding alterity. This otherness is retained, at least as a problem, in Plato. But with Aristotle, this female corporeality is transformed into a mere internal specification that somehow renders inferior a paradigmatic male body.

Antigone's body is thus always and ever more outside the political walls, but its constitutive figuration within the category of the terrible has now become merely the degenerate consequence of an overly tepid concoction of sperm in a badly calibrated womb. Aristotle assures us that when the uterus is at the right temperature and no other disaster occurs, the embryo should reach its telos and become a male body. That is, it becomes a human body in the true sense (DuBois 1990, 252). The body, however, cannot completely escape the unpolitical fact that it is *also* mere life, weighed down by necessities of the biological cycle, and thus entrusted to a woman's care. But it is already perfectly shaped, in all its virile splendor, for the polis to reembrace it finally as the image of its order.

# 2

# THE BODY POLITIC

I<small>THE GREEK HERITAGE</small>t is well known that the *body politic,* as a generic term still used today to indicate the state, owes its origin to an ancient metaphorical tradition based on the analogy between the human body and the political form of the community.[1] Both the name and the idea of the community obviously vary according to the age—*polis, res publica, realm,* and lastly *state,* while the images of the body, which medieval science and general culture provide for the formation of metaphors, vary as well. The history of this analogy and its figural potential are also recognized as bound especially to a specific period ranging from the early Middle Ages to the late Renaissance, a period that insists on an organic image of the body. On the paradigmatic nature of the body, it models a political order divided into different parts and functions that are the members or organs of the community. Conceived as a collective body, a supraindividual organically and internally divided whole and not the mere sum of the individuals composing it, the body politic finds its greatest expression at this time (Rigotti 1989, 24; 1992).

The success of the metaphor during the Middles Ages has its precedent in ancient tradition, starting with the Greek tendency (especially in philosophy) to illustrate the political order through frequent analogies with the body (Struve 1978, 11–21). In addition to the endurance of its language of analogy, the peculiar aspect of Greek thought is its central location of the soul, which controls the form of the body and subordinates the meaning of bodily form to its own logocentric framework.

As we have seen, the Greek concept of the body tends to deny it that vital autonomy needed to substantialize the organological metaphor. The body is instead defined as a living thing, or even as something that possesses a form, only because it is granted life by the soul. Indeed the body is designed for the needs of the soul. For the Greeks' concept of the living organism, the soul must be present in the body. The presence of the soul accounts for the specific relationship between an essentially passive fleshly material and an active principle, centrally identified with the logos, that grants it life. The organic model featured in the analogy between the body and the polis thus depends more on the activity of this vital principle than on the autonomous configuration of fleshly matter. That is, it depends more on the psychological foundation of the body than on its physiological and anatomical makeup. And the order of the polis is indeed founded on the order of the soul, as Plato clearly points out. The order of the body intervenes only indirectly and is shown, in any case, to possess no figural autonomy or efficacy by itself. For the Greeks the soul is not, as the medieval metaphor would have it, an organism, and thus the natural model for the political version of itself. Rather what orders the body and its form is the vivifying principle that is the soul. Suffice it to recall Plato's *Timaeus,* where the task of the soul as regards the body is not at all merely to give life to preformed matter but to determine the very design of that matter. This is the job of the gods, who proceed like artisans in giving a rational and supersensible order—a morphology and function—to their raw material.

Both Plato and Aristotle posit a soul that governs the body, and they both assign it the task of disciplining the body's form and constructing a corporeal model on the logocentric projections of the male sex. Indeed "life is introduced into the body by means of the soul that governs it" (Brunner 1970, 66–67), so that everything the body is and signifies, in its form as well as its function, depends on the philosophical qualities of the soul within. Leaving aside the potential for troubling hybridizations and unresolved textual paradoxes, Greek anatomy thus appears structurally to be a form of psychology. The unity of the organism itself has its vital and constitutive principle in that psyche shaped by the philosophers.

The bodily image—as the paradigm of a natural order upon which politics can also be modeled—is necessarily figured, for the Greeks, in the many-sided power of the soul over the body.

Even the central role of the head results from this framework's psychological foundations. If the soul is rational, or if, as *logistikon,* it is the location of thought and speech, there is no better place for its placement in the body than the head. This fact has many consequences for present and future metaphors, in which the head stands for immaterial rationality. It comes to be posited as both a part of the body and an incorporeal entity, or at least as a bodily organ that is, in its function as in its substance, distinct from, and above, mere physiology.

Beginning with the Greeks, the constitutive dualism between the soul and the body prevents the body from being presented as the solely material paradigm of an order that is all-inclusive and coherent. On the other hand, in the ordered composition of the human body the decisive role of the rational soul is inscribed within a cosmos that is also considered to be a great organism, with its divine, noetic soul animating and governing it.

We know that for the Greeks, the entire visible world, from the movements of the heavens to the bodies of animals, bears witness to a "durable order of existence" (Brunner 1970, 58), whose origin is the supersensible order. Thus, this durable order may serve as model or analogy for the political community, insofar as that community is the material expression of the divine order that shapes it. There is a correspondence between the macrocosm and the microcosm, which can also be called a correspondence between the macrobody and the microbody. Both are sustained by the principle of the psyche, and therefore by that nous which, from Anaxagoras on, is at the center of Greek thought. This is a part of a conception extending from Plato and especially found in Aristotle, which assigns unquestionable validity and clarity to a hierarchical order descending from heaven to the animals. In this order, the immediate presence of the body—that material existence of animals, perhaps capable of thought, which would make the body itself the prime paradigm of the entire metaphorical operation—risks becoming invisible.

Within the ancient organological metaphor that spans from cosmos to politics, the human body, despite its role as the implicitly foundational metaphorical referent, is nearly obscured if not negated by the centrality of the soul. This results from the human habit of representing the species by reference to intellectual faculties not content to be merely *found within* the living human being (and thus within the constitutive corporeality of that being). The faculties instead claim to be the vivifying, shaping, and even generative principles of the body. In this way Greek philosophy fashions an image of the body that clearly stresses its elementary physical givenness, but at the same time it imagines this givenness to be the result of an intellectual principle that "produced" this and every other body. It does this according to a primitive, immaterial model designed by that intellectual principle itself (as set out in the *Timaeus*). It is precisely the soul that renders the body organic, having constructed it and breathed life into it. The basis of this organic quality consists precisely in the government of the soul over the bodily material.

It is difficult to provide detailed proof of how much the particular Greek notion of organism and the relative problem of a hypertrophic psyche have influenced subsequent organic imagery for the body politic. We can at least claim that within medieval and Renaissance political doctrines the organic body, more or less capable of autonomous life, is strongly marked by the rational nature of the head. As the nexus between the microcosm and the macrocosm, it often serves to defend that doctrinal system.

In Greece, the weight given to psychology over anatomy doubtless prevents the similitude between the body and the political community from developing in a fully corporeal direction or in any form that would be of rigorous physiological interest. Aristotle, indeed, quickly abandons the analogy involving animal parts he used in classifying various types of constitutions; the *Republic* too speaks clearly of the soul's parts rather than of bodily limbs or organs. This results, among other things, in weak attention to anatomical detail and organic functions within the political state and in a preference for the spatial coordinates of "high" and "low." Overall we find suggested a symbolic system tied to the mind's superiority, the impetuous nature of the heart's passions, and the unruliness of sexual urges.

As we have seen, the problem especially for Plato in the *Republic* does not concern a physiology of the body and its inscribed balance (unitary or whole divided into parts) that might serve as model for the political order. It involves, rather, a conflict between reason and the impulses, which must be resolved within a hierarchical model containing subordinate and superior parts. This is as true for the individual as it is for the polis. Any partial analogies and linguistic reciprocity between the bodily and political spheres come from the frequent recourse to medical knowledge that does not involve an idea of the body we could call organic, even within the corpus of genuine Hippocratic theory. The medical body is taken to be a hollow receptacle where fluids clash, mix, and react in a sort of battle (Vegetti 1983, 41–58). Nonetheless, beginning with Plato (who was probably influenced by Pythagoras), a new idea of medicine begins to spread, which borrows from politics the image of a hierarchical arrangement of body parts. Thus a system of metaphorical exchanges is set up between the two disciplines, in which hierarchical order is defined as health and any disturbance of hierarchy is considered a disease. This view then translates into a general cosmic vision in which the cosmos is aware of its infinite potential for balance or loss of equilibrium, and in which right reason is the cosmos's sole physician.

The fundamental problem is the persistence of the organic metaphor short of its true and proper corporeal material (which would be autonomous and sufficient). It is a problem rooted in the history of a body devitalized to serve an overwhelmingly logocentric view of the world. This view marginalizes corporeality and attempts to dominate it, only to find the body constantly within the folds of language and among order's obsessions, lurking in the nightmare of nocturnal impulses that upset not only the Platonic tyrant. These nighttime monsters only seem to be tamed by Aristotle, who models the body definitively on a virile, logical, and political specimen, while as always expelling the female body from the city as a failed male, naturally illogical and therefore unpolitical.

## THE FABLE OF LIVY

Livy's celebrated and influential "fable" concerning Menenius Agrippa comes between the Greeks and the medieval theorists of the body (Nestle 1968, 502–16). Livy writes that when the Roman plebes revolted against the Senate, Menenius Agrippa regaled them with a sort of fable. "Long ago," he told, "when members of the human body did not, as they now do, agree together, but had each its own thoughts and the words to express them, the other parts resented the fact that they should have the worry and trouble of providing everything for the belly. They plotted together to rebel, and thus the hand stopped bringing food to the mouth, the mouth refused to swallow and the teeth refused to chew. The purpose, evidently, was to subdue the belly by starvation, but the unforeseen result was the weakening of the entire body. By then it was apparent that the belly, too, has no mean service to perform: it receives food but also nourishes in its turn the other members, giving back to all parts of the body, through its veins, the blood it has made by the process of digestion" (Livy 2.32). This comparison "between the internal revolt of the body and the anger of the populace against the senate," Livy assures us, was so successful that men's resentment was mollified.

It appears Livy's account decisively expands and develops the corporeal metaphor applied to politics, at least in this instance that clearly refers to anatomical detail. The Greek tradition proves incapable of conceiving a pure and simple bodily anatomy not based on the order of the soul. Nor can Greek medical language, to which the text often has recourse, compensate for the physiological shortcomings of Greek political discourse.

Livy's analogy, in any case, has the merit of basing itself on clear anatomical references. It is also original in its recourse to a bodily image that places the stomach (*venter*) at the center without mentioning the head and its usual dominance in the most common forms of this political metaphor. Strengthening the organic message of Livy's analogy is his image of a stomach clearly more suited to a purely physiological structure than the head could be. Furthermore, the metaphor is based on the notion of cooperation (reciprocal nutrition) between center and periphery, rather than upon an idea of some hierarchical arrangement between a superior, ordering element and subordinate parts. Clearly the organic principle Livy sets out coincides with the order of the entire body. This order is explicitly identified with health, while the claim of autonomy for the various parts is figured as health's opposite, disease.

Despite the anomalous central position of a prosaic organ like the stomach, Livy's metaphor aptly suggests the triple metaphorical horizon that the image of the body lends to the political treatises of the Middle Ages. This is essentially the symbolic context of an *anatomy,* a *pathology,* and a *therapy,* all applied to politics. The Greek texts had already used these, albeit in passing (Peil 1983, 306).

The history of the organic metaphor is primarily the history of anatomy, whose variations in general structure affect conceptions of political order as well as the detailed identification of the various social members or parts. The fact that the stomach, the head, or occasionally the heart holds center place will naturally be of primary importance for the political use of the body's figure. Each of these parts is bound to a different image of the body and to different coordinates of its general functioning. Each is apt to invoke (and not only in medicine) a different horizon of value. If the stomach alludes to a nutritional context in which, beyond pure physiological fact, the moralizing tone of the words *pleasure* and *insatiability* necessarily comes into play, the head in its turn cannot but evoke the high spiritual values of *reason* and *wisdom,* coinciding with the most accredited definition of humans as a species endowed with thought and language. The heart is another matter: it is often the seat of good feelings and the vessel of truth, but it is also an organ whose measurable beating signals the body's life. In addition, the heart in seventeenth-century medicine becomes the principal motor of blood circulation, according to a new view of the body as a "natural" machine. These considerations, however, pertain to a modern, mechanistic context (that of William Harvey and of Hobbes, for example) representing a drastic change in the real and proper organological metaphor that interests me here.[2]

Intermixtures involving different notions of the body are not in short supply during the long history of the organic metaphor. The metaphorical flexibility of this material even in the field of medicine is related to the uneasy nature of the image and to the body's capacity to activate an infinite number of symbolic cross-references. In keeping with the figure inaugurated by Plato, the hegemony of the head is, however, the central element of the most durable metaphors. In fact, with few exceptions, it becomes a sort of obligatory image throughout the Middle Ages and the Renaissance, above all in the frequent equation of the head with the functions of the king. Yet this unquestionably successful equation does not travel through the centuries without shifts in meaning brought about by the metaphorical system itself. Hence we note changes in the ideas of the body considered most functional to different political forms.

Although the bodily metaphor is generally called "organic" or "organological," the idea of a body made of organs is absent among the Greeks and probably begins in the Middle Ages. The Middle Ages inaugurates the image of an organism mirrored in a hierarchical social order that is divided into various roles and functions, supposed to act in coordination and reciprocity. In this scheme the head plays the main role, but it also participates in the balance of the whole, with no possibility for its own independence. Its post of command is neither absolute nor even marked. Beginning in the late Middle Ages and extending into the Renaissance, however, monarchical doctrine reshapes the bodily metaphor so as to make the role of the head more and more independent. It begins to govern the collective body that is largely dependent on and dominated by it. Organicity in the strong sense, implying reciprocity and the interdependent articulation of parts, is thus replaced—and in one sense simplified in the direction of absolutism—by a sort of bipolar, composite image of the body (Archambault 1967, 21–53). It is now composed of a royal head that commands and a collective body of subjects, which serves as the extension, or instrument, of the head. Still, the peacemaking function of the organic figure persists in its attraction, and it is repeatedly invoked to justify drastic interventions of the head to ensure the proper functioning of its members.

A significant problem of lexical ambiguity appears, however, in this particular monarchic version of the metaphor. It lies in the indeterminate use of the term *body,* which denotes both the human body in its entirety (including the head) and the lower part of the body from the neck down. This points to the difficult position of the head. It has claimed autonomy from the body (in its metaphorical role of Renaissance king), yet at the same time it is hesitant to relinquish the medieval organic figure that places it *within* a unified bodily order and better justifies its natural, if not (for the Middle Ages) absolute, preeminence.

Given the importance of anatomical detail within an organism of articulated functions, it is no surprise that medieval texts dwell on the various correspondences between the members of the human body and those of the body politic, while in the Renaissance this symbolic exercise seems to lose its edge. We may note, in fact, a decrease in attention to anatomical detail as the metaphor passes from its full organic meaning, with reciprocity and interdependency among the various functions, to a second, monarchical meaning that merely alludes to a body. The newer figure is not well articulated and is unilaterally dependent on an extremely powerful head.[3]

We are in any case still dealing with political anatomy, which more or less aims at distributing the roles of the hands or feet to subjects, or simply calling them a body subject to a royal head. The inevitable result is a political pathology that inscribes itself on the collective body.

Given the basic contribution of medical science to the conceptual framework of the metaphor already as early as the Greeks, it follows that a body politic, by now named as such, must anticipate the risk of disease and hence death. The metaphor is, in fact, ripe for a vocabulary of political pathology, organized around the category of health as order in the entire organism, to which may be opposed disease as disorder. Disease is generally due to an infection in part of the body resulting in breakdown through contagion. The source of infection is increasingly located in the peripheral parts of the body politic, since it is clear that a metaphorical structure that emphasizes the central position of the head, in the monarchical model, will identify order and disorder (health and disease) with the obedience and disobedience of the various parts of the body to orders coming from the head. The head will come to claim that it cannot be the source of infection, but fears it from various members in revolt. Such peripheral disease, transposed into the political sphere, is almost always called rebellion in regally sympathizing treatises. It is usually rendered metaphorically as a disease of the body *against* the head, according to a lexical ambiguity typical of the figure's use in the late Middle Ages.

Logically enough, this commonly found pathology calls for a political remedy. Medical language here becomes increasingly precise, suggesting cures vaunting the drastic measure of surgery. Operations often prescribed by the crowned head, these procedures cut away the infected part in order to avoid contagion, thus saving the body and setting it on the road back to health. In perfect correspondence with its political pathology, this therapy works in a metaphorical body that can become diseased only in its nonvital parts: obviously the head is vital and cannot be cut off. Anatomical detail in such cases is almost always lacking or generic; usually it is replaced with imprecise references to "members" that must be cut away and whose vital functions are not identified. In the body politic, both pathology and therapy pertain to an imbalance in the organism, characterized by an internal conflict presaging total ruin. Medical science, in such cases, appears to find the drastic measure of the scalpel more effective than mere palliative remedies.

### JOHN OF SALISBURY

The celebrated fable of Menenius Agrippa is amply quoted, as well as refashioned, by John of Salisbury in his *Policraticus* (6.24). In mid-twelfth-century England, the metaphor of the body politic finally receives its most noted and durable form in this work, where the head sits in the chief position. The quote from Livy (although unchanged regarding the central role of the stomach, in keeping with the spirit of the fable) appears to be a sort of digression or incidental variant within the overall plan of John's treatise. The book descends into anatomical detail concerning the various parts and illustrates the metaphor of a perfectly organic body politic that places the head in a position of hegemony. Thus John affirms a model of exemplary "organicity" and assigns interrelated functions to each corporeal part. These specialized functions he groups within a collaborative structure, in which the head too plays a specific and interdependent part.

The idea of a collective body composed of members and a head able to ensure guidance and unity, was already present in the work of the jurists of John's time, as well as in the theological tradition of the church's *corpus mysticum,* which dates back to St. Paul (Kantorowicz 1957, 193–272). For this reason John, who is usually called the chief inspirer of the metaphor in the Middle Ages, must be recognized not as the originator, but the proponent and developer of the organic meaning of the figure (McIlwain 1959, 391; Struve 121–48). He chooses as his authority a work of Plutarch (which has not come down to us) called the *Institutio Traiani.* Critics consider it to be either lost or a mere invention devised by John in order to invoke Plutarch's authority for his argument. With this inspiration, John details how the state *(res publica)* is a sort of body modeled on the human figure. The prince is its head, the senate its heart, and the judges and governors its ears, eyes, and tongue; soldiers serve as its hands. The discussion proceeds to identify financial experts with the belly and intestines and farmers, "who are in constant contact with the ground," with the feet (5.2).

Aside from the question of anatomical detail more or less integrated into argument, we find configured here a fully organic conception of the body politic, capable of entrusting a hegemonic role to the head while refraining from giving it absolute centrality (Bianchi 1985, 21). Moreover, the *Policraticus* is open to figural overlap but not to the dominating role of a privileged organ, be it the stomach of Livy's fable or the head whose fortunes past and future will be more enduring.

The organicity of the corporeal metaphor appears here still capable of containing that irresistible tendency of the head to become autonomous from a now instrumentalized body, which will raise more than a few problems in the subsequent development of monarchical doctrine. For if it is true that for John of Salisbury the head guides the entire body with the mind's judgment and reserves for itself a primary role, it is also true that this head must avoid swelling and crushing the members with its weight. The head too is subject to a specific pathology, and its disease is often revealed to be incurable, a fact that makes the death of the body politic preferable to life (5.7). Given that according to the organic principle of life the head must also be faithful in solidarity with its members, for John of Salisbury it enjoys no special immunity to life-threatening infections. Indeed, in these pages political pathology comes to recognize in cephalic illness its most serious clinical predicament.

Such adherence to the material context of the metaphor leaves its mark as well in the author's preoccupation with distinguishing the mere carnality of the body politic from the immaterial soul it possesses and that gives it life, just as it animates every human body. John, in fact, accepts the usual distinction that sees man as composed of a rational soul and corruptible flesh. But with a certain originality he detaches the soul from its usual location in the head and assigns its role to God and to "all those who preside over the religious faith" (5.2). Obviously, beneath this reasoning lies the thesis deriving temporal power from that of the papacy. We have seen, on the other hand, that the vitalizing role of the soul need not necessarily imply a religious referent, since it belongs to the whole long history of the corporeal metaphor. In Greece this metaphor had been crucial to the marginalization of a physiological image of the body, and it showed its adaptability to the later function of the monarch in frequent figural exchanges between the soul and the head. What remains truly interesting—leaving aside the immediate historical context of John's arguments—is that already in the *Policraticus*, in view of the evident *carnal* nature of the body politic, we can see with particular clarity the link between corporeality and ephemerality. This link necessarily counts among the metaphor's most problematic, if inevitable, figural consequences.

It seems that in all its iconological variants the metaphor of the body politic is displayed so as to grant itself a peculiar freedom to accept or refuse some of the given facts of the natural carnal conditions that pertain constitutively to bodies. Admittedly, we are dealing with a figural register; but it is also true that any bodily image must necessarily contend with a fundamental material realism inherent to the thing represented. The symptomatic result is a metaphor that tends, in its historic progress from the Middle Ages to the monarchies of the Renaissance, to ignore ever more of those facts of bodily experience that pertain precisely to the flesh's transitoriness and the measure of time. This is especially true of those undeniable aspects of the body that at a certain point cause it to die; but also to be born, to grow, to mature, and to age. The body politic instead chooses to represent itself in a *static* conception of the body: in a figure of the adult body at the height of its mature powers. This body appears perturbable only by eruptions of disease and not by the obvious law of a life span that has reached its natural terminus.

This problem is no small matter, for from here we can trace the distinction between two models of the corporeal metaphor applied to politics. One is the cyclical model—let's call it Polybian—of a body politic that degenerates "realistically," as illustrated in the flesh's developmental stages and its decline. The other is a static model, taking the organic figure of the body as evidence of a nearly eternal life span for the particular form of the body politic it exemplifies.

It is not for nothing—and one thinks here of Machiavelli—that the organic significance of the body image is usually ignored in the cyclical model of history. That model instead emphasizes the inevitable ruin of a material that requires an extraordinary effort from the "head" to preserve, at least temporarily, the life of the state.[4] It is the opposite case in the organological model—and hence in the fully developed medieval version of the metaphor offered by John and, later, especially during the age of the monarchs. This model affirms an image of the body that provides neither for old age nor for death by natural causes. It stresses the dangers of predatory illness, but also methods for therapeutic intervention and cure.

The idea of "nature," in all its possible senses and ambiguities, is employed to full advantage in the case of the real and proper organological figure we are examining here. As we move through the age of the great monarchies, the metaphor deriving from the "natural" body tends to emphasize the significance of the model and to reject signs of death. Likewise, it ignores phenomena linked to temporal development in the life of the body. This is curious, to say the least, because the organic image of the body

III

seems to bring with it references to a natural order that is irrefutable and good precisely because it is natural. But at the same time this nature can only underline the reality of a body made of mortal flesh, corruptible, marked by life's seasons, and subject to decay. Political anatomy thus always drags with it a pathology and a therapy, using a set of discursive tools that must oscillate between the paradigm of a bodily order called health, and the forces of disorder, called disease and death. These are inscribed in that very body which has been raised to paradigmatic status.

In other words, the image of the body that feeds the organic metaphor is both positive and negative, and it ends up meaning both good and bad things. The positive meaning clearly posits an organism as a *natural order* that by its very nature can ensure a stable and lasting, as well as just and good, model for politics. The negative, whose ambiguous implications are kept hidden and yet are constantly surfacing, cannot help pointing out all the elements of the body that dash the hopes for stability and longevity in which the metaphor itself is invested. Beginning with the transitoriness of the flesh, this model acknowledges a life cycle that, *by nature,* includes not only the risk of disease, but also the moment of birth, the fragility of infancy, the weakening of old age, and the closure of death.

The body politic is certainly mortal for those medieval authors who, like John of Salisbury, design the first, completely detailed organological figurations of it. Yet early and ever more frequently, they begin to reason in their doctrines as if the "naturalness" of the body, so essential for the metaphor, could be ignored regarding precisely those bodily characteristics bound to time, which guarantee death at the end of a development by stages. The metaphorical body of politics is always an adult in full flower, who is neither born, nor grows, nor dies of old age. Rather, it risks death by traumatic disease or sudden infection. The sort of naturalness that ought to imply a precise life cycle, including growth and deterioration, is rarely part of the metaphorical meaning of the organic model. The metaphor instead attempts to preserve the organic balance of a body that knows all too well the continual threat of traumatic circumstances that might lead to its dissolution—a body that remains, however,

# The Body Politic

largely static with respect to the temporal arc of its nonmetaphorical development.

## A BODY NOT IN PROCESS OF BECOMING

A description of the genesis of the body politic, however it proceeds, balks at metaphorically rendering the *natural birth* of the human body, even though the organic metaphor uses the body precisely because it is a natural object. This is not so much because the grotesque prospect of the birth of a collective body is unimaginable, or because there is any difficulty in rendering the event of such a birth in metaphor. There is, indeed, a sort of embryology of the body politic. The famous jurist John Fortescue comments that "as the physical body grows out of the embryo, regulated by one head, so does there issue from the people the kingdom, which exists as a *corpus mysticum* governed by one man who as its head" (Kantorowicz 1957, 224). Rather, a natural birth remains symptomatically unrepresented because of the well-known androcentric foundations of politics. This foundation renders superfluous, indeed unthinkable, everything female that pertains to the body's materiality: not only birth, but also the woman's upbringing and care of bodies.

Here as elsewhere—more than elsewhere, in fact, since we are dealing with the body—the *sexualizing* of the subject is crucial. This sexualizing places the subject within a precise context, orienting its discourse and its imaginary. A body politic comes to be modeled upon the natural body of an exemplary rational and political man, whom Aristotle not coincidentally identified with the free, adult male. The body recognizes its image in the ideal of a male in good health and in the full flower of maturity, but it does not pose the problem of its origins or ask itself who raised it to such splendor. The therapeutic part of the metaphor uses only medical language, totally ignoring what is traditionally the woman's part in caring for the body's health: raising, nourishing, and tending it.

It would not be irrelevant to note that political doctrine often sets organological and paternal metaphors side by side, without making precise logical connections. The very same king who is the body's political head appears as the father of his subjects, yet the maternal metaphor seldom occurs, even when a queen occupies the throne (Axton 1977; Jordan 1987, 421–51). Moreover, there are frequent metaphorical constructions inspired by biblical sources that transpose Pauline doctrine also into this political framework. In Ephesians 5:21–31 Christ stands at the head of the body of the Church, in analogy with the husband, who is the head of his wife (viewed as the body of her spouse). In the political extension of the analogy, the king was declared both head and husband of the collective body, the commanding part of his realm (Kantorowicz 1957, 216; Descimon 1992, 1127–47). In full evidence is a male perspective's logical manipulation of the metaphorical material, not to mention a strong, if perfectly predictable, misogynist accent. The use of the term *fatherland* here to indicate the political community is too familiar to require further discussion.

This body politic, which seeks guarantees in its natural paradigm, is indeed symptomatically an already fully grown body, within the rootless self-sufficiency of its perfect and mature form. Death, as the end of a life cycle in accord with nature's ordered cadence, is absent. Yet the body runs the constant risk of death by some terrible disease of its members, threatening it from within. This body, remarkably never born nor begotten, *exists* from time immemorial in the fullness of life.[5] If it really fails to avoid death, it dies an adult, just as it has lived. All the body's forces compete to avoid this death, concentrating themselves in a therapeutic exercise of self-preservation, which increasingly tends to convince the body of its own eternal nature. At least it becomes convinced of the eternal duration its "form" seems capable of winning, as it outlives the brief corporeal lives of those who materialize it through the ages.

In the organic metaphor the theme of death is thus twofold. The first part concerns the collective body, which tends to displace death by positing itself as eternal. The second concerns individual mortal bodies of the subjects of every order and rank that compose it, especially that of the king himself. As Aristotle was well aware in *The Politics*, there is also the problem of a political form *(politeia)* that endures unchanged, while men die and are replaced by those born, who are no longer the same

(*Politics*, 1276a, 35). The political community is thus conscious of the mortality of its members. The same problem was faced in the second century by radical Christianity, which saw simple mortality as a realistic, though strange, way to "flatten the social landscape of the Roman world" (Brown 1988, 94). These Christians preached a chastity that by interrupting births would have deprived the empire of its lifeblood. In the Middle Ages, Aristotle's positive meaning is taken up again: an infinite continuity of the body politic is imagined. This body remains constant, despite the fact that new living beings replace the dead every day. There remains, in the end, the insoluble problem of a metaphor that refers to the natural life of a collective body politic, whose flesh is furnished by the mortal individuals who serve as its model.

The organological concept, which takes the head and the members of the body politic "mainly as they were represented at a given moment, but without projecting beyond the Now into Past and Future" (Kantorowicz 1957, 311), must reconcile its static vision with a human material that is always in the process of becoming. Before the immobile perpetuity of the body politic, by now a celebrated metaphor, the bodies of those who ground it ontologically and make it sociologically useful are instead consumed within the cycle of birth and death. Nor can any relief come from the theological notion of the mystical body, which posits the body politic as people living in one community "achieved . . . in view of the successiveness of its members" (Kantorowicz 1957, 309). For despite the obsession with the eternal life of a political body, always adult and thus untouched by time, death—individual and collective—concedes to each only a brief season.

Nor is it a matter of indifference whether, in a body politic, death comes to the subjects or to the king. This is true especially in the Renaissance, when the head is dominant and responsible for the health of the entire organism. The king is also a man of flesh and blood who inevitably dies. It appears that the figure of a body politic desiring eternity must be adapted to handle the recurrent deaths of its supremely important head. It is almost as if the metaphor were forced to admit the essential transience of the material of which it is composed, as well as the great paradox upon which this whole iconic fiction is based. The solution is to grant the king two bodies. One of these is the natural body, subject to all chance infirmities, to infancy, old age, and death. The other is a political body, perfect and immortal, lacking infancy and old age. Of this body the king is head, his subjects the members. It is to the jurists of the English Crown during the second half of the sixteenth century, the glorious reign of Queen Elizabeth, that we owe this vision (Kantorowicz 1957, 7–23).

### THE KING'S TWO BODIES

This curious variant of the organological metaphor is eminently English. It passes into history as the theory of the king's two bodies, which is also the title of Ernst Kantorowicz's distinguished book on the subject. The theory attributes to the sole body of the king the entire body politic. He thus no longer acts the part of the head alone, and from the *part* that he was, he becomes the *entire* collective body, materially composed of his subjects. This is a body politic that is perpetual, composed of the immobile and immortal monarch joined to his natural and physically perishable body and forming an indivisible unit, "each being fully contained within the other" (Kantorowicz 1957, 9).

This notion is said to originate in the thirteenth century with the Christian theologians' use of the corporeal metaphor. They used it to explain how Christ possessed two bodies in one person: the individual, physical, flesh-and-blood body that died on the cross, and the mystical collective body of St. Paul's doctrine (the *ecclesia* of which Christ was the *caput*).

Among the many difficulties with this metaphor is not only the uniqueness of that person who possesses two bodies, but also the figure of the mystical corpus (a body plus a head) in which the entire body of Christ (once more, a body plus a head) serves only as head. The problem lies precisely in the chiasmus between, on one side, two bodies coexisting in one person, and on the other, one of these being presented as both an entire body and the head of that body. This problem is linked to the theological conceptualization that reuses the metaphor of the body politic, while adding to it a number of previously unseen complications. Despite the theory of Christ's two bodies, the familiar organological metaphor of the body politic, for example in John of Salisbury's use of it, presents only fairly minor structural difficulties. Beyond the different contexts and diverse institutional divisions, there recurs the quite simple and effective idea that someone plays the role of the head and others play the parts of the members or various internal organs. Complications arise when the Christological reworking of the metaphor passes from the realm of theological debate to that of politics and constitutional issues. This occurs especially in England with the Crown jurists' doctrine of the two bodies of the king.

The English Tudor king, by this point the secularized figure of Christ, is the privileged possessor of two, inseparably joined bodies. There is a natural body of flesh and blood, which is clearly born and dies, according to the cyclic parabola of human life. And there is also a political body, collective and composite, which does not ponder growth, decay, or death. The mysterious amalgam of this extraordinary figure evokes the destiny of the mythical phoenix, which also becomes the emblem of Queen Elizabeth I (Yates 1990, 39–104): a being who is mortal as an individual, but immortal insofar as it is identified with the entire species. The phoenix is always new, always the same, rising up again after death, just as the new king is born out of the dead one by dynastic succession. They are two individuals and yet the same person. Whatever the creative stages of this ideological apparatus might be, it now adds a personal physiognomy to the impersonal constitution of the larger political body. This personal image precisely resembles the king's natural body: a fleshly face and a recognizable effigy (Boureau 1989, xx).

Kantorowicz also describes the passage from the old formula to the new. The old consists of "the subjects plus the king," incorporated and together forming the body politic of the realm. This formula is replaced by a "body politic of the king," who is now incorporated within "the political body of the king" (Kantorowicz 1989, 367). This second formula is truly curious, for it involves the incorporation of the king with himself, and it shows moreover how by this point the head has invaded the entire body. Now, in fact, through the survival of the ancient figure of the collective body, the king is the head of the body of his subjects, and at the same time he is this same body, which has now become his political body, obviously including a head.

Whatever the historical vicissitudes of this overpowering regal head at the expense of subject members, the main purpose of the new metaphor of the king's two bodies is clear (Brenot 1991, 441–66). The image attempts to resolve in the king's favor the tension between the king and his subjects, even if not through an absolutist closure. It connects, but also distinguishes, the head and the members: a relation for which the old organological metaphor is no longer serviceable. The iconological history of the human body, rewritten by the political imagination, thus passes from the wholly organic imagery of the late Middle Ages to the disproportionate centrality of the head, contrasted with a substantially instrumental body. Ultimately, the body is completely absorbed within its crowned head.

It comes as no surprise that the doctrine of the king's two bodies found little favor among supporters of the English Parliament in its conflict with the monarchy. The doctrine does not merely exploit the inherently pacifist valence of the ancient organic bodily metaphor, its organic character, which tended to resolve every conflict and potential for dissolution in the political order. The doctrine of the king's two bodies rather seeks to transfer this pacifying force to only one side in the struggle: to the king, and the head. For the king is now that part incorporating the rest of the body, in order to block, at least figuratively, any opposition. This body politic also coincides with the natural body of the king, thus closing the circle of regal incorporation in an absolute immanence for the monarch.

At a crucial moment of the epoch, thus, the theory of the two bodies of the king appears to play a preservative role with respect to a political form on its way toward decline and even collapse. It provides a compact representation of a collective body (compressed into the figure of a single king) on the point of losing its organic unity, or at least the hierarchical unity figured in the original metaphor of the king as head and his subjects as members. During the course of the Middle Ages, that metaphor had already increasingly been marked by an emphasis on guaranteeing that the body politic would endure forever. Such emphasis reveals the presence of disturbing symptoms of instability in the period, and in response the metaphor's preservative side was reinforced.

It is curious that as the Middle Ages are waning, a doctrine is consolidated that projects the body politic as immortal, yet bound to the corruptible fortunes of the mortal body. It is almost as if both the desired perpetuity of a political order founded on the Crown and the clear contradiction of that perpetuity were celebrated in the emblematic figure of a single person possessing two bodies. Moreover, precisely this dogmatic indivisibility of the two bodies places death in the foreground, since the king naturally dies, and the doctrinal denial of this crude event is extremely laborious. The body's decay wins out; it is only apparently defeated by the asserted eternity of a body politic supposed to transmit its qualities to the natural body of the king. A force of dissolution effectively maneuvers the body politic, controlling the chessboard of epochal transition. In response, a political form, seeming to sense its promised end, chooses to reformulate itself through the bodily metaphor. But in so doing it eliminates every reference to the intrinsic fallibility of the body and instead stresses its preservative capacities with palpable obsessiveness.

## ROYAL TOMBS

The doctrine of the king's two bodies resulted in odd changes in the funeral rites reserved for the monarch. The death of the king separated his natural body from that political body to which he was incontestably bound while he lived, and this fact of course required adequate representation during the last rites. The custom arose of conspicuously carrying in the funeral procession a wooden effigy dressed in full regal splendor next to the corpse, which remained concealed in the coffin. In this way, the natural body, albeit in the guise of its simulacrum, "realistically" acted the part of the body politic. It was identical to the corpse, yet survived it in the immortality of the reign it incorporated.

Evidence suggests that the ceremony began in England with the funeral of Edward II (1327), but it is in France especially that the rite bursts into full splendor, above all in the triumphant tombs of Saint-Denis (Brenot 1991, 361–65; Bertelli 1990, 197–

207). In these two-tiered, monumental votive chapels we find a powerful, nearly sculptural metaphor of a metaphor. A statue of the monarch stands on top, in full regal pomp and in the eternal dignity of his office, while on the bottom level lies the pitiful stone effigy of his corpse. Yet the entire mise-en-scène is of course a tomb. It is almost as if sepulchral destiny were already inscribed in that human body, mortal by nature, which for thousands of years has informed political metaphor. Never as here, however, has the Western world shown itself to be "so keenly conscious of the discrepancy between the transience of the flesh and the immortal splendor of a Dignity which that flesh was supposed to represent" (Kantorowicz 1957, 436).

Ultimately, the surprising thing about this highly successful metaphor is that the aspired perpetuation of a political form would represent itself from the beginning with the figure of a body that is, by definition, mortal. This is a crucial blindness, which the Greeks had somehow escaped by "psychologizing" the body, but which the religious foundation of medieval imagery—even in its notorious enamorment with death—cannot fully explain. A paradox nests inside the metaphorical artifice that adopts a corruptible body in order to evoke a political order desired as stable and long-lasting. This paradox becomes absolute in the game that joins, in one person, both the collective and the natural body, thus redoubling the symbolic code of death. Yet English jurists claim that "the king never dies," and in so doing they illustrate the most authentic aim and result of the two-body doctrine. In effect, the doctrine consents to the ambiguous symbolic game of a dead man who does not die: as if the mortality inscribed within the very notion of the body did not contaminate the figure of the kingdom, but rather the postulated eternity of the kingdom passed into the body and freed it from death. The natural body of the king dies in the end, but it nonetheless lends itself in effigy to the immortal body politic, which it temporarily incarnated.

Let posterity come to see the monarch's tomb: it will find a body in all the royal dignity of its metaphorical function, be it only of stone, a lid atop weightless dust, much resembling nothing at all.

# 3

# THE BODY OF OPHELIA

HAMLET

*Hamlet's Double Mask*

Thus was I, sleeping, by a brother's hand / Of life, of crown, of queen, at once dispatch'd" (*Hamlet,* I.v.74–75): so speaks the ghost of the dead king Hamlet to the young son who bears his name. Another fratricide rises up on the tragic stage. This one, however, is not a reciprocal murder, for Claudius, the brother who resorted to the inglorious weapon of poison and hastily wed the victim's wife, now securely rules Denmark. The relationship between Claudius and Gertrude is not one of blood, and only figuratively can it be called adulterous. Still, "that incestuous, that adulterate beast" (I.v.42) tore the crown from his brother and entered into a marriage that, given the crime that enabled it, can be labeled incestuous. To look for correspondences between *Hamlet* and *Antigone* would not, however, get us very far. There are twenty centuries of European history separating one tragedy from another, and the avenger in the background of Shakespeare's play is more likely Orestes.

From this fratricide and incestuous murder the theme of revenge classically follows, but postponed, suspended, and made the object of Hamlet's philosophical inquiry rather than openly and courageously acted upon by a conventionally avenging son. This very paralysis of gesture makes the play famously tragic in the eyes of modernity. This is the enigma that docilely lends itself to infinite readings, that makes Hamlet *a* Hamlet and allows us to celebrate an anomalous figure who is the exact opposite of the avenging hero.

The absence of decisive gesture opens a space in which many other murders will take place. It is as if an accumulation of corpses were needed to prove that Hamlet is capable of killing. No lack of physical daring, or of strategic wit, keeps him from murder. Rosencrantz and Guildenstern, the betrayers betrayed,

die by his keen strategy. By mistake, he stabs the poor but conniving Polonius instead of Claudius, in a sort of rehearsal of the
absent revenge. Above all, Ophelia dies, in an unwitting suicide
triggered by madness. In the final analysis, she is also another of
Hamlet's victims: the Ophelia of the beautiful, floating death,
crowned with flowers as her body is drawn into the dancelike
embrace of the waters.

The scene of the final hecatomb is much more horrible and
cruel, a rapid concatenation of vendettas and punishments.
These cohere with the indirect progression of homicidal gestures
that guide *Hamlet*. Each character meets the sort of untimely
death not meant for him and that he himself had readied for
another. Thus the sequence that crisscrosses multiple murders
founders in a blind (but effective) mechanism: a trap of traps, a
paradox that wrenches homicidal intent away from its object. In
the general confusion every body finally becomes a corpse.
"Such a sight as this / Becomes the field," Fortinbras exclaims at
the end, as he orders the bodies raised up for the people's view-
ing of the spectacle of death (V.ii.401–2). The scene is indeed
more fitting to a battlefield than a court, but the story of the
kingdom of Denmark is one of dead bodies.

The theme of the body takes center stage once more in *Hamlet*.
But this is not only the dead body as such, or the corpse that
imposes its presence in so many different variations. These individual inanimate bodies are nearly de rigueur for the final blood-
bath of canonical theater; yet through their spectacular materiality, the body appears in *Hamlet* as a symbolically packed
metaphor for the plot itself. Critics agree that a corrupt royalty
headed for internal collapse is one dimension of *Hamlet's* plot.
But also well recognized is the "Hamletism" of a conscience as
fascinating as it is enigmatic, a madness capable of playing out its
duplicities and retaliations at the crossroads of truth and fiction.
Above all there is the Hamlet-like female mask of Ophelia, which
thrives on deep estrangement from the political context: a figure
almost capable of telling another story and creating its own
iconographic destiny (Showalter 1985, 77–94).

Certainly *Hamlet's* status as a masterpiece is not unfounded.
The text's multiple stratifications, the resultant infinite her-

meneutic work it inspires, and its irreducibility to a single reading all attest to its rich complexity. One important key to the play's interpretation seems to be the theme of the body, or rather the body's metaphorical power. The oft-noted, massive presence of bodily metaphor throughout Shakespeare's work develops in *Hamlet* as an obsession with corpses and decay. The heavy materiality of the body as flesh stands out against a grotesque background of inner organs and their end as food for worms. If, given the traditional metaphor of the body politic, the comparison of this carnal decay to the rottenness infecting the Danish realm appears obvious, it is nonetheless worthy of careful analysis.

Of course, in approaching what Carl Schmitt calls the "boundless sea of *Hamlet* interpretation," we risk falling into the "impenetrable jungles of Shakespeare studies" (1983, 119–20). What might be a foolhardy adventure for nonspecialists, however, will in my case be guided by Schmitt himself, who unabashedly leads the way and fends off the English scholars whose monopoly we will violate. Without scrutinizing Schmitt's highly unorthodox interpretation for accuracy, we might sum it up as an analysis of the connection between the role of Hamlet and the historical English king James I. Schmitt's is a political reading that links the play crucially to events in the early seventeenth century, when it was originally staged.

It was an age of transition in many ways: from one century to another; from the conflicts of war and religious disputation to the neutralizing power of the state; from sacred to secular foundations of sovereign power. The period signals, in short, the twilight of the late Middle Ages and the rise of the modern state. England, however, lags politically behind the rest of Europe in this process. Its passage toward modernity travels by other roads, which Schmitt locates in the development of naval power and the consequent industrial revolution, that specifically Anglo-Saxon answer to the "barbarous Middle Ages" (Schmitt 1983, 116). Early-seventeenth-century England offers an interesting vantage point from which to observe this irregular transition, especially if we discern in England's anomalous passage to modernity the model of the state proposed shortly afterward by the Englishman Thomas Hobbes. According to Schmitt, the problem—or better the political backdrop—of King James's presence behind the mask of Hamlet is that England does not take the road of monarchical absolutism in leaving the Middle Ages. Though the absolutist model is current on the Continent, England chooses a different path out of the medieval world that is coming to an end.

In Schmitt's view, James I fails to see this development and obstinately refuses to move beyond the medieval religious and feudal notions of sovereignty. James's reluctance seals his unhappy fate and that of the entire house of Stuart. His end is tragic, precisely because it is experienced by a king in flesh and blood in objective historical time and not by a character in some artistic game (*Spiel*) of theatrical invention. James's destiny, transfigured in the mask of Hamlet, allows tragedy itself to erupt in Shakespeare's play (*Spiel*).[1]

Schmitt credibly demonstrates the relationships between Hamlet and James: the game and the tragedy, drama and history. James I, like the Danish prince, is the son of a queen who joined in the murder of her husband. He is the son of Lord Darnley and Mary Stuart, queen of Scots, who hastily remarries her husband's assassin Count Bothwell only three months after the murder. The story is even more complicated than the dramatic action in the state of Denmark, for it is none other than the great Elizabeth, the orderer of Mary Stuart's decapitation, who wants to place James on the throne. Not to mention that James displays great filial devotion to the memory of his mother on every public occasion. Schmitt believes that Shakespeare's odd reticence—his "taboo of the queen"—concerning Gertrude's complicity in the murder of her husband, Hamlet's father, derives from this real history.

In any case there is no shortage of parallels between the events of James's life and *Hamlet*. Given their encouraging number, it may prove useful to seek similarities between James's reflections on power and those of his dramatic double. If Schmitt is right, and these similarities are the political key to Shakespeare's tragedy, it behooves us to look at both figures in a political light. Since it is the theme of the body politic and its fortunes that interests us here, we shall seek the parallel fortunes of this long-lived metaphor in Schmitt's adventurous scenario.

## James I and the Body Politic

We know that King James I, a Stuart and Crown of England and Scotland, was one of the great men of his age for other reasons besides his rank. A learned scholar of the political treatises of his day, he also authored various political writings. In these writings James does not shrink from dealing with the tortuous debate over the rite of confession, nor from the question of demonology, which resulted in the shameful fury of the seventeenth-century witch-hunts. This is the age in which Bodin bids his famous farewell to the medieval political order depicted in the six books of the *Republic,* but also writes the less modern (to our eyes) *Demonologie des sorciers* (1580). It is not surprising, then, that James produces his own *Demonologia* (1597), as well as the *Basilikon Doron,* a work on the duties of the king. The most important of James's works is the treatise called *The Trew Law of Free Monarchies* (1598). Here he claims the absolute power of the king, based mainly on divine right and then on the king's superiority to the law, since he is the metaphorical father and natural master of his subjects. Aside from the medieval tenor and theological background of his arguments, James's treatise seems to be an English response to continental absolutist models of transition to the modern state. In this regard, Schmitt's opinion that James does not move beyond medieval doctrine may require revision or even overturning. James's writing appears to be part of the decisive premodern absolutist doctrine in vogue in the rest of Europe. True, the tragic situation of this first Stuart to reign over England would become more acute, projecting its eccentricity in relation to the island's history not just forward toward England's nonstatist entrance into modernity but also backward into the ancient English tradition that boasted its freedom from absolutist rule.

In fact, little in that older constitutional tradition would support James's claim that the king is above the law, as his enemies in Parliament tirelessly reminded him. But James's advance on older political doctrine is beyond the scope of this book.[2] It would require that we also discuss the Catholic Scotland of his birth, which was also more favorable to absolutist claims, and which contributed heavily to the sorry end of the Stuarts. One thing we can say for sure about James's writings is that however medieval Schmitt may find them in their religious and theological dimension, they are also influenced by continental absolutist doctrine. This fact makes James's work doubly eccentric compared to the past and future political history of England.

In James's writing, there is, however, something specifically English, if not in political theory, at least in its use of symbols. This is the author's recourse to the ancient metaphor of the human body, which English tradition takes up from all of medieval Europe, recycles persistently, and re-elaborates in new ways within the debate on royal power. The survival of the metaphor in England, "at a time when in other countries that particular notion no longer was current" (Kantorowicz 1957, 448), is due to the doctrine of the king's two bodies. This doctrine accompanied constitutional debate from the time of Elizabeth and had come down to the first Stuart (but also to Shakespeare) as an obligatory metaphor in political argumentation. Unlike Shakespeare, however, James does not appear to appreciate the fine points of the figure of the king's two bodies, and in this respect he manages to move away from English tradition. Thus James writes in his greatest work:

> [T]he proper office of a King towards his Subjects, agrees very wel with the office of the head towards the body, and all members thereof: For from the head, being the seate of Iudgement, proceedeth the care and foresight of guiding, and preventing all euill that may come to the body or any part thereof. The head cares for the body, so doeth the King for his people. (1965, 64).

At first glance, this is a conventional organological metaphor. It considers the body as a whole, granting the head, as locus of intelligence, the task of guiding every part or member and of providing for its health.

The anatomy of this figure and the entire symbolic weight of its original organic structure are reworked by James, who asserts the central placement of the head prevalent in monarchical doctrine. Indeed, in other writings he does not hesitate to require both the devotion of the soul and the service of the bodies of his subjects, in keeping with the usual definition of a collective body that has by now been made part of the head. James appears curiously capable of coupling with himself, when he claims he has taken the entire English isle as his wife (Ciocca 1987, 23, 31). He affirms the regal principle again when he shows that every part of the body must not only perform its function (known in legal terminology as its *office*), but it must also follow orders proceeding from the head in the form of "discourse and direction" (1965, 65). Here we note also a reference to the common logocentrism of politics, which is absent in the silent rapport between the head and the bodily functions. The natural and physiological guidance of the head is transformed into explicit command, which avails itself of written or spoken orders, in a familiar adaptation of the organic metaphor to the Renaissance monarchy's needs for self-representation.

James's originality lies in his use of surgical language. As he discusses political pathology and cure, he repeats over and over that any part "affected with any infirmitie" must be amputated in order to save the rest of the body from infection. The decision to amputate naturally lies with the head, which cares for the whole. Only the head can fully guarantee a healthy life for that whole, since "what state the body can be in, if the head, for any infirmitie that can fall it, be cut off, [he] leave[s] it to the readers judgement" (65). The tragic element so dear to Schmitt seems to invade James's sober political tract with bloody irony at this point, for history will soon echo his language: Charles I, James's immediate successor and heir, will himself be decapitated.

Drastic and prophetic as James's proposed cure may be, its primary image is that of a body that has abandoned the organic model of the Middle Ages. The interdependent nature of the body's functions appears to have changed to unilateral dependence of the subject members on the head.

The heavy emphasis on the unidirectional and absolutist center position of the head suggests a distancing, almost a radical removal, of the head from the body. It is more than probable that James's insistence on the surgical metaphor indicates a prophetic fear of decapitation. James was certainly aware that many apologists for rebellion and treason were capable of authorizing subjects to "cut off their king at their owne pleasure" (66). He also knew that the problems of his reign must be faced in just these terms: of cutting, amputation, and bodily dismemberment that seeks logical justification in the organological metaphor (and not vice versa). These are terms that recycle the image of political anatomy not to illustrate an organic social order, but to detail a pathology that will tolerate drastic therapeutic measures for the infected collective body. For this body, the surgeon's individuating cure inspires more fear than the illness.

James certainly sees the early symptoms of crisis, or at least of transition, but he cannot predict their outcome. Amid this crisis, the bodily metaphor is forced to solidify into an image that makes the power of the head over the body absolute, well exceeding its usual role as coordinator. The metaphor thus risks detachment from the vocabulary of the organic structure within which it still maneuvers. Instead of harmony and interdependence, we now have tension and conflict between the head and the body. The forms of command and amputation appear to overshadow the organic ordering of roles and functions, which nevertheless continue to be part of the metaphor's conventions.

It is thus plausible to suppose that the age itself is responsible for this surgical emphasis in political discourse. Although the theme of amputation is part of the metaphor's traditional baggage, James's insistence on it suggests he was aware of a serious political illness and of the impending catastrophe, despite the confidence of some in the curative powers of the royal scalpel.

This illness lies, however, in the outer "members," who are rebellious and infected. The inner sickness and irreversible bodily decay that subtend so many of Hamlet's speeches are not present. For the Danish prince, there is no cure for the body politic, nor is there any faith in the surgeon, because evil is situated in the crowned head of the fratricidal king, and the problem lies in the resolution to cut it off.

Shakespeare, like James, knows how the question is traditionally formulated, and in his theatrical practice he tries every possible rhetorical version of the corporeal metaphor, often representing the realm as a body with a head in central command.[3] These figurations draw especially on the contemplation of transience and the painful experiences of the flesh.

In *Hamlet,* there is also an example of the familiar organic metaphor, but free of any anxious references to surgery. Notably, the figure is pronounced not by the Danish prince, but by the defenders of the court, as a contrast with Hamlet's obsession with catastrophic bodily decay.

Laertes first alludes to it in a speech in which he tries to disillusion Ophelia regarding the possibility of marriage between her and the enamored Hamlet. The prince, Laertes observes, is not like other men, who may follow their hearts in choosing a bride. As heir to the throne, the young prince is ruled by his birth and by the other dictates of his royal role, which do not allow him a will of his own in the matter. For

> on his choice depends
> The safety and health of this whole state,
> And therefore must his choice be circumscrib'd
> Unto the voice and yielding of that body
> Whereof he is the head.
>
> (I.iii.20–24)

Laertes' uses of the metaphor include the traditional notions of the "health" of the entire organism and the identification of the head with the king. Here the metaphor tends, in fact, to emphasize the ancient organic principle of the body as a *whole,* despite the Renaissance tendency to grant an ordering function to the head. This emphasis allows Laertes to place the head under the rule of the voice and of the consent (the "yielding") of the body. This esteem for the body/people, coming from the mouth of a king's subject, may not be casual; but the metaphor is completely traditional, and it underlines the organic tie between the order of the kingdom and the actions of the king. This tie is taken for granted and involves no conflict or sign of infection. It is as if the king's function were inscribed within the well-ordered body of the realm. The king is at the head, either by nature or by birth, and nothing seems rotten in the state of Denmark.

As Hamlet well knows, however, there is something rotten, and it lurks precisely in his uncle, King Claudius, fratricide and usurper of the throne. It is quite strange, therefore, to see the way this unworthy occupant himself calls on the metaphor's positive, traditional valence. Claudius's words to Laertes express the metaphor not in its explicit form, but through a familiar play on words involving the bodily vocabulary on which it is based.

Claudius wishes in this speech to show royal benevolence to the son of Polonius. Referring to Laertes' father, a faithful counselor to the Crown, Claudius says that "the head is not more native to the heart, / The hand more instrumental to the mouth, / Than is the throne of Denmark to thy father" (I.ii.47–49). Here the metaphor functions in the background, although it meaningfully compares the relationship between the king and his counselor to that between interdependent bodily organs. This relationship is the medieval commonplace that seems to admit only health and harmony, excluding conflict and illness.

Onstage, Polonius is as tireless a counselor to the king as Laertes is faithful as subject. By all appearance and at least from the court's point of view, the body politic truly "holds together" in its hierarchical structure of organic interdependence. Shakespeare's innumerable plays with the scene's duplicity reveal also the paradox of a court that moves as an internally coherent body politic, while the head itself is rotten through and through, and its subject members are scheming accomplices. This conflict, however, this decay-promoting illness, is not lodged in the members but spreads from the head to those members. The illness is *within* the body politic, a body rotten at the core, whose flesh collapses under its own weight.

For this reason, Hamlet is not the direct agent of a royal disintegration that could be accelerated by means of some vengeful action. He is, rather, an *outside observer* of intimate dissolution. For this reason too he does not use a dagger to cut off the crowned head, but instead carries on about a grotesque body that is content with its own rotting apotheosis and offers philosophical metaphors of a body politic that, by its own means, is being devoured by worms onstage.

Generally the rhetoric of the grotesque, in emphasizing the festive side of catastrophe (and thus, perhaps, reminding us of the regenerative cycle of decomposition), is a kind of dissolute sign pointing to a new life, and thence, in historical context, to a new political order (Bakhtin 1979, 61). In hindsight, this is as true of Shakespeare's theater as it is of the ruin of the Renaissance monarchies and the birth of the modern state. But in trying to read Shakespeare within its historical context, we must admit that *Hamlet* concentrates entirely on the disaster of collapse, with no glimmer of any new political order. The collapse is deafening, pure and simple. No phoenix appears ready to rise from its ashes; much less does it anticipate that improbable form of impersonal rule, the mechanical monster yet to be born in the mind of Thomas Hobbes.

### Hamlet and the Grotesque Body

Whatever the profundities emanating from the most famous soliloquy of the modern theater, the grim threshold of the body's death is central to Hamlet's speech. Encapsulated in his opening, "To be, or not to be," is Hamlet's fear of contemplating what comes after bodily existence. He confines his question to the fleshly material of life, to a body that seems to supply a solid foundation for "being," however heavy the burden of its unhappiness, a body posited as the necessary vehicle of suffering and action (Hunt 1988, 28).

Action is the key. Action for Prince Hamlet is the heroic, traditionally theatrical form of revenge: in the crucial form of murder, of taking life from a body and, with one gesture, transforming it into a corpse. A not-to-be? Though Hamlet's hand is certainly not stayed by worry about sending the living murderer of his father into the world of nonbeing, his soliloquy indirectly blocks his plan of revenge against Claudius. Hamlet's dagger is stopped once again when he sees the king intent at his prayers. He hesitates because, in killing the king at that moment, he might send him not directly to hell, but to heaven. And it was from hell, that "undiscover'd country, from whose bourn / No traveller returns" (III.i.78–79), that his father's ghost rose up to ask his son for revenge. Hamlet, it seems, like any conceivable philosopher of his age, must reserve a place in his philosophy for the beyond.

One side effect of this philosophy that dwells on the threshold of *nonbeing*, where a corpse can be made out of a living man, is a sort of renunciation, for fear of the unknown, before the full expression of an otherworldly form of *being*. This renunciation confines discourse concerning both being and not-being (or at least concerning their normal verifiability) to the sphere of bodily life. In other words, the choice "to be, or not to be" is here equivalent to the empirical alternative between living and dying. The eternal being of the bodiless spirit after death is in this context a thing unknown and terrifying, not a simple locus of doubt. The choice not to be, for Hamlet in this soliloquy, is the choice of suicide. It is this act that fear of the next world paralyzes, just as it paralyzes Hamlet's revenge, which would also be an action to inflict death. It is not only the fear of an afterlife, or of an inevitable divine punishment, that halts the extreme gesture. A certain delight in subjective *inaction* plays a role, even concerning death, which slowly works even without our help: "O that this too too sallied flesh would melt, / Thaw, and resolve itself into a dew" (I.ii.129–30).

We are not dealing here with a philosophy that may easily be molded to boldly anachronistic readings, or with a doctrine that will neatly resolve as either final or only apparent the threshold of nonbeing. Hamlet's reflections are wholly imprisoned within a bodily material that envelops both existence and action in one substance. "My thoughts be bloody, or be nothing worth!" (IV.iv.66), he exclaims, but this is precisely the aspect of the question that cannot be resolved. There is a kind of void between thought and the body; and it is the same gap that separates the immateriality of thought from the corporeality of action.

Thus, if action, in the crucial form of killing—regardless of the promise or intention of revenge—is always an act of the body, suicide is also such an act. Even that which, with self-procured death, robs action of its necessary bodily dimension, is itself an action. Here we may almost discern that the choice is between consciously robbing oneself (or another person) of life by an act of the body, or dying (entering nonbeing) by the internal bodily decay that is completely independent of our will. This decay is unfortunately not so swift as the words "resolve itself into a dew" imply. It is exactly the expectation of this internal decay that opens the space of inaction.

Decay is at work in the body politic as in the single body. The death of the political organism is in fact under way, and the stench of decomposition is perceptible everywhere. Although *Hamlet* is saturated with the melancholy caused by the awareness of transience, it would be a mistake to consider the play, or Shakespeare's work as a whole, as dealing above all with the inevitability of death. *Hamlet* offers itself as a reflection on killing as an act, either one's own or another's, which takes, cuts short, or robs bodily life. The body seen as active or passive protagonist of the homicidal gesture is the problem. The royal characters who embody the problem shift it toward its probable root: the crucial sphere of the political order.

In Shakespeare, the body of the king is the natural and political body where power and life coincide. Dynastic murder, that is, violent death as the means of gaining the throne, is its most effective law. The specificity of *Hamlet* lies in its reflection on this oft-described phenomenon, and on its remarkable *interruption* by means of internal and observable collapse. The vengeful act would merely repeat the old story of royal succession through murder, while *Hamlet* is the tale of the body politic ruined from within. Typically for Baroque drama, the play holds up the "idea of catastrophe" (Benjamin 1980, 48), and it is catastrophe, in its unstoppable and almost casual occurrence, that moves Hamlet. In the words of Walter Benjamin, Hamlet wishes to "breathe in deeply the destiny-laden air, the suffocating substance," of this *idea* of catastrophe (1980, 135).

Being a student at Wittenberg and a habitual, solitary reader of philosophy, Hamlet has plenty of time and passion for theorizing. Death, rotting corpses, worm-eaten bodies, and fleshless bones seem to be his favorite topics. In contrast with the traditional use of the bodily metaphor by the advocates of the court, Hamlet uses the image of the body to focus on the grotesqueries of illness and decomposition, as in his speech to Polonius: "The satirical rogue says here that old men have grey beards, that their faces are wrinkled, their eyes purging thick amber and plum-tree gum, and that they have a plentiful lack of wit, together with most weak hams" (II.ii.196–200). The reference to the rot that pervades the kingdom of Denmark is explicit, as Hamlet varies the traditional metaphor in every possible way, playing on the contrasts organic/inorganic, health/disease, outside/inside, conservation/decomposition, whole/dismembered, and so on. Hamlet looks at a body whose external form is more or less inessential.

This is not only because its real substance lies in its innards, but also because Shakespeare's very language seems to delight in an anatomical dismemberment that isolates and renders self-sufficient various bodily parts for metaphorical use. This tendency is carried to such a degree that the play itself might be "'considered curiously,' . . . like a dissecting room, stocked with all of man's limbs, organs, tissues and fluids" (Hunt 1988, 29).

In the play's scheme of correspondences, Hamlet has inherited his taste for anatomical fragmentation from his father, who is similarly eloquent. The ghost of the old king, in fact, warns his son that the story of his infernal tortures would chill the blood, make the eyes pop out from their spheres, and cause the hair to stand on end, not being fit for "ears of flesh and blood" (I.v.22). After these words, the ghost itself willingly narrates how his brother poured into his ears, as he was sleeping, a poison

> whose effect
> Holds such an enmity with blood of man
> That swift as quicksilver it courses through
> The natural gates and alleys of the body,
> And with a sudden vigor it doth [posset]
> And curd, like eager droppings into milk,
> The thin and wholesome blood

until a "vile and loathsome crust" covers the body (I.v.64–72). Hamlet rivals his father in the passion for frightening anatomical detail, even if his passion for the grotesque is more targeted at his mother's body. Her body is described by the son for her sin of requiting the love of her murderous brother-in-law, as having "eyes without feeling, feeling without sight, / Ears without hands or eyes, smelling sans all, / Or but a sickly part of one true sense" (III.iv.78–80). Hamlet begs her, moreover, not to cover her fault with an unction that "will but skin and film the ulcerous place / Whiles rank corruption, mining all within, / Infects unseen" (III.iv.147–49).

Examples from Hamlet's speeches concerning abscesses, festering wounds, and the stink of rotting flesh go on and on, nearly a Shakespearean echo of the horrible plagues that arrived in regular waves over Europe. Hamlet's taste for imagery involving worm-eaten corpses is no less evident, as in the lines "For if the sun breed maggots in a dead dog, being a good kissing carrion—have you a daughter?" (II.ii.181–82). The daughter is Ophelia, and Hamlet's mad, disconnected syntax amply attests not only to his grotesque predilections, but also to his misogyny. Hamlet's eloquence is not void of sarcasm and humor; a certain lightness of language tempers the heaviness of the flesh and renders audible the deft and melancholy strains of Shakespeare's grotesque (Calvino 1988, 21). But such grotesquerie is constant and may be included in that undoing of the organic which appears to have invaded the political, as well as the flesh and blood, person.

Philosophical observer and passionate narrator of catastrophe, Hamlet finds himself at the center of a "time out of joint" that he suspects he was born to "set right." Perhaps in his role as passive chronicler and illustrator of the collapse of the royal body, he is the best mask for a theatrical canon that restores to "the very age and body of the time his form and pressure" (III.ii.23–24). Yet there may be too much perfection in this role for him, as Hamlet seems overly seduced by bodily introspection, metaphorical explorations of matter, and baroque visions of worm-eaten bodies. It is as if the prince were caught up in his own visceral investigations, which compel him to exaggerate his role as the *other* of Ophelia, in the play between the outside and the inside that the body allows.

The virgin Ophelia is contrived as a figure of completely external, visible, and delightful bodily beauty. She is a flower maiden, as beautiful as a mermaid in the story of her watery death. More than Baroque, she is ornamental, as the Pre-Raphaelites were quick to perceive.[4] More than a body of flesh and of obscene lusts (as Hamlet, prey to his fear of sex, sees her), Ophelia is a whole body, made up of gentle surfaces that seduce the eye. A flower among flowers, her body floats on the river, mirrored in an incorruptible nature. But only for an instant, before "muddy death" (IV.vii.183) swallows her up.

At this point the funeral of the drowned virgin becomes a good example of the spectacular theatrical excess that builds the opposition between Hamlet and Ophelia around the theme of the body. Not content to offer innumerable comic puns regarding the flesh's obscene destiny and the horror of death, Hamlet seizes the chance to appear onstage with a pair of gravediggers, who outdo him in Hamletic philosophy by handling actual corpses. They show themselves to be well acquainted with the time it takes various types of bodies to rot, and they pique the prince's curiosity with speeches as sophistic as anything he has to offer. Meantime, unbeknownst to Hamlet, it is for Ophelia's innocent body that they dig this grave. This is a tragic paradox, deftly handled by Shakespeare through insertion of a comic scene that heightens the situation's tension. But it is also the final fall of Ophelia's virginal body, a surface of beautiful female forms, into the gravepit of Hamlet's fantasies of decay. The circle of excess closes, and corruption triumphs over the external, transient beauty of the female body.

"Lay her i' th' earth, / And from her fair and unpolluted flesh / May violets spring!" (V.i.239–41), exclaims the young Laertes shortly after, ready for revenge. The image is delicate, but we cannot help noticing that the maiden's body, which was so beautiful in its pure forms, is now become fertilizer.

### The Two Bodies of the King as Food for Worms

If there is one character who especially unleashes Hamlet's fantasies of putrefying stenches and pullulating worms, that character is Ophelia's father, Polonius. The favored target of Hamlet's grotesque jokes as well as much of the tragedy's comic derision, Polonius is the conniving courtier Hamlet kills by mistake, a fool taken for Claudius and stabbed in his stead (Thatcher 1990). Hamlet takes care to hide Polonius's body by the stairs into the lobby where, in a month, anyone will be able to smell it and easily trace it down (IV.iii.33–37).

The joke about finding Polonius by following one's nose is only one of many about his body. These jokes are repeated in a widening verbal overflow concerning flesh, worms, and guts. Every possible variant on the theme of the body, especially that of the king, is allowed into the play. Hamlet, when asked where to find the body for burial, famously answers Rosencrantz: "The body is with the King, but the King is not with the body. The king is a thing . . . of nothing" (IV.ii.27–30). The answer grows clearer if we recall the doctrine of the king's two bodies, which Shakespeare knows well and often uses in his political plays.

The doctrine of the two bodies is most evident in *Richard II* (for example in act IV, scene ii) (Kantorowicz 1957, 24–41). But we should not underestimate its impact in a general Shakespearean context where royalty appears most often in the human catastrophe of the king. Above all there is the metaphorical intermingling of nature and politics evoked by the doctrine: a fragile, mysterious, and ultimately unresolved boundary from which Shakespeare's imagination does not shrink. He looks at it especially in the context of a body that dies. It sometimes seems, in fact, that Shakespeare's art is inspired most by the catastrophe of royalty, of monarchy as a political form. In this case the king's weaker body represents that catastrophe. The king's natural body should go beyond the human into the divine perpetuity of the body politic, as the doctrine appears to claim. Instead, the very nature of the body involves unclean carnality and makes the catastrophe wholly human, hence profoundly tragic.

The body as corpse appears immediately, as part of the doctrine of the king's two bodies modified by Hamlet. His jesting artfully places the king's body on the side of the festering corpse: the body is with the king, but the king is not with the body, and the king is a thing of nothing. The pun clearly refers to the two bodies doctrine, a fact probably recognized by the Elizabethan public, who needed no gloss to appreciate its multiple allusions. In joking about Polonius's corpse, Hamlet uses the notion of the double body and hits on the image of multiplication. From the start, the prince speaks of a body approaching the riot of rotting and its accompanying stench. The metaphor of the two bodies is thus inscribed within a discursive register dominated by death. The king's body, both natural and political, is first and foremost a worm-eaten corpse. Polonius, moreover, is part of the body politic, since he is a prestigious member of the court. He is thus part of the king's body, though the king is no longer with the body of his faithful subject, which is a corpse, and now even stolen away from the ceremony of burial. Not to mention that he appears to be the king's involuntary substitute, stabbed by the revenge-seeking Hamlet. The rotten double body is here substituted by that of Polonius and so becomes dismembered in many senses. Hamlet visibly enjoys this little game, underlining his passion for dissolution by hiding what he calls the *parts* until they stink.

The political and natural aspects of the body are indistinguishable within the joke's many levels. What connects the two aspects is the theme of corruption contained in both. In the end, the king is nothing: bones, dust, or even the ghost of a beggar. Or in yet another comparison with Polonius's body, he is flesh, eaten by a worm, which is in its turn eaten by a fish, which is then consumed by a beggar. This goes to show that "a king may go a progress through the guts of a beggar" (IV.iii.30–31).

A very inglorious end indeed for a royally founded order that the doctrine of the two bodies hopes to preserve forever. Mortal matter not only drags political matter into its own fate, but all poetry concerning its transience is rendered null in the squalid celebration of the grotesque.

Buried according to Christian rites (which Hamlet wants to deny Polonius), the mortal remains of the Stuart king James I lie in Westminster Abbey without a "proper" tomb. His body was placed, like an intruder, in the elegant sepulchre designed by Bartolomeo Vivarini for Henry VII and his queen, Elizabeth of York. It is they who are sculpted in marble and have lain there for centuries, sealing the tomb with their fine regal raiments, while no simulacrum of James appears. There is only his name on a faded and nearly illegible plaque.

This absence, the lack of effigies of the king, is remarkable, for it renders invisible both his natural and his political body. James's absence is all the more odd when compared to the small but striking tombs of his daughters: the two-year-old Marie, and Sophie, who lived for only one day. They gaze like porcelain dolls from their eternal cradle sculpted in marble. Not far away stands the sumptuous tomb of Mary Stuart, previously buried in the cathedral of Petersborough following her outrageous beheading. Her son James wanted her remains for the royal chapel at Westminster, so that his mother's effigy might shine in marble there. By a paradox of time, the same sort of effigy, the durable sign of that metaphorical king's body that James had so passionately defended from the symptoms of serious illness, was denied him.

The historic "double" of the mask of Hamlet thus lacks a sepulchral image. Through an irony of history, he seems to have become merely an all-too-human corpse, and to belong to the all-too-mortal aspect of the metaphor. Beyond all the simulacra and fictions, there is no spectacle more fit to indicate the mortal sustenance of the incarnate body politic than that of the royal tombs that contend for the sacred ground of a cathedral. In the series of coronations and deaths, there is a sequence in which the body of a king generates through his seed the body of the next king, who is crowned just after his father's death. This is why the French subjects exclaim, "The king is dead, long live the king!": a sort of rhetorical variant of the English "The king never dies." The root of the problem lies in the patriarchal lineage of royal bodies that remains immortal within the species. The body of the king, transmitted from father to son, does not die as a breed, though individuals, of course, perish. This is the royal twist of the ancient principle of individual mortality that locates its redemption in the survival of the species.

## Genealogies of Royal Bodies

Hamlet also features dynastic mysteries. After the father's death, the son should probably assume the crown. But Hamlet's obsession with paternal genealogy strangely has little to do with dynastic succession. His rapport with his father borders on identification with him, already signaled by their shared names and the dealings with his ghostly projection (Fusini 1981, 149). This relationship is strengthened by their common use of bodily imagery. In contrast, the son's hostility toward his mother Gertrude is continually stressed. That Freudian criticism has had a field day with the play comes as no surprise. One thing is clear: Hamlet's prolonged mourning for his father, connected to his failed revenge on the usurper who would give him the crown, is also linked to the fact that dynastic succession has not passed from father to son.

Claudius himself complains of the excessive length of Hamlet's mourning. He reminds him that "your father lost a father, / That father lost, lost his" (I.ii.89–90). He thus appeals to the inevitable law of human mortality, read in the light of the paternal line of the succession of generations. The problem is that the anomalous place of Claudius himself in the hereditary line creates a mismatch between patriarchal and dynastic succession.

The central place of the natural body of the king, as the vehicle of the continuity of the realm, is obfuscated. Yet it does not completely collapse, since Claudius sees his rule as temporary and recognizes Hamlet as his legitimate heir to the crown. The dynastic aberration (constitutional law, rather lax at the time, plays little part) functions onstage as a metaphorical allusion to a corrupt royal body that has crept into the patriarchal continuity of the realm. It thus represents an interruption in the body's health. Within the temporal unity of the drama, this expedient may also represent the sudden fracture, the thunderous collapse of the body politic.

The catastrophe of the body politic that *Hamlet* places onstage is effective as drama because the germ of decay is introduced so quickly. The rotten corporeality of the new king corresponds with this decaying realm just as the splendid appearance of the old king stood for the perfect form of the old monarchy. Hamlet's praise for his father's deeds comes close to the mythologizing of the divine Renaissance sovereign (Ciocca 1987, 47). Praising the splendid harmony of his father's body he recalls "what a grace was seated on this brow: / Hyperion's curls, the front of Jove himself, / An eye like Mars" (III.iv.55–57).

The symbolic horizon favored by Shakespeare is direct comparison between the two brothers on the Danish throne. We see this in particular when Hamlet forces the queen to look at the portraits of her first and second husbands, in order to make her *see* their contrasting features. The first is "a form indeed, / Where every god did seem to set his seal / To give the world assurance of a man" (III.iv.60–62); the second is "a mildewed ear" (III.iv.64).

The fracture that has replaced the old balance, and that introduces the catastrophe, now seems irreparable. If the doctrine of the king's two bodies made it possible to claim that the king never dies, now the old king Hamlet seems to have dragged the whole universe, of which he was the stable center, down with him into the grave. No system of sovereign centralism survives his natural body. As the treacherous Rosencrantz says with an uncanny mechanical metaphor:

> The cess of majesty
> Dies not alone, but like a gulf doth draw

What's near it with it. . . .

.  .  .  .  .  .  .  .  .  .
　　　　　　　　　. . . which when it falls,
Each small annexment, petty consequence,
Attends the boist'rous [ruin]. Never alone
Did the King sigh, but [with] a general groan.

　　　　　　　　　　　　　　　(III.iii.15–23)

In addition, however handsome he may be, Hamlet is certainly
not the living image of his father. He lacks the predatory eye and
that "fair and warlike form" (I.i.47) of the old king. This is
especially true after he assumes his mad attitude and falls into
thoughtful melancholy. The masculine fixation of every patrilinear culture, the norm of males born resembling the father
(Bettini 1992, 213ff.), is thus disappointed for this reason also.
The whole ancient splendor of the Danish monarchy is dead and
buried with the king (Hertzbach 1985). And so the doctrine of
the two bodies, of the correspondence between the king's human
flesh and his royal functions, has yet another meaning: that the
corruption of the body politic not only works deep within the
king's natural body, but also on the surface, in his carriage and
his facial features. In other words, the catastrophe affecting the
political form is represented in the realistic image of the natural
body of the king who, internally and externally, shows swift,
visible signs of his undoing.

From the divine and splendid natural body of the old king, a
son is indeed born, but not a new king. The continuity is broken.
A rotten body insinuates itself into the line, not a stranger generated by other loins, but a brother of the same flesh and blood.
The body that sits decaying on the throne is thus a kindred one,
and its intimate proximity spreads its infection to the bodies
closest to it.

Thus the queen now lives in "the rank sweat of an enseamed
bed, / Stew'd in corruption" (III.iv.93–94). The opposition between the brothers' two faces as illustrated in their portraits is
reflected in the change taking place in her female body in its
passage from the first to the second husband. It is as if woman's
inherent nature were to adapt, as if her chastity or lustfulness
depended on her accompanying mate. At least this is how Hamlet

sees things. His jests abound concerning the contamination of his mother's body through the new relation, going so far as to call the new king "my mother," since "father and mother is man and wife; man and wife is one flesh" (IV.iii.51–52) and hence his naming of the stepfather as mother is perfectly consistent. The corrupt body becomes one flesh in Claudius and Gertrude. That limit which gives an individual form to the body gives way, becoming other living material, according to a conventional rule of the grotesque (Bakhtin 1979, 33, 347). In a stench of decomposition and a feast of worms, corporeal fusion and confusion seem to be the rule here: from Claudius to Gertrude to Polonius. This is the exact opposite of that patrilinear rhythm of births and deaths, that orderly succession of natural bodies that gives the body politic its handsome head and knows neither interruptions nor mixtures.

Patrilineal succession is the sacred principle that joined patriarchy and monarchy for thousands of years in the West. In England, too, the throne is exclusively a man's domain, although numerous exceptions disturb this historic rule. James I, in fact, found himself surrounded by the unexpected coronations of women, born as he was between his mother, Mary, Queen of Scots, and the great Elizabeth I, who left him her reign. In this context, some critics have pointed out the notable impact on the doctrine of the two bodies of the king when it must adapt for a queen. In that case, the generative power of the royal body is, in a sense, fully visible; the natural body of the heir is born of the natural body on the throne, in a much more straightforward manner than occurs with the king's powers of generation. The queen's gestation and her giving birth mean that the continuance of the realm is literally founded in her body (Robertson 1990, 26; Jordan 1987; Axton 1977). Clearly the incorporation of the body politic within the natural body of the king is radicalized when that body is also maternal. An absolutely perfect figure of this coincidence occurs when a royal body is heavy with its heir.

This did not take place with Elizabeth, but James's mother was Mary, Queen of Scots, the symbol of a gravely unfortunate and controversial female royalty. In a version of *Oreste* written at the time by John Pikering and staged repeatedly, this symbol was represented symptomatically in the role of Clytemnestra, enabling a dramatic contemporary allusion to the "problems posed to the son by the body natural of an adulterous and murderess mother" (Robertson 1990, 29).

As we can see, Shakespeare's Gertrude—or at least the Gertrude of Schmitt's interpretation—is not far off. Nor are we far removed from T. S. Eliot's reading of *Hamlet,* in which the excess of the prince's disgust for his mother's wrongs becomes the aesthetic motor of the drama (Eliot 1992, 367). And yet we must also note how the events of Mary's life, tragic and thus fit for the stage, provoked the political imagination of the time to pose many questions concerning a female royal and ruling body. Her body, unlike Elizabeth's, had given birth to an heir.

The body politic, for all the detail its metaphors may allow, is apparently sexless. Obviously it cannot be pictured as a female body, since it is men who incarnate it and serve as its model. Yet though it is a male body, it has no sex; at least the sexual organs never figure in the metaphor. Despite this modesty regarding the body politic, the sexual organs of the king's natural body were so important as to inspire the custom of *ostentatio genitalium,* a showing of the genitals, which occurred on the occasion of the birth of a prince, in order to prove to the court the maleness of the next monarch. The ceremonial display of that diminutive phallus connected the past and future of the natural body of the king, since the baby proceeded from royal loins and was part of a paternal genealogy. Through the maleness of the infant, the natural body of the king passes through future incarnations.

It seems plausible to suppose that the *ostentatio genitalium* that is so very frequent in sacred images of the infant Christ derives precisely from the political dimension of this sexual question via divine imagery. Just as famously, the official portraits of the time featured a certain emphatic swelling of the king's codpiece. The phallus is meaningful in this imaginary not only as a symbol of power, but as the material instrument used to generate heirs in a continuous male bloodline. Using his sexual organs to get his bride with child, the king commits a genuine political act. And that act takes on compounded meaning when supported by the doctrine of the king's two bodies.

One reason why the metaphor of the body politic need not express that body's sex (hiding it, or not using it) is that the natural body of the male, on which the metaphor draws for its material, renders the point obvious. Hypotheses concerning the effect of a differently sexed royal are consequently of intense interest. If the apparent neutrality of the body politic might suggest its adaptability for a queen, the idea of mystical union between the queen's natural body and the body politic is more problematic. The female body does not generate in or through another, but in and by itself. In this way, at least, it seems to be more suited for the doctrine of the two bodies than a male body. Matrilineal succession seems better adapted to the figure of incorporation of the body politic. In the case of a female monarch, the doctrine's ambiguities are, if not resolved, then at least simplified.

It seems, however, that the jurists of the age in question (including those serving Elizabeth), versatile as they were at legal cavils, were not up to this conceptual challenge. The theater, for its part, dealt more willingly with homicidal and adulterous queens in examining the effects of power on the female sex. Far from untangling the knots contained in the double metaphor, power to women brought only blood and ruin. As great as the "virgin queen" Elizabeth was, she could not combat this trite misogyny of political virilism.

Apart from the bloody Lady Macbeth, it appears that Shakespeare was more interested in presenting the more traditional aspects of a virginal femininity, which he embodied in roles of fragile and impotent maidens completely ignorant of politics and the glories of the throne. These figures seem perfectly willing to remain within domestic confines, appearing predestined to the absolutely nonpolitical role of the innocent victim.

### The Body of Ophelia

Of all the characters in *Hamlet*, Ophelia seems most fit to dissolve theatrically into pure symbol (Lyons 1977, 61). From the outset she appears in the iconographic tradition of the maiden: intent on some pious book, urged on her by her father who seeks to naturalize in her a good girl's virtue. There follows the image of female melancholy madness, which will be crucial for the history of both theatrical and medical representation. Then we have the enigmatic language of flowers, symbolic code par excellence. And finally comes Ophelia's death by water. Ophelia's figuration of other things, her dwelling within the symbolic play of femininity, seems to correspond for Shakespeare with her docility before the orders of her father and brother. Indeed, at least in the first part of the drama, she functions as a mere pawn moved by other hands within the complex game of the court.

A female body beautiful with youth, virginally innocent yet potentially seductive, Ophelia functions here merely to rouse the amorous fervor the prince so obviously feels. Not much more than a girl, ignorant of male desire and of the untamed law of the flesh, an object with a pretty surface rather than the subject of inner passions, she is ready to believe Hamlet's sincere expressions of affection for her and the sacred promises of marriage that accompany them. In short, she expects a future nuptial crowning of this love. Up to this point, we seem to have the age-old story of the male seducer and the innocent virgin. But between Hamlet and Ophelia things are different. Because if he loves her with a sincere heart and is willing to legitimate his love in lawful marriage, the prince fully expresses his sincere love and (purported) nuptial intentions only after her death. Hamlet swears he felt more love for her than forty thousand brothers could, but his declarations are a bit forced, and anyway they come too late. While Ophelia was alive and could speak, their drama seemed to tell the usual story of male desire couched in sweet and deceptive language.

But Ophelia and Hamlet do not tell this story: we get our information from Laertes and Polonius, the girl's brother and father. Like every self-respecting heroine, Ophelia has no mother. From the first appearance of the love-stricken girl on-stage, the men of the family never cease to warn her against the light promises masking Hamlet's "boiling" desire. It is not that Hamlet is not sincere. But the men of the family remind her of the difference in rank that makes marriage between her and the prince impossible. Her brother warns her not to open her "chaste treasure" to Hamlet's "unmast'red importunity" (I.iii.31–32), and her father follows suit, echoing the imagery of commerce as he stresses the value of Ophelia's virginity: "Set your entreatments at a higher rate / Than a command to parle" (I.iii.122–23). Her father's orders, which are based on the criterion of virginity well spent, are therefore not to speak to Hamlet and to refuse to see him or receive his letters. As a mere docile pawn moved by others, by the author, and by Polonius, Ophelia obeys. The stage is thus set for unrequited love to appear as the plausible reason for Hamlet's madness.

In the first part of the play, thus, the obedient Ophelia moves onstage either as informer, reporting Hamlet's actions and notes to her father, or as an "actress" under her father's direction. A meeting to sound the depths of Hamlet's passion is contrived. In act III, Polonius tells her to walk where Hamlet will come by, pretending to read a book: a religious book suitable for well-bred girls. This pose recalls the iconography of the Annunciation over the centuries, in which the Virgin Mary reads a book: a model for virginal conduct well suited to the style of the court.

Ophelia therefore possesses a docile character in a seductive body, or so it seems to her cunning father, who moves her as he pleases. He plans the meeting with Hamlet to watch her act from behind a curtain, in a sort of anticipation of the "play within the play" of act IV, in which none of Ophelia's words or actions are really hers. She possesses the treasure of virginity, which attracts but must not be given. In its service, her father puts words in her mouth, but these words are strangely altered by those Hamlet forces her to utter in answer to the eloquent discourse of his feigned madness. For precisely because Ophelia's amorous interlocutor is only pretending insanity, and his apparent overheated desire is not accompanied by a corresponding perspicacious mind, his turning of the screw of dissimulation puts him at risk of actually losing his mind.

The prince's comedy of madness, together with the virginal charade of devout reading, traps Ophelia in a conversation in which she can neither keep up with the illogical tone of Hamlet nor follow the logical script forced on her by her father. A double Ophelia thus takes the stage, divided between a body that by itself moves desire, and an intellect that labors to deliver speeches that do not belong to her. This discourse, moreover, oscillates insistently between the specular themes of her virtue

146

and her vice, sounding her female body, which supposedly is capable only of absolute virginity or absolute sin. Both categories are products of a misogynistic male imagination that regards the woman's body as an object of beautiful but penetrable surfaces.

Polonius and Laertes are experts on the subject of the hot-blooded male. For them, Ophelia is a virginal body of good commercial value, exchangeable in marriage. That body can also be manipulated in order to sound the depths of madness caused by the male's ungratified desire. Only the male seems to have an "inner" body for these two courtiers, and only the man may experience that "toy in his blood" and that "hot blood." At most, they fear that it may be a "contagious blastment" transmissible to the maiden in bloom.

Hamlet, on the other hand, seems to be an expert on females in heat. He shows himself convincingly cognizant of the obscene sensuality hidden in the bodies of women, thus confirming a Pauline misogyny, perhaps studied at Wittenberg, that makes him a man of the Reformation and a strange ascetic of the flesh (Rothwell 1988, 80–99). This irrepressible if youthful expertise concerning the carnal licentiousness of women seems to have come to him mostly from observing the behavior of his mother, the queen. Only two months after her mourning as widow, she has readily succumbed to the "filthy lust" of the new king, his brother's murderer. And Hamlet appears only too ready to model his idea of the nature of women after his mother's behavior.

Whatever the real behavior of Queen Gertrude—and the play tells us nothing of her fleshly sins except through the imaginings of her son—Hamlet looks at Ophelia with a recently acquired misogynistic prejudice. He sees her as a body of virginal appearance and surface candor, artfully dissimulating the obscene sexuality common to women.

If Hamlet ever loved Ophelia, as the pure heart of the maiden seems to deserve, his love occurred not only before the appearance of the ghost, and hence before his plan of madness, but also prior to his mother's marriage to his murderous usurping uncle. The figure of the mother, in fact, functions like a lens of aggressive misogyny through which Hamlet's gaze falls on Ophelia. It is brought between them by the date of his mother's second marriage, which sets the time scheme of the play, and by her ignoble haste "to post / With such dexterity to incestious sheets" (I.ii.156–57), in which she wears mourning for less than two months, like a "beast that wants discourse of reason" (I.ii.150). Hamlet recurs many times in the course of the play to his mother's rotting in vice and her enjoying "reechy kisses" and the "paddling in your neck with his damn'd fingers" (III.iv.184–85). But all his conversations with Ophelia are likewise full of violent misogyny and an obsession with the female sexuality he considers obscene by nature. This behavior ranges from his advice that she enter a convent, viewed as the only cure for the uncontrollable immodesty of women, for whom marriage is no obstacle; to his famous question, "shall I lie in your lap?" (III.ii.112), which draws Ophelia into a series of double entendres, including that "nothing" defined by Hamlet as "a fair thought to lie between maids' legs" (III.ii.118–19).

Nothing indeed. In the slang of the Elizabethan age, *nothing* is a euphemism for the female genitals. Most especially it means *nothing* in place of the absent phallus, which, if we accept the famous etymology of Jacques Lacan, is contained in the name O-phelia/O-phallus (Lacan 1977, 20).[5] In his obsession with seeing into the body in order to contemplate its stench and decay, Hamlet's words tear away the lovely surface of Ophelia's body and make of it a receptacle for lust, to the point where the comedy of madness no longer appears sufficient to justify the persistently obscene tone that mocks the virginal role of Hamlet's interlocutor with pitiless sarcasm and excessive immodesty. Of course there are only two women onstage, Ophelia and Gertrude, and in Hamlet's eyes, Ophelia is a distant second in importance. His negative judgment of women—embodied by Gertrude—is the cause of his aggressive misogyny toward Ophelia.

As in ancient tragedy, the political element of *Hamlet* is based on a royalty completely reticulated by family ties and woven of ambiguous relationships between mothers and fathers, sons and daughters, brothers and sisters. In an age before the impersonal character of the modern state largely removed the family from the sphere of politics, Shakespeare's theater thus necessarily represents family ties in which the dichotomy between male and female must be canonically expressed. And expressed it is, in the squaring off of two women of different ranks and fates, who are united nonetheless in the misogynistic gaze directed at them by the prince.

It is therefore not odd that, joined to Gertrude by Hamlet's impudent misogyny, Ophelia finds affection and support only in her. Gertrude neither commands nor uses her. For the queen alone, she is not a pawn to maneuver, but the bride she hopes her sincerely beloved son will marry. The flowery and pathetic description of Ophelia's drowning in fact comes from Gertrude, who supplies the play's only sympathetic and gentle portrait of Ophelia, the only one that frees her from the context that binds her throughout the play. Gertrude's description contrasts with the play's usual misogyny, of which the virgin's suicide is the symbolic restatement. At the same time, it immortalizes the positive image of a female body that is difficult to kill off (Leverenz 1978, 303; Wilt 1981, 95).

Though she is only a pawn, Ophelia's role seems to move the play's dramatic machinery more than Gertrude's. A false hypothesis that attributes Hamlet's madness to her rejection of him entangles the multiple events of the play's first part. And the final hecatomb results from her madness and death, which furnish Laertes with the motive for revenge. The word *pawn* is appropriate for Ophelia as perhaps for no other pawn in Shakespeare or in the literature of the theater as a whole. After having spoken and acted not on her own initiative but on her father's, and after becoming the embarrassed butt of Hamlet's obscene jokes, Ophelia appears onstage again *out of her mind*. She is now a body with no intellect, not even one guided by others.

In contrast with Hamlet, Ophelia is genuinely insane. This new specularity will have its own important function in Shakespeare's complicit geometries. The real madness in the play finally occurs in the woman who is the presumed cause of the (false) insanity of the spurned prince. Ophelia had already tamely relinquished her wits to the wills of others. Now her words, pronounced in fits of madness, *belong* to her more than those she spoke while sane and obedient. Indeed, again mirroring Hamlet's methodical madness, her words "would make one think there might be thought, / Though nothing sure, yet much unhappily" (IV.v.12–13).

In all this we see the theme, cherished not by Shakespeare alone, of the truth in madness. No less significantly, the specularity between Hamlet's and Ophelia's madnesses puts onstage, in the former, an insanity feigned in order to utter truths about the intrigues of the Danish Crown, and in the latter, a madness that expresses the truth precisely because it is authentic. In either case we are of course dealing with an inherently theatrical *truth* that carries only the pretense of *sense* and *thought,* and hence is completely based on a play of relations among masks or roles. Through insanity Ophelia reveals the theatrically true sense of her character: the thought of her body or the symbolic order of her existence as a woman. That order, as we know, is expressed entirely through the language of flowers.

### Like a Mermaid

The central scene of Ophelia's madness is her giving of flowers to those around her in act IV. She gives her brother Laertes rosemary and pansies for remembrance and thoughts, probably recalling their recently dead father. She gives Claudius fennel and columbines, perhaps because they are herbal intestinal medicines, cures for those deep illnesses affecting the "body" of the monarch. To Gertrude, besides a daisy, she gives rue, also called herb of grace, keeping a little for herself. It is probable that she means to give grace, which is appropriate to women; but the main sense of the gesture is perhaps the sharing of the same type of flower between the queen and herself. It is true that she asks Gertrude to wear it differently than she does, but the scene nonetheless points to their common sex and to an increasing mutual affection.[6]

The importance of this language of flowers lies not so much in its botanical symbolism (probably known to the Elizabethan audience, although even then there were variants in meaning), but in Ophelia's very choice of flowers as symbol—that is, in her impersonation of Flora. Critics have suggested that Shakespeare wished to allude to two noted figures of Flora of the time: the mythical, pastoral nymph of Ovid, who was associated with fertility and spring rebirth; and the Roman prostitute Flora, who appears in both Plutarch and Boccaccio (Lyons 1977, 63). The flowers would therefore be a stereotypical allusion to woman as mother and as courtesan. The importance of the figure of Flora seems in fact to lie in her ambiguity, for a persistent ambiguity likewise characterizes Ophelia throughout her madness.

In other words (and leaving aside the fact that Ophelia would have been played by a man in Shakespeare's time), Ophelia mad is doubled: she is the totally innocent, virginal creature, and the sensual woman who offers her body. Ophelia is both the pure maiden and her opposite, even in those scenes that present her with her hair and clothes undone. She is the symbol of a female nature in whom hidden sensuality has come to the surface. It has revealed itself precisely because it was in her, as in all women. Then there is the distribution of flowers, which functions as a virginal "deflowering" (Showalter 1985, 81), accompanied by her ambiguous song. The song veers from poetic allusion to a lost love, a person dear to her and now buried, to vulgar references to sexual intercourse and the lusty language and double meanings more befitting a soldier. The song plays on equivocation between the chaste and the vulgar, the poetic and the prosaic, which is underlined by Ophelia's portrayal of Flora the nymph and Flora the prostitute. All of these meanings rely on the ambiguous language of flowers, a language stretched even further in Gertrude's description of Ophelia's death.

In a scene justly celebrated for its poetic beauty and which is the main inspiration for the iconographic tradition surrounding the figure of Ophelia, the queen tells how the virgin, now insane, sang on the banks of a stream, weaving whimsical garlands of crowflowers, nettles, daisies, and long purples. Shepherds call these last flowers with a "grosser name, / But our cull-cold maids do dead men's fingers call them" (IV.vii.170–71). In this nearly Botticellian image of a nymph at home in her natural habitat, the mention of the flowers' double name (long purples) adds an ambiguous, vulgar touch. The "grosser name" traditionally alludes to the male genitals, especially the testicles (Otten 1979, 397–402). The intrusion of the obscene symbol within the graceful picture of the garlands is tempered with an evocation of death: the stiff fingers of the corpse or "dead men's fingers," the name given to the flower by "*cold* maids." The figure of Ophelia remains contradictory and unclear in this juxtaposition of flower-crowned virginity with the image of a woman provocatively adorned with phallic symbols and the sarcastic counterfigure of stiff and cold "fingers."

Death is about to seize this virgin, who is cold in two senses: on the one hand she awaits the chilling embrace of death, and on the other the virginal body is itself cold, an effect it transmits to a phallus reduced to a dead man's finger. The piling up of symbols and allusions, in a language that shifts between erotic carnality and virginal frigidity, seems here pushed to a culminating excess of ambiguity before consigning Ophelia to her death, which is finally narrated in clear, natural, and melancholy tones. The enchantment of the instant when Ophelia hesitates before the water's mirrorlike surface is beautiful indeed. The garlands fall with her into the stream, while her clothes swell around and keep her afloat: "mermaid-like . . . / Or like a creature native and indued / Unto that element" (IV.vii.176–80). Ophelia sings calmly and without fear of her proximate and inevitable death. It is as if, in her unwitting madness, Ophelia has been able to recognize the water as her native element, where, for a fleeting instant, she feels at home, outside time and the history of Denmark.

The metaphorical logic of doubling and contradiction—a logic that places Ophelia at two extremes of the male gaze upon the young female body—seems in the end to produce a character that escapes its own structure. In addition to the interpretive phantasmagoria occasioned by the heaping up of symbols and by the suggestive power of Shakespeare's language, a side of Ophelia's icon seems to be produced that exceeds the control of the text. That icon proves able to migrate, so to speak, toward an autonomous history. In the Western tradition—one thinks, of course, of the Pre-Raphaelites—an Ophelia exists who can stand completely by herself, not only without Hamlet, but without *Hamlet,* or at least in spite of *Hamlet.* But this is not the point.

The point is that in Ophelia as nymph, mermaid, siren, Shakespeare cannot help alluding to an originary *sign* of the female sex in its natural connection to water. Even Shakespeare, it seems, cannot resist citing this association, in a sort of poetic surrender to the autonomous power of the ancient image. The enduring tradition of water-bound women points constantly to the seductive power of an image that, perhaps more than any other, evokes the enigma of a different sex. For thousands of years, an unresolved alterity based on the female *monstruum* of that liquid element has left traces within the androcentric universe that has dominated texts. The persistence of the aquatic sign, which is reserved for mythical creatures of the other sex, is so evident and so ancient that we cannot trace it back to any stereotypical strategy of a patriarchal culture, though of course that culture also weaves its plots, even in *Hamlet*.

The stereotype (or, if we will, the effect of the male gaze on the different sex, which categorizes female characteristics for its own purposes) is in fact present in *Hamlet*. It is present in the desire for a dead female body that is infinitely available and passive. This body also has an intense connection with flowers, water, and bestiality, and it offers itself up in a sacrificial ecstasy (Dijkstra 1986, 51).[7] Such is certainly not the *totality* of the representation, and it does not mean that there is *nothing* irreducible within the reality of the thing represented, which in this case involves the link between women and water substantiated in the figure of Ophelia. Hence in addition to the hermeneutic exercise of ferreting out familiar stereotypes from the patriarchal macrotext and aligning them within the now-classic category of gender, we might add another, probably more productive operation. We might attempt to separate the essential core of such a figure from the stereotypical deformations that have encrusted it.[8] In this way we may gauge the figure's resistance to changes in cultural context. In the case of the aquatic woman, the image passes—almost slips—from myth to fable, from the wild and terrible key of bestiality to harmonious nature. On its way, it illustrates how the kernel of its meaning can adapt to different narrative styles without losing its original substance. Its substance—or its mystery—is evidently pliable to stereotype, yet capable at its core of a certain resistance over time.

The mermaid comes down to Shakespeare from a very ancient tradition of half-animal, half-female monsters, originally related to birds, then given serpents' tails, then finally formed like fish. It reaches him as the female whose voice, as early as Homer, is that of seductive song. Even more probably Shakespeare gets the figure from that of the medieval Melusine, which was famous throughout Europe at that time and found in many written versions known in England.[9] The image as Shakespeare receives it, whether water nymph or mermaid, comes inevitably laden with stereotypes handed down from the patriarchal tradition. These range from a sensual abandon that appears to fit well with male desires, to the debasement from human to animal in the theriomorphic woman. This degradation seduces and terrorizes at the same time, attracting the flesh as it puts the male intellect on guard. Ophelia in the stream is also this type of figure. Her clothes, swelling about her, keep her afloat, but the thousand properties attributed to the mermaid by the male imagination push her underneath the water's reflecting surface.

Ophelia, however, also represents the female subject's enchantingly brief homecoming to the watery element that appears native and originary to her. Hamlet had called her a nymph in a previous scene. And she appears, in the end, as a nymph in the scene that momentarily delays her death. Here Ophelia reclaims for herself, beyond all the layers of stereotyping, a character that belongs to the welcoming waters, irreducibly alien to everything around her that rots away in the political realm of Denmark.

The complexity of the Shakespearean text allows a reading of Ophelia's adventures as a progressive alienation from the material of the drama, which is evidently and inevitably androcentric. She thus gains a female alterity that resists assimilation and leaves her finally within the sheer beauty of her own enigma. This is true despite the trap of the stereotype that continues to work around her. The commonplace workings of woman-nature against man-politics almost turn her fleeting victory into a banal formula. Yet an irreducible something, coming from very far away, puts its *unyielding mark* on the writing, leaving to posterity the image of an aquatic and floral Ophelia who is infinitely reinterpretable in an imagery belonging to her alone, outside any memory of *Hamlet*.

The alienation that, in the end, brings the maiden to her peaceful homecoming in the waters of the stream follows a precise itinerary. Her path is clear from the first, from her initial role as a pawn ensnared in political machinations (and therefore not a conscious subject of them), to her subsequent madness and abandonment of all the political and courtly "rationality" that had been imposed on her by her father. This very rationality continues to function onstage, gradually working itself into its own trap. To that which is commonly considered logical discourse, as well as to Hamlet's bizarre logic, with its oblique and seemingly mad method, Ophelia opposes a discourse of free associations, turned to song in a fragmented syntax that dislocates sense (Charney and Charney 1977, 456). The otherness of her language to that which circulates in Denmark is confirmed by the floral language she adopts as a ciphered code. This code is not only botanical and unpolitical, but also thoroughly Shakespearean, interpretable by a theatrical public (which recognizes in her the ambiguous design of the two Flora figures). Yet there is also another decoding that seems to be understood only by Ophelia herself in the undecipherable world of madness.

Having found her language in song, in flowers, and in the disconnected syntax of insanity, Ophelia in this sense thus also becomes Hamlet's *other*. Hamlet's discursive style, given to introspection and philosophical musings, seems to want deliberately to turn death itself into words, so as to control future events:

> O, I die, Horatio,
> The potent poison quite o'er-crows my spirit.
> I cannot live to hear the news from England,
> But I do prophesy th' election lights
> On Fortinbras, he has my dying voice.
>
> (V.ii.353–56)

There seems to be an immeasurable difference between this self-narrated, politically loaded death and the unconscious death of Ophelia, who drowns in an exquisite nature totally divorced from the world of the court (Fischer 1990, 8).

The poor Ophelia, whom Claudius calls "divided from herself and her fair judgment, / Without the which we are pictures, or mere beasts" (IV.v.85–86), in the end is particularly divided from her role as obedient daughter. She is now completely alienated from the court, within a *self* that no longer communicates according to courtly logic. Meanwhile Hamlet's language of the madman still communicates tangentially, as he reshapes his own self in opposition to that very court (Rothwell 1988, 88–89). Ophelia will soon become in image a beast, half-beast, or mermaid, as Gertrude's account suggests, but not before having crucially found herself in the water's mirror.

Reflecting the branches of the willow where she hangs her garlands and into which she will later fall, only to float on its surface singing and covered with flowers, "the glassy stream" has naturally been an important part of critical interpretation of Ophelia's character. The story of Alice and the looking glass will not appear for some time, but the image of the mirror offers a compelling hermeneutic key (Philip 1991, 73–84; Bettini 1992, 113), one that cannot fail to capture the reader's imagination in its age-old figural schemes.

The dynamics of Ophelia's doubtful suicide are fully mirrored in that stream, in a doubling play of her death scene. Separated from the plane of reality, she falls into that of reflection, suggesting a kind of drainage of the referent into its image. Or perhaps we could say that in the aquatic mirror Ophelia finally recognized her true reflection, merged with it, and came to possess it at last. Not like Narcissus in his fatal embrace with his double: Ophelia does not immediately *cut through* the plane of reflection, dragging herself and her own image to the bottom. She floats on the surface of the reflecting waters, herself becoming the incarnation of the mirror. She becomes that aquatic and floral image the mirror had shown her, and with which she finally coincides. In short, she is a bodily materialization of her true *self,* caught sight of and captured in the reflected figure. The dream of all identity dreams comes magically true: this is the eternal illusion of the human race as such, but especially of that unrepresented female subject who succumbs all too readily to the desire for perfect correspondence with an image.

In this densely symbolic situation, the question of voluntary suicide or accident is irrelevant. The gravedigger's sophistry concerning whether she has gone to the water or the water to her becomes secondary. The fact is that the female body and its own reflected image have come to each other, in a watery element that belongs to them both. Here a final incarnation of the mermaid that resists being captured in stereotypes claims its space on the stage and takes on a significance and life of its own. But its time is brief, and death by drowning intervenes to break the mirror's spell. The noted polyvalence of the iconography surrounding Ophelia—the swelling clothes, the crown of flowers, and the placid rise of song—interrupts the logical sequence that will change the mermaid into a drowned woman, and the mirror into a dark and muddy whirlpool. Thus despite her pitiful fate, the metamorphosis of Ophelia into a melodious aquatic creature resembles more a scene of birth than one of death, at least insofar as birth here is, in theatrical terms, the character's finding herself in the image that most belongs to her. This image in the end renders visible the ancient enigma of the aquatic woman, a figure that endures beyond its thousand stereotypical permutations.

The spell is perfect but brief. After the mermaid's purity comes muddy death for Ophelia's body. This body, moreover, immediately becomes a corpse, subject to the predictions regarding rotting and worms that the gravediggers swap with Hamlet. It is thus soon torn from the beautiful and natural setting that would have the female body at home amid flowers, water, and melodious song. In this context, it is also important to note that Shakespeare's nature, and not only in the scene of Ophelia's drowning, is a spontaneous garden, beautiful and orderly. Nature thus assumes a positive significance of beauty and order, in clear contrast with the disorder and filth invading the political realm.

The difference between Hamlet and Ophelia, between male and female, is underlined again by this opposition, one of a "bewildering array of mirror relationships that make up the substance of the text" (Rothwell 1988, 92). This dichotomy risks descending into the stereotypes of nature versus politics that for thousands of years have dominated the symbolism of sexual difference. Yet the very simplicity of this binary structure works to the play's advantage. Within the relationship between macro- and microcosm so important to Renaissance thought, Shakespeare inscribes an extraordinary metaphorical permeability between the body, seen as nature, and nature understood as a garden. When the biblical Eden serves as inspiration for the image, that garden is spontaneously beautiful and well ordered in all of its manifold forms. But it often becomes an earthly garden, in need of care, always ready to return to wilderness, and suffering the effects of the climate and of disease (Ciocca 1987, 110–12). Like the human body, the cultivated garden is an organism possessing a fragile beauty that can go to rot and be destroyed by illness.

Compared to the paradisiacal, natural setting that welcomes Ophelia in the mermaid scene, the world appears to the nauseated Hamlet as "an unweeded garden / That grows to seed, things rank and gross in nature / Possess it merely" (I.ii.135–37). This is part of the soliloquy in which Hamlet complains that his too sullied flesh cannot resolve itself into a dew. He calls his mother, who has succumbed to obscene passion, a beast that wants discourse of reason. There is thus an explicit transition from the metaphor of the abandoned garden and the courtly world of politics to that of the body disordered by the passions, unable to change into the poetic form of dew. For Hamlet and for the realm of Denmark, nature, especially its plant and animal species, is a theater of illness, mildew, and putrefaction. It is disorder and ugliness, in short. This earth is reduced to a sterile promontory beneath the majestic beauty of the starry heavens, which themselves appear to Hamlet to be "a foul and pestilent congregation of vapors" (II.ii.302–3). Hamlet's melancholy obviously plays a part in this nature permeated by decay, so dear to the saturnine gaze. It supplies a cosmic setting for the collapse of royalty (Benjamin 1980, 186). This collapse is the political manifestation of a general decay, which the grotesque tonality of the bodily metaphor aptly describes as it allies itself with corrupt nature in shared metaphors of inexorable ruin. Ophelia's fluvial body, gently embraced by the quietly beautiful flower garden that furnishes her most famous image (and that restores Ophelia to her true *self*), becomes all the more meaningful seen in juxtaposition with Hamlet's bodily imagery.

The female heroine is pointedly reinstated within a natural and consequently unpolitical realm. Beyond the stereotypes and dichotomies that function here, this realm gives back an aura of ancient mystery to the aquatic figure. In the image of the mermaid, briefly located outside temporal and historical logic, the body of Ophelia is saved. Her female body lies outside the political ruin whose metaphor is the worm-eaten body; it moreover takes no part in the clearly masculine substance of the metaphor itself. The millennial and foundational expulsion of women from politics, which is disturbing enough when a queen sits on the throne, cannot help but leave its traces in a body employed as the metaphor for politics itself. This is so not only because that body, as we have seen, is plainly sexed as a male, but above all because, from time immemorial, politics is built upon a distancing from the body. And this body, in its *natural* substance of flesh and blood, and in its generative womb (to which the aquatic element alludes), is felt to be, at bottom, female.

We are all born of a woman, and every body comes from a woman's body, as Plato, despite his logocentric fantasies, well knew. The entire culture of the West confirms this, including Shakespeare's Macbeth and his celebrated riddle. It comes as no surprise, then, that the female is expelled from an idea of politics created in order to keep at bay *birth,* which instead assumes death as its training ground.[10] Such a politics of course risks a definitive estrangement from birth, which may return only in the form of an enigma.

Buried alive, Antigone's body had been significantly held outside the political walls. She is kept in that realm of untamed nature, wild and animal, from which the polis in its greatest glory separates itself, fearing, however, its siege from without. In Shakespeare's text, where an era recounts its own political collapse, the female body in the guise of Ophelia poses crucial questions. In one sense, her body is received as a corpse, for the customary funeral belonging to the social order. In another sense, however, her body gains immortality with an aquatic image, which expresses both her estrangement from a political history of crime and ruin, and her resistance to the patriarchal codes of this world.

In contrast with the corpses that are the subject of Hamlet's descants, the mermaidlike body of Ophelia (above and beyond her corpse, given over to decay) discloses a type of figure that stands immutable in its iconic autonomy. The dissolution of her body underground is described gracefully: Laertes hopes that violets may spring "from her fair and unpolluted flesh" (V.i.238–40). These are the same violets she had wanted to give the Queen in the scene of the distribution of flowers, but which had all withered when her father died (IV.v.184–85). Violets here seem to be a type of flower mysteriously sensitive to the vicissitudes of life and death, similar to bodies in love, since the lover's warm blood is like "a violet in the youth of primy nature, / Forward, not permanent, sweet, not lasting, / The perfume and suppliance of a minute— / No more" (I.iii.7–10).

In the language of flowers recodified by Ophelia, her flower seems to be the violet. Melancholy and ambiguous in its beauty and evanescence, it brings her corpse back to the setting of the natural garden that, by all appearances, seems to belong to her truest image. In the perfume of violets we may almost sense the posthumous trace of a female and unpolitical body. That body continues to be born and to die elsewhere, in the silent realm of the waters. The body politic, meanwhile, collapses noisily amid stinking decay, in the twistings and turnings of a history that has always been choked with words.

Like many aquatic women before her, the mermaid Ophelia perhaps sings for other, less greedy ears. For since the beginning of time, or at least "since the fortunate misfortune of Odysseus with the Sirens, all songs have fallen sick, and the whole of Western music suffers under the absurdity of singing in civilization, which nevertheless gives art music its power to move us" (Horkheimer and Adorno 1989, 59–60, translation modified; cf. Horkheimer and Adorno 1992, 124).

LEVIATHAN
## Mechanical Body

Hamlet presents a political body that suddenly collapses into the black confusion of the worm-eaten corpse. This is not yet a void, but the grotesque site of catastrophe, a perspectival view of the slide into formlessness. Although Hamlet's "modernity" now makes him unable to reconcile past and present (Colaiacomo 1993, 30), an exemplary royal splendor from the very recent past remains constantly before his eyes, in the passage of the scepter from one brother (his father) to the other (his uncle). And this splendor, it is intimated, could yet return triumphant, perhaps with Fortinbras, thus revealing the catastrophe as only a temporary if disastrous misfortune.

A few decades after the composition of *Hamlet*, when civil war spread through England and all of Europe, Thomas Hobbes took the widespread disorder as the point of departure for an entirely new type of body politic. The chaos of the preceding age, with its old forms of domination, gave way to a state that would subsequently be modified with the adjective *modern*. Hobbes conceives this new form both as an artificial body and as a monster modeled on the biblical Leviathan. A prepolitical scene of radical and constitutive disorder necessitates its construction. Saturated to the point of nausea by religious struggles and bloody wars arising from the irreversible crisis of an old political model, the system was unable to resolve the conflict from within (Schmitt 1986, 92). It appeared that nothing that might reestablish some form of political order could be salvaged from the historical present. Indeed, precisely the present was lived in most people's experience as endemic disorder. The medieval image of the world as a hierarchically ordered, self-sufficient whole had disintegrated into a confessional fanaticism rekindled rather than quelled by the principle of monarchy (Schnurr 1979, 25–26).

Given this unresolvable situation, Hobbes's theory—radical as it is—is extraordinarily simple. He attributes the bloody oppressiveness of the age and its endless wars to an original state of nature characterized by the total disorder of a war of all against all. He thus postulates the radical opposition enemy/enemy as the *normal* basis of all human relationships (Biral 1987, 58). In this way the "state of nature" as starting point assumes an exemplary philosophical position outside of history, while at the same time it explains all of history's despairing outcomes.

In his doctrine, Hobbes offers no regretful narration of the unexpected collapse of late medieval society. Much less is he nostalgic for an ancient monarchy capable of flourishing anew in the sixteenth century. His point of departure is instead a pure and timeless disorder; and chaos without memory is the institutional void with which his theory begins.

Against the background of the state of nature, which functions both as a logical category of foundation and as a transparent image of the civil war, Hobbes traces his famously pessimistic and atomistic anthropology, in which men are depicted in permanent war with each other. This situation, however, is neither chosen nor desired by individuals guilty of malice; it is the inevitable and innocent essence of human nature. Hobbes understands human nature to be mechanically moved by a perennial and inevitable desire inscribed in corporeality. Everyone naturally desires what he considers to be to his own good and concentrates all his power on acquiring it, employing any means to this end. All obstacles are perceived as bad and must be removed, even if this means the physical elimination of competitors, the murder of anyone whose movements oppose one's own.

The only law of Hobbes's universe is that of the local motion of bodies; and man, as body, is not exempt from this law. He is in fact attracted to the object of his desire and urged to eliminate any impediment. "This he doth by a certain impulsion of nature, no less than that whereby a stone moves downward" (Hobbes, *De Cive,* I.7). Natural impulse dictates action, in a situation where all men have the right to all things. This right proves ineffectual and self-contradictory, however, because it is nullified by reciprocal and unregulated impediments within a mechanical and murderous game where "every man, as much as in him lies, endeavours to protect his life and members" against the attacks of others (*De Cive,* I.7).

These lonely, unhappy, and brutish men, following the notorious principle of *homo homini lupus,* are substantially equal in their fate of violent death. According to Hobbes's dry reasoning, those who can act equally against each other are equals, "but they who can do the greatest things (namely kill) can do equal things" (*De Cive,* I.3). Since, according to Hobbes's *Elements of Law,* "it takes only a small effort to eliminate a human life" (XIV.2), murder even levels differences in bodily strength, as well as differences of intellect, which structurally depend on the diverse constitution of the body (X.2).

Equality, therefore, is founded on the violent horizon of death. This most crucial category in the modern political vocabulary—

one of the most alien to the previous political lexicon—is based on death predatorily given and received; corporeal death cuts off a life conceived, according to Hobbesian mechanics, as nothing but "a motion of limbs" (*Leviathan,* intro.). Propelled toward ever new objects by a "perpetual and restless desire of power after power, that ceaseth only in death" (*Leviathan,* XI), and thus comparable to one running a race where "to abandon the track is to die" (*Elements,* IX.21), man in a state of nature is subject to constant movement, which is the whole of life. In this progression entirely projected into the future—never satisfied in the present because unstoppable—death, as the cessation of all movement, becomes the thing that everyone most fears. All men are equal to all others not only in fearing death, but also and especially in giving it.

Hobbes's state of nature, governed by murder in a vast, generalized warfare conducted by lone wolves, is presented as a form of disorder so severe as to be nearly beyond the pale of metaphorical representability. Feeding the war of everyone against everyone else is a continual, chaotic, and general movement; it has neither rules nor collective formations that might allow it to be communicated through images, thus simplifying its design. It is merely the turbulence of crazed fragments that stop others or are themselves stopped by death in unpredictable encounters. If the life of every person consists not only of movement but also of ensuring by any means the possibility of future movement, this disorder of incalculable aggressions becomes totally counterproductive and unbearable. It merely guarantees a high probability of violent death, which contradicts the basic urge for self-preservation.

The natural freedom to move according to one's own desires, which aims "not to enjoy once only, and for one instant of time, but to assure for ever, the way of his future desire" (*Leviathan,* XI), results in the constant and dreaded danger that movement itself will cease. Men's bodies, left to the mechanical law of their actions, produce war and death. This is a life that is nasty, brutish, and short, full of fear, loneliness, ignorance, and cruelty (*De Cive,* X.1).

Thus it happens that "fear of death; desire of such things as are necessary to commodious living; and hope by their industry to obtain them" (*Leviathan*, XIII) are the passions that incline men toward peace. Having grown conscious of the aporetic mechanism of reciprocal self-annihilation, men understand that "peace is good" (*De Cive*, III.31). Not only good, but necessary, if they wish to escape the founding paradox of a life-preserving movement that generates death. Within this paradox in which the natural abnegation of an individual life in its very biological basis is held up as the supreme point of reference (Arendt 1989, 232–33), the problem of the "passage" from a state of nature to political society emerges. The problem is how to instill and maintain peace; how to create a situation in which peaceful behavior can be made obligatory for everyone. In fact, while the state of nature exists, it is not enough for some to desire peace and to consequently give up their right to everything, if everyone else does not follow suit, "for that were to expose himself to prey" (*Leviathan*, XIV), followed by certain death within a natural condition where "every man has a right to every thing; even to one another's body" (XIV).

The problem is solved with the passage from a state of nature to an artificial political state, which is created by means of a *pact*. Everyone exchanges with everyone else the promise to give up his right to everything, that is, to the natural right to use his power, transferring it to someone who declares that he accepts it. The reduction of many wills, capable of reciprocal harm, to only one, which represents everyone and possesses the power to oblige everyone to obey, resolves the problem: with the removal of the plurality of wills, there is no longer any place for war. Peace finally reigns within a single body politic. This body politic is, of course, surrounded by war, which determines international relations with its equals. But within, it is strong, cohesive, and endowed with one will, manifested by a sovereign who governs his subjects.

The sovereign is nothing more than that man or assembly of men on whom the makers of the pact have conferred all power. As Hobbes specifies in the *Leviathan*, it is as if each of them had said to the other: "I authorize and give up my right of governing myself, to this man, or to this assembly of men, on this condition, that thou give up thy right to him, and authorize all his actions in like manner" (*Leviathan,* XVII). Thus the sovereign is born: he is born out of the pact, yet remains alien to the logic of the mutual promise of those convening. The sovereign has stipulated no pact with anyone, but has merely accepted the *summa potestas* resulting from everyone else's renunciation of their natural right. The transfer of force, pronounced in words, takes place concretely in each man's renouncing its individual use; the supreme power, or sovereignty, which is its name and substance, thus consists of each subject's renunciation of his right to resist the sovereign. The pact of renunciation is enough to force each man to obey, since it is necessary and obvious that only the sovereign retains the compelling use of the sword.

The sovereign is by universal agreement unopposable, insofar as he makes no covenant with his subjects. Therefore there can be no breach on the part of the sovereign, who is made irresistible by the use of that power rendered concrete by the sword: "He hath the use of so much power and strength conferred on him, that by terror thereof, he is enabled to form the wills of them all, to peace at home, and mutual aid against their enemies abroad" (*Leviathan,* XVII). The crucial problem of war is resolved, in the end, through the absorption of many conflicting forces into one, absolute, and irresistible force, held by the sovereign. Made obedient through their pact and the terror of the sword, the subjects are no longer a mere multitude in which each man moves according to his own will, clashing with every other man in a violent and murderous mechanism. They are now incorporated into a people, a union that moves with one will. This union "by the compact of many men, is to be received for the *will* of them all" (*De Cive,* V.9). Each man must recognize it as his own will and cannot oppose it, lest he oppose his own will.

In other words, subjects and sovereign constitute a sole person; a single civic person generated artificially by the pact and called the state. Thus many people are linked and transfigured (*De Cive,* V.12). Peace is finally ensured, if only because there is a single will, which all are compelled to recognize as their own and which no one can resist.

The key to the entire structure consists of a logic that goes from a natural multiplicity to an artificial unity: in other words, from an absolute disorder, numbered on the many, to an absolute order, founded upon the one (Cavarero 1991, 313–19). According to Hobbes, it was earlier philosophers' ignorance of the fact that human nature is founded on conflict that let them believe one could build a society in which many powers, and thus many forces and wills, perhaps balanced into hierarchies, could coexist. But where there is pluralism of powers, there is nothing but the war and anarchy that is the *normal* state of nature. The just and peaceful society, in which the power of reason, wealth, splendor, and the refinements of art will finally rule, speaks the language of the *one:* one state, one body politic, one sovereign, one people. In Hobbes's discourse, these things seem to fade into figures of one another, strengthened by a corporate logic that assigns them substantial coidentity. In the end they seem to be different names for the same thing, merely seen from different perspectives.

The reasoning that structures this political theorem is quite clear: an absolute, contradictory, and thus unbearable disorder gives way to an artificial absolute order in which the cohesive, and therefore pacifying, power of *unity* cannot tolerate any *other* if it is to be true and effective. Not only is no other power admitted (else all peace would be lost), but, more importantly, no other thing may intrude that claims to be autonomously definable: having a sense of its own outside of the unity of the political form. Such a thing, in that case—whether it be the people, the sovereign, or even the state—could possess an identity isolatable from that unitary form itself, and therefore something *other* with respect to it. Instead, not only is the sovereign (whether king or assembly) "one people" (*De Cive,* XII.8), but there is nothing that can be called people, or sovereign, outside that artificial person, the commonwealth. Similarly, nothing merits the name of commonwealth outside this perfect coincidence of people and sovereign. The theory of a unique and irresistible will tends to engulf in its representational logic all the different notions, old and new, in the political lexicon. It thus leaves no logical, intermediate space for conflict between sovereign and people. Everything is swallowed by a giant body politic that moves in one direction, without contrast from within.

One of the most curious features of this rigid logic of unity—which is, moreover, neither simple nor seamless in its obsessive insistence on identity—is the variety of metaphors Hobbes employs. He resorts to images that describe the state in four ways: as a gigantic, artificial body, as a machine, as a person, and as the monstrous, biblical Leviathan. Obviously these metaphors strain to form an internally coherent symbolic framework. If the shift from *body* to *machine* to *person* in this gallery of metaphors already poses some problems of figural change and incongruent evocative valences, the additional image of a giant, fishlike *monster* (the Leviathan) seems to annul any reassuring effect of the other three figures. Since the idea of a machine may be inscribed within that of a body mechanically envisioned, the first three figures appear to spring from a single, anthropomorphic network that can include even the concept of the person. The image of the monster, however, connotes not only animality, but even an extraordinary, irregular and unpredictable bestiality (Rigotti 1992, 169).

It is thus inevitable that the image of the state as Leviathan, a mythical monster, should be opposed to that of the state as a fundamentally rational body-machine, which belongs to a predominantly rational framework. A drastic opposition appears to hold between the rational and the bestial in the Hobbesian imagination: an opposition between organic monstrosity and mechanical corporeality, between the irregular and unknowable body of the monster, on one hand, and the mechanically constructed and therefore knowable (and artificially reproducible) body of man as normal animal, on the other.

From whatever way one looks at it, the question revolves around the concept of the body. In Hobbes, the body does not appear simply at the end, so to speak, as a metaphor for a mechanized body politic. It appears from the start of the discussion as the carnal machine, active and reactive, of that unlimited desire which is the horizon and cause of the war of every man against every other. It is a body, then, and precisely a mechanically constructed body, inscribed in the universal law of movement, which holds together the threads of political discourse and which orients that discourse toward the new solution of an artificial form for the state. This new state will once again be figured in the mechanical body. This new body is light years away from that medieval, organic body that implodes in the catastrophe of *Hamlet*. But it is also far from the mythical, strange, and uncontrollable bestiality of the monstrous Leviathan. This new kind of body owes its mechanical features to the conceptual innovations of the distinguished seventeenth-century English physician and anatomist William Harvey. Harvey's great success in England enabled a rapid reorganization of contemporary science around his ideas and constituted a fundamental turning point in the history of medicine.

### Harvey's Heart

William Harvey published his *Exercitatio Anatomica de Motu Cordis et Sanguinis* in 1628. There he presents a revolutionary theory of the circulation of the blood, which he developed further in his *Exercitationes Duae Anatomicae de Circulatione Sanguinis*. Harvey studied at the medical schools in Canterbury, Cambridge, and Padua, but he declares that he prefers to use his own eyes, rather than rely on "the books and writings of others" (1968, 23). Harvey's eyes look at the cold truth of bodies on the dissection table but also endeavor to see inside the living body. He tells, with some satisfaction, how he personally fished shrimp out of the Thames and how he could see in their fragile, transparent bodies, as through a window, the small, beating heart that causes the blood to circulate, and thus "the beginning of life" (38).

The similarities between the bodies of animals and those of man unfold a single physiological structure centered on the heart. Its rhythmical movements cause the blood to circulate in an orderly fashion. Life consists in this circulation; life is generated by it and, as long as the heart beats, life is preserved. Harvey notes that this process can be compared "to what occurs in machines, in which, since one wheel moves another, all seems to move together" (1968, 39). The foundation of Harvey's thesis is his description of the cardiovascular system considered as a sort of hydraulic complex (Webster 1979, 21–22) and, in general, a mechanical notion of the body, in which the scientist does not hesitate to use analogies between various bodily functions and the structures of certain exemplary "machines." The act of swallowing is thus surprisingly compared to the mechanics of firearms, in which the pressing of the trigger and consequent explosion of powder and firing of the projectile are compared to the tongue's pressure on food. Together, Harvey says, the movements of the tongue, larynx, and epiglottis with their relative compressor muscles push the nutriment finally to the stomach (1968, 39–40). Similarly, the heart's formation consists of a "sort of swallowing and transmission of blood from the veins to the arteries" (40).

An analogical framework is evident in which everything is related, from the hydraulic pump to the gun and from the act of swallowing to the heartbeat. This framework permits a conception of the body as a natural machine, which has precise echoes in man-made mechanisms. The natural and the artificial, far from being counterposed as the organic and the mechanical have been, are only two anamorphic versions of the machine principle. The order of the machine explains that of the body, and the metaphorical exchange between them suggests a universe of predictable and regular movements that both explain and contain each other. There is, therefore, a single principle of truth, which holds the great advantage of being empirically observable in nature as well as applicable to the products of technology.

A sort of central motor initiates a chain of movements upon which everything else depends. In the bodies of animals, this is the heart. The heart is more material than the head and in any case is necessitated by the mechanical structure of the body. The heart is indeed nothing but a perfect device consisting of the rhythmic beating of diastoles and systoles, the organization and action of its auricles and valves. The mechanical nature of the heart does not make it any less important, for as Harvey says, "this organ merits the name of the beginning of life, and is the sun of our microcosm, just as the sun merits the name of the heart of the Earth . . . , since the heart is the tutelary god of the body and the root of life" (59).

Thus, the ancient and familiar metaphors return in Harvey, having already served to form the organic notion of the body cherished by tradition. The metaphors of the microcosm and macrocosm also reappear, apparently adapting easily to the new mechanical model. Yet within this traditional language, everything has changed. Everything has become an enormous, intricate contraption in which life, understood mainly as movement, circulates and pulsates, transmitting a motor energy from the center to the outside and back again to the center in a cycle that repeats as long as the device holds up.

Harvey was a well-known champion of the cause of the monarchy in an age of constitutional crisis. It comes as no surprise that he dedicated his writings to Charles I and inserted the figure of the king in his metaphorical universe, where the heart held the central position. The king, like the role of the heart in the bodies of animals, is described as "the basis of his reign, the sun of his microcosm, and the heart of the state." Moreover, given his eminent role, the king, as monarch and man, is in a perfect position to see simultaneously the human body's central organ and its correspondence with his own royal power (3).

Interestingly, this political recycling of the organological metaphor in a cardiac and mechanical version causes Harvey's pen to run away with him at times. Compared to the rigor of his science, his vocabulary often appears excessive. This happens especially in a page dedicated to his beloved monarch, where Harvey does not hesitate to compare the king, as first and highest authority of the state, to the heart, which governs the whole body. He goes so far as to define the heart itself as "the source and root from which all power derives in the creature, and on which all power depends" (108; Hill 1964). The circulatory system is thus described in terms of "government," "power," and "authority"; that is, in terms of a political lexicon that seems to contaminate that of science unnecessarily. The heart and not the head is at the metaphorical center of this new body; and that heart appears, in its role as the body's sole mover, to obey the necessary laws of a perfect machine. However important he may be, thus, the king as heart is wholly internal to a preexisting and preformed structure: a natural, collective machine whose origins are not investigated, and which has been built by no one, it seems, but God.

Problems regarding nature versus artifice inevitably arise, however the hermeneutic model of the machine combines mechanical and organic concepts to describe animal bodies. For machines are obviously built by men, while fleshly bodies are not. Within the wide playing field afforded by the metaphorical exchange between the human body, the machine, and the body politic, a new problem thus ultimately arises concerning the natural or artificial origins of the body politic itself. This question certainly does not trouble the prose of Harvey's dedication. He reserves the central role of the heart for the king, without worrying about details. But the question necessarily arises within Hobbes's examination of the state as artificial macrobody.

The enormous influence of Harvey's work in Hobbes's time is well known. Hobbes was the junior of Harvey by only ten years and admired his work, which he may have come across through his contacts with friends such as Kenelm Digby and Walter Charleton, members of the prestigious Royal Society and authors of mechanistically inclined treatises on the human body (Sawday 1983). The cultural horizon of a body considered as machine is therefore the backdrop to new scientific categories, in which Hobbes feels right at home. Life becomes not only a machine, but a controllable and predictable apparatus capable of self-preservation. This model ultimately proves extremely useful in addressing the obsessions that newly characterize the telos of the political order (De Giovanni 1981, 36–40; Cohen 1944, 187–210). In addition, philosophy too has now at its disposal the Cartesian, mechanical conception of the human body (Descartes 1994, V). Thus by the time Hobbes's *Leviathan* is published in the English version of 1651, followed by the Latin version of 1668, the image of a mechanically structured body politic is already supported by a widespread vocabulary endorsed by both science and philosophy.

## The Great Artificial Man

In his introduction to *Leviathan*, Hobbes employs the new corporeal grammar of the animal machine, placing it importantly at the start of his reflections on the state. We thus read, in the first line, that "nature, the art whereby God hath made and governs the world, is by the *art* of man, as in many other things, so in this imitated, that it [the art of man] can make an artificial animal."

This artificial animal, a giant body politic with a mechanical framework, is none other than the state, whose construction, by imitative human art, is made possible thanks to the mechanical art that had already characterized the divine creation of animal bodies. God, evidently considered a sort of Great Mechanic, forges animal bodies in which he projects a heart that functions like a spring, nerves that work like strings, and joints that operate like wheels giving motion to the entire body. Hobbes's precise and synthetic definition of life is "but a motion of limbs" (*Leviathan*, intro.). It thus comes as no surprise that the entire body, having been planned and built by God, is controlled by the mechanical principle of motion. Indeed this is the very reason why human art can imitate the divine. The ability of men to build "*automata* (engines that move themselves by springs and wheels as does a watch)" (intro.) has moreover already been proven: the technology of the time is not opposed to nature, but imitates it, using the clear strategy of a natural, and therefore divine, projection of the machine. *Homo faber* has placed himself at the center of the world, and he no longer hesitates to think of the world itself, and God, according to his model.

We have, therefore, the affirmation of a general principle of life as mechanical motion God followed in creating the bodies of animals. Men imitate this principle in producing self-moving objects like clocks. The political disorder of the age, the catastrophic civil warfare that Hobbes "normalizes" in an original state of nature, urgently calls for art that "goes yet further" (intro.). That is, further than the technical imitation of partial objects, to imitate that rational and excellent work of nature which is man. Thus the *artificial man,* the state, is created by human art: it is a gigantic political automaton, modeled on the divine masterpiece. Hobbes performs yet another metamorphosis of the Platonic figure of the city as *macroanthropos,* giving us a new state that is none other than an "artificial man, though of greater stature and strength than the natural, for whose protection and defence it was intended" (intro.).[11]

The body politic is clearly artificial, not because it is conceived and functions as a machine, but simply because it is built by the *art* of men. God's art is also mechanical, founded on the principle of life as the movement of limbs. Nature and life are, in other words, already mechanical in a conception of the organism that tends to see them as hybrid rather than opposed. Strangely, Hobbes, in reconnecting his new metaphor with the old figure of anatomy, identifies the center of motion of the body politic neither with the head nor (as we might expect) with the "spring" of the heart, but with the soul. But this is now an "artificial soul, giving life and motion to the whole body" (intro.), and it corresponds to the basic concept of sovereignty, around which Hobbes's political doctrine revolves.

Hobbes's renunciation of imagery based on the concrete materiality of the body, which the heart as "spring" would have provided, in favor of a hazardously immaterial imagery based on the soul, results from the difficult translation of the concept of sovereignty into metaphor. Sovereignty is, in fact, the important cohesive power behind the logic of the *one*. This power embodies everything in a single form, since sovereignty itself is not an element, role, or part of that form, but the form itself, insofar as it is a unity. More than the heart (what Harvey calls the *beginning of life*), which as a simple part, pump, or spring, starts and supports the vital motion of the body politic, sovereignty is the life of the body itself, spread into every part, holding all together within a single and specific form.

Even better than the heart, then, as a metaphor for the great artificial body politic found at the start of *Leviathan,* is the notion of the soul, in which life and form once again coincide as they did in Aristotle. John Locke, who criticized Hobbes's notion of sovereignty and weakened its absolutist overtones, defined the legislature as a supreme yet resistible power, as the soul that gives form, life, and unity to the state (1952, 212). In the new metaphorical apparatus of these natural jurists, therefore, a soul reappears that, though it has lost all Christian pretence to immortality in the artificial nature of its birth, still retains its Greek valence as form and reason for the cohesive unity of the body politic. This soul, especially for Hobbes, is in no way a part or organ of the body politic and is therefore not one element of its anatomy among many.[12] It is the whole, the order, the form and principle of that living totality; the whole of that artificial mechanical body whose parts were assembled and united by the fiat pronounced by those entering the pact, in imitation of the divine fiat.

*Fiat* is only a word, a promise spoken by those making a pact. Although Hobbes uses metaphors based on a mechanical model, which are dear to the *homo faber,* he leaves little room for the material act of building. That would involve forging and assembling single elements, as a watchmaker does, for example. It seems that inventing the machine counts more than empirically building it: the idea of the watch is more important than its actual assembly. Moreover, "the art of building and preserving states consists of certain rules, as in arithmetic and geometry" (*Leviathan,* intro.), Hobbes assures us. He thus underlines the importance of the intellectual aspect of the task; that is, the formation of the idea of a machine based on rational criteria.

God himself, implicitly defined as a sort of Great Mechanic, does not so much forge the machine of animal bodies, as conceive them in a certain manner and create them by means of the fiat. This fiat, pronounced by those entering a pact in imitation of the creative word of God, puts into words the great idea that is capable on its own of creating sovereign power and hence the entire form and life of the artificial body politic. This idea's effective existence is indeed rivaled by that of the utterly material sword; but this follows logically from the mechanism created by the word of those who forge the pact, rather than being something prudently added to it.

It is also curious that, aside from the first page of *Leviathan*—which clearly compares animal bodies to the automatons built by man—the rest of the work falls back on the usual metaphors involving bodily organs, including a language of political pathology. If the organism is now indeed that body understood as a machine by Harvey and the scientists of the Royal Society, the comparison to "machines which move by themselves by means of springs and wheels, like a watch" works only up to a certain point within the complex reasoning of *Leviathan.*

Already in the introduction, we read that in the body politic the analogy spring-heart could only correspond to the sovereign who is, however, the soul: a pervasive and very different thing, not just a part of the machine but its sole, true form. The metaphor then goes on to compare wheels-limbs-judges and strings-nerves-punishments by mechanical analogy. Soon, we instead read that the wealth of all the individual members is the force of the body politic and the security of the people is its task, while the counselors are its memory. We also read that equity is the reason of the body politic, the laws its will, agreement its health, and sedition its illness; civil war, finally, is its death. In the swift flow of the writing, we go from a machine in the strict sense to the image of a man whose body is mechanistically formed (and has been thoroughly discussed under the topic of the state of nature), but who nonetheless transcends the model of the moving machines built by men.

Both the natural body created by God and the artificial body politic created by those entering into a pact seem to exceed the material reality of the machine that serves as hermeneutic model for them. The recourse to the notion of the soul for the figure of the sovereign, instead of the heart as spring and principle of movement, bears witness to a figural undermining of the mechanistic framework. This is probably due to Hobbes's obsession with a pervasive unity and compact solidity not possessed by the machine. It is strange, however, that elsewhere in the text the new theory concerning the circulation of the blood—from the outer limbs to the heart at the center—is used as a metaphor for the circulation of money. In this case the heart corresponds to the public funds administrated by the sovereign's treasurers, which, by initiating the flow of money, "enliven, and enable for motion all the members [of the body]" (XXIV).

The artificial man is not built part by part and then assembled; he comes alive immediately following the fiat of those who make the pact. He is born completely whole and in sovereignty has his life. Likewise, when the sovereign power is diminished or incapable of guaranteeing peace and security (mainly due to intestinal or external conflicts), the artificial man suddenly dissolves and dies. The commitment of the members dies with the death of the soul: the body politic is now a corpse, and it dissolves (XXIX). It is dismembered or disordered, and men fall back into a state of nature. The irreducible composition of the state's unity and personhood in one sovereign implies that when the sovereign is rendered impotent, a collapse from above will occur, with no possibility for continuity and no halfway remedies. The great machine does not break down in such a way that one can simply replace a part, as a good mechanic might do. It comes crashing down when the principle of its form, the sovereign, collapses. The sovereign and the people disintegrate together, as they have coincided in life.

Hobbes's pathology of the body politic does not contemplate curable illnesses of the soul. Either sovereignty is the form of the state, a power that obliges all men and that ensures peace through internal cohesion, or there is no state, nor order, nor form. Either sovereignty exists full and irresistible or it does not exist at all; in which case there is neither body politic, nor people. Every illness of the body politic, for Hobbes, must be attributed to errors committed during the institution of the body politic itself (XXIX). It is never due to the weakness of the material, to men and their irresponsibility, which Hobbes, in any case, presupposes. Here what counts is the initial act of inception, the geometrical criterion of the design ensuring a rational model, rather than the inferior quality of the materials.

In order to illustrate the most common political maladies, Hobbes furnishes a long survey of imperfect institutions. A negative result is certain, for example, when whoever governs "is content with less power, than to the peace, and defense of the commonwealth is necessarily required" (XXIX). In this case, like the bodies of children born of sick parents, the body politic is destined to die a premature death. Another mistake consists of admitting a spiritual power alongside the civil power. This provokes epilepsy, which is not by chance considered a spiritual illness of the artificial body. Another error is the formation of a government of three distinct powers, as occurs in mixed monarchies. In this case, with three representative persons and three sovereigns, the artificial man is but a monster with three bodies growing out of a single torso. Hobbes does not pass up the chance to list the most serious or irksome illnesses found in the medical treatises, most of which are incurable. One thing is certain: the secret of success consists of the geometrically perfect conception of the body politic, founded on a unique, unopposable power. This power brings its members together, binding and obliging them within a single form, so that by banishing any internal differences it also excludes conflict. When, in spite of all these forces, intestinal conflict occurs, death is the inevitable result.

Hobbes's state, conceived by art in opposition to civil war and in fact created out of civil war as a historical referent for the state of nature, likewise dies of civil war. It can also die through outside attack by another state that moves against it and annuls its sovereignty. But death arises especially from intestinal conflict. War stands at the beginning as well as at the end of the theory of order that sustains this structure; its horizon anticipates both the birth and the rapid dissolution of the state. Indeed Hobbes's state may be defined as a peace presided over by absolute order, suspended between two wars. These wars are essentially one and the same, because the war that dissolves the body politic merely reopens the way to the state of nature, the war of all against all that is the only alternative to the body politic. Since that natural disorder is intolerable, one must begin all over again and convene to obey a new sovereign.

The great man created by human art is mortal, but his mortality may be postponed in time, if the structure is well built and the sovereign is able to guard against collapse. The sovereign should be able to discern the symptoms of internal conflict and suppress its effects immediately. The only remaining problem is the death of those natural bodies (one or more than one, depending on whether the sovereign is a monarch or an assembly) in which sovereignty is temporarily materialized and sustained.

In this context, Hobbes writes that "as there was an order taken for an artificial man, so there be order also taken, for an artificial eternity of life" (XIX). The eternity that the mortal body politic may paradoxically enjoy is based on the rules and rights of succession. In the monarchical form, which Hobbes prefers to all others, succession means that the state is not dissolved with the death of the natural body of the king. A successor designated by the king immediately assumes sovereignty, which thus passes to the natural person of the heir without any interval or void of power. Even a very small interruption—pictured in the old organic metaphor by a body momentarily without a head—would mean immediate return to the formless state of nature.

The eternity spoken of here is a relative concept: an artificial eternity that surpasses the terms of the bodily deaths of sovereigns, but which must itself die if sovereignty is lacking and the body politic dissolves. Oddly enough, Hobbes does not exclude women from the criteria of succession. If there is a son, women come after him because they are less suited "for actions of labour and danger" (XIX); yet the daughters of a king lacking sons may be preferred to a male heir of less direct relations.

In the right of succession, as throughout Hobbes's treatise, the body assumes a decisive role, starting with the natural inclination toward offspring that comes from having produced them. There is furthermore in the state of nature a "right of dominion by generation" of parents over their children. This is the *mother's* right, according to Hobbes even if it is conventionally called *paternal*. It is so defined, he says, not by natural but by civil law; that is, the law of states, which "for the most part . . . have been erected by the fathers, not by the mothers of families" (XX). In the state of nature, by contrast (and thus in a prepolitical sphere in which the institution of marriage is not supposed), the mothers, rather than the fathers, have the right of dominion over children, because "it cannot be known who is the father, unless it be declared by the mother," and above all because dominion over children belongs to whoever nourishes them. A child, Hobbes writes, "ought to obey him by whom it is preserved; because preservation of life being the end, for which one man becomes subject to another, every man is supposed to promise obedience, to him, in whose power it is to save, or destroy him" (XX; Conti Odorisio 1987). The dominion of mothers over offspring thus derives more from their nutritional than their procreative function in Hobbes's unusual recuperation of their natural role.

Hobbes seems little interested in the scene of birth in his natural and political philosophy. In the *De Cive,* before dealing with the mechanical creations, human or divine, that open *Leviathan,* he indicates that his method in describing the state of nature will be to "consider men as if but even now sprung out of the earth, and suddenly (like mushrooms) come to full maturity" (VIII.1). In his crucial, logical construction of this fundamental hypothesis, Hobbes thus denies birth by the maternal body as an influence or even considers it a disturbing detail of bodily life.

Hobbes's reasoning, however, does not lack coherence, at least in his consideration of life as mere survival. On the basis of the elementary principle of self-preservation, Hobbes grants the right of dominion in the state of nature to the one who provides nourishment, while in the civil state he grants this right to whoever assures peace by unopposable command, thus enabling the continuation of life. There is a striking inconsistency, however, in Hobbes's historical note that "for the most part commonwealths have been erected by the fathers, not by the mothers of families" (*Leviathan,* XX), which seems to be valid also for the geometrically founded state that inaugurates a new age. The question is not developed further, despite Hobbes's usual thoroughness and clarity. His revolutionary theory retains the ancient concept according to which only men, as fathers of the family, are the founders of states. This implies, then, that family patriarchs are the ones who enter into the pact, despite the fact that the state of nature does not foresee any institution of marriage, and therefore any family. We again note a certain imprecision regarding the problem of the family, whose position, both in a state of nature and in the civil state, remains ambiguous (Mancina 1991, 105).

Only slight notice is given to the theme of the sex of those entering into a pact. They are, in general, identified as the fathers of the family, while the inclusion of women in the hereditary line of sovereigns (even if it is for lack of male heirs) seems to indicate a certain recognition of human sexual difference within Hobbes's political philosophy. But sexual difference is not explicitly addressed, nor is the usual discriminatory discourse against the female sex present. Sexedness is simply not visible in the egalitarian sphere of the pact. The makers of the pact are identified as the fathers largely out of habit; that is, because of the automatic *invisibility* of women on a basic, foundational theoretical horizon that has always been cast in male terms.[13] Considering the revolutionary novelty of the modern concept of equality, this is no small matter in Hobbes's theory, and the exclusion of females is, moreover, undermined by the absence of reasons in Hobbes's theory concerning any arguable difference of powers between men and women in a state of nature. Later developments in the theory of social equality will in fact succeed—after a hardly negligible two hundred years or so—in turning the sexist blindness of this absence in favor of emancipation.

As for Hobbes's text, the historical presence of certain queens (most pointedly, of course, Elizabeth) renders visible the category of sexual difference only where history itself makes it so, in the holder of the scepter of monarchy. In the construction of the body politic, or rather in its institutions by pact, the problem is never posed, although it is in a sense "resolved" by the conventional and unexplained designation of fathers as creators of states. Thus, the traditional division of competencies attributed to the two sexes is repeated for the thousandth time. Mothers give birth to and nourish natural bodies, ensuring their survival; but from fathers comes the fiat that gives birth to an artificial, already adult, and perfect body politic that ensures the survival of everyone.

After all, with his word of creation, God makes adult bodies, and it is his fiat that the pact makers imitate in order to form an artificial body politic. The human body is a well-built natural machine and thus a model to imitate. It is, as always, the divine prototype. Like the machine, the body is without growth or development, lacking sexed birth or infancy. It is fully adult in its static form, and its artificial copy is as perfect as can be.

### A Monster Named Leviathan

Beyond its status as an indirectly divine artificial body (since it is a copy of the prototype made by God), the state is worthy, according to Hobbes, of the name *mortal God* (*Leviathan,* XII). Like God, it is the bearer of peace and security, and the creator and dispenser of justice. It is animated by a potent and irresistible sovereign. In the domain of earthly concerns, its power equals that of God, although like everything on this earth it is mortal. It is more durable than natural bodies but destined, all the same, to decay.

For Hobbes, it is especially the feature of constitutive and invincible power that makes the state comparable to the biblical Leviathan, who is animated by the terrible force of which God himself says, "There is nothing on earth, to be compared with him" (*Leviathan,* XXVIII). The Leviathan, Hobbes says, quoting the book of Job, "is made so as not to be afraid. He seeth every high thing below him; and is king of all the children of pride" (XXVIII). Hobbes's metaphors, more or less frightening or reassuring, are mixed and juxtaposed: from the giant body to the machine, from the mortal God to the great beast. The monster's constant feature is gigantic size, while his distinctive omnipotence gradually increases as the aura of myth contributes to Hobbes's writing.

Though he claims the title of *Leviathan,* and despite the association of Hobbes's book with his awful and monstrous figure, the biblical giant is barely sketched in the text. Nonetheless the frightening force invoked by the name of Leviathan soon comes to stand for Hobbes's *entire* political doctrine, contributing in no small measure to the negative reputation immediately earned by the book and that endures today. These negative judgments have in large measure been handed down to posterity. It thus appears that the power of the image surpasses the intentions of its user, overshadowing "with its suggestive strength, all the author's other arguments, precise as they may be" (Schmitt 1986, 50).

Though still passionately debated, the question of whether Hobbes's political philosophy truly deserves its reputation as totalitarian lies beyond the scope of this book. It is curious that Hobbes's choice of title in some way foreshadows the work's negative reception. It overpowers a discourse concerning the precise construction of an artificial body politic and puts a monstrous and terrifying face on a supreme power that guarantees the advantage of peace through the invincible nature of the sword. The parallel between the images of the body/machine and Leviathan seem both too incongruous and too prophetic to be casual or unimportant. More likely, the giant is a symptom of a dark side of power that may exceed the rational structure of political order, lending it a monstrous aspect. This dark side of power gets confused with political order, or perhaps, gives it all its irreducible materiality.

The metaphors Hobbes chooses for the state might be considered separately, like a gallery of images that do not imply absolute congruence but illustrate different sides of the question. In this case we would simply bow to the author's imagination and to the free, searching play of his language. Seen in another light, however, the choice may be a deliberate metaphorical grouping that claims internal coherence. Now, the rational aspect of the machine will become one with its monstrous aspect, and the artificial body created by men to organize the uncontrollable motion of natural bodies reveals the uncontrollable and terrifying power of *its* soul.

We know that the biblical monsters used by Hobbes are Leviathan and Behemoth.[14] They give title to two different works: *Leviathan,* which treats the construction of the political order, and *Behemoth,* a work describing the civil war. It thus seems that in Hobbes's work as a whole, a rational, symbolic, and metatextual strategy posits a monster of war, which can be tamed only by another, more powerful monster, the unconquerable Leviathan. This all comes about in a play of animal figures, each of which is, in itself, rationally intelligible. The civil war is terrible and monstrous insofar as it is the consequence of the general and intelligible law of local motion obeyed by human bodies. In an analogous but inverted manner, the power (one, absolute, and invincible) of the sovereign has an ordering and pacifying effect, inasmuch as it concentrates within itself the force of all, inculcating terror in all.

What Hobbes manages to evoke with his polymorphous metaphorical construction is a sort of seminal, and thus mythical and ineradicable, political *object.*[15] This terrifying object seems to be rooted in the very possibility of political discourse and has always assumed the name of force, war, conflict, fratricide, and the thousand other terms for violence among individuals: literally fatal disorder. This is the true object of a politics that, at the very instant in which it posits itself as the order of human cohabitation, also takes the idea of the enemy as its foundation. Hobbes's metamorphic icons seem to suggest, however, that violence, war, and conflict do not remain objects to be tamed and *resolved* by the political structure; rather they seep into the order itself, contaminating and transfiguring its peaceful face, presented as just and good, into something terrifying. Hobbes's metaphorical system is peculiar not because it has strange incongruities, but rather because it renders absolute an order capable of enlarging both itself and its object. Contamination and constitutive over-lap become ever more visible between the political structure and its terrifying object.

Hobbes's doctrine has been judged by history as a justification of absolute power. It proves, however, to be a theory that takes the traditional form of politics (order) and its equally common object (fatal disorder) and renders those concepts *absolute* in order to reach the extreme limits of their representability at a threshold where their metaphors meet. War, for Hobbes, is the absolute conflict of all against all, where violence and murder are in fact natural, and thus *normal* and innocent. In Hobbes's vision of war, the first term of the binomial friend/enemy is definitively eradicated in favor of the pair enemy/enemy. Likewise, the politi-cal category of order is made as absolute as possible through the logic of the one, which eliminates all alterity, and thus all con-flict. The force that created the conflict has not, in the end, simply disappeared, but is concentrated in the soul of the *one*. It remains what it is and has always been: pure force, basic and natural, prepolitical and violent in its divine and inscrutable origin.

Hobbes's structure is thus founded on a concept of human nature as substantially oriented toward murder and war. To call this *realistic* is perhaps not sufficient. In this realism there is, of course, the disenchantment that comes from a direct experience of civil war. There is, in short, the tragic and cold aura of moder-nity. But in a profound sense there is also the entire history of the West and its self-representations. Present, in other words, is the West that begins to narrate itself with the story of the Trojan War, a story where men are measured by the sword, and the gods take sides with one or the other group of warriors. Alongside these practices is the rite of fratricide, which has been celebrated over and over as the foundation of the city, together with a thousand other past and future atrocities. In Hobbes's self-examining vi-sion of politics, different epochs are irrelevant. Their particular cultural motives for killing, their reasons for defining various models of collective order as justification and remedy for human ferocity, are of no importance. What counts is a political *realism* that appears to capture the persistent pattern with which the West has woven its own history. Machiavelli too, another writer damned by posterity, knew how much blood and how many tears have soaked this eternal and (not by chance) masculine power game.

*Leviathan,* then, is an apt title for Hobbes's famous work. Uncontainable monstrosity, yet meticulous order; savage violence, yet rational machine: these are the two aspects that political discourse may wish to separate, or to juxtapose as the two sides of a radical alternative. But they inevitably blend together again in the very modes of discourse, when discourse *surrenders* to the reality of this alternative.

Carl Schmitt is in this sense unconvincing when he claims that Hobbes's use of the sea monster in the Book of Job is consistent with the many medieval reconfigurations of the image and is meant to invoke the pacific and familiar English picture of the "great whale." Hobbes's humorous intent, Schmitt says, has been badly misunderstood by posterity (Schmitt 1986, 76). But Hobbes's own quote from the Old Testament directly alludes to the terrifying and invincible force the philosopher uses as the symbol of the state. The biblical passage cited by Hobbes seems to leave little room for light humor. In the Book of Job, we read that no one can resist the Leviathan and no one has ever escaped him, since his scaly armor is impenetrable, his teeth are terrible, and blazing flames issue from his mouth. Fear spreads around him in all directions (Job 40–41). The Leviathan, in short, as monstrous and mythical animal, is the symbol of unparalleled and terrifying power. Its image is absolutely alien to that of the human body, as well as to the artificial body that men build in imitation of the machine. The image of the monster, unexpectedly, does not increase the frightening aspect of the artificial body-machine, as is often claimed, but rather gives a face to the monstrosity that the mechanical machine seeks to contain and eliminate.

Hobbes's polyvalent metaphorical imagery seems to take on a life of its own. The monstrous body of the beast overpowers the organic body of tradition, despite attempts to liquidate the monster through the grotesque metamorphosis of a mechanical body. The body returns, now grown monstrous and bestial. It returns as a body whose monstrous, irregular, and anomalous features trigger not the liberating laughter of the grotesque, but terror and absolute obedience, and this to a much greater degree than had the secular, regular machine. This great sea monster of inscrutable origin and inexplicable force is unequaled in its compactness, unity, and invincibility, covered as it is with a double armor and impenetrable by any tridents and arrows that dare to challenge it: they will only break on the monster's skin. The Leviathan, we read in the Book of Job, has a body of which "his scales are his pride, shut up together as with a close seal. One is so near to another, that no air can come between them" (41:15–16).

## A Giant on the Frontispiece

On the frontispiece of the first English edition of *Leviathan*, there is a celebrated engraving that is extremely effective in its symbolism. It shows a giant man holding in one hand a sword, and in the other, a shepherd's crook. On his head he wears a crown, and before him extends a peaceful countryside that he seems to regard with a protective air. His body appears as a suit of armor composed of thousands of tiny men with their faces turned inward, thus showing the nape of their necks to the reader. Each man seems a single scale in a coat of armor, and the effect of their combination is clear. At the top of the page there is a Latin inscription from the Book of Job, in the Vulgate Bible: "Non est potestas super terram quae comparetur ei" (see Schmitt 1986, 72).

The figure in the frontispiece thus seems to combine many of the images and conceptual links of Hobbes's text. The figure evokes, at once, the man of giant stature, the sovereign in the semblance of the king, the body politic as a collective body, and even the biblical animal, recognizable in its armor of close-fitting, impervious scales. This last recognition, in any case, is lent authority by the quote of the Latin verse: "There is no power on earth that can be compared to him," and by the eloquent title under the image: *Leviathan*. The machine is missing in explicit form, but it is identical to the body understood as mechanical movement and is supposedly part of the image of the body itself.

In any case, it is very significant that the figure inspires both reassurance and terror. His expression toward the countryside over which he looms is benign, but his size and his scales composed of human bodies are still monstrous. It thus seems that the ambivalence between peaceful order and threatening force (which is not confined to this figure alone, but characteristic of Hobbes's whole political discourse) is given fitting shape in the image, also effectively suggesting the terrible and monstrous elements politics always rediscovers in its object. Another excellent feature of the image is its capacity to render the obsessive logic of the one, since the small men who make up the body are none other than the people, and these people are none other than the sovereign, in a perfect and cosubstantial identity. Both the people and the sovereign are then identified with the body politic of the state. It may lack the form of a sea monster, but it does, at least, have its scaly skin.

Like the traditional organic metaphor, which ended up engulfing and embodying its subjects, the body politic now possesses only one, perfectly homogeneous element, which makes up its artificial flesh: single individuals. Those individuals are equal by nature, and each has value and enters into a pact on his own, without first being joined into distinct castes or corporations. This means that if they subsequently come to form some specific organ or precise part, role, or function within the body politic, that fact will have nothing to do with any previous membership in a class, whether by birth or by trade. In the Hobbesian body politic, any possibly prejudicial tie between caste and function is broken; the medieval mirroring of the hierarchical system within the design of the organism disappears. There are neither ranks nor any other collective forms prior to the state, only equal, individual men. The state itself is therefore the only *form* able to incorporate individuals. It transforms them into a people, and at the same time, it creates the various functions of the body politic that the members of the populace carry out, as judges, counselors, law officials, and so on.

In the image of the frontispiece, this essential uniformity of the material of the body politic is well conveyed by the small men who compose the giant figure. They constitute the skin, or rather the scaly surface that seems to be a monstrous coat of mail, but they also may be imagined as internal flesh; that is, as the sole material of the body politic. This may be why we see them from behind, instead of from the front: they look into the center of the body, because only within it do they have their reason for existing as a people. In fact, nothing outside the body pertains to them, and so they have no interest in looking elsewhere.

There is, however, a sort of exception to the image's logic, or rather an extraordinary reiteration of the ancient, metaphorical inconsistency that often figures the body without a head. Only the body assembled of tiny men, in fact, appears in Arcimboldesque fashion, while the head itself is all of a piece, with smooth skin and (perhaps even recognizable) human features.[16]

This is the head of the sovereign, the face of a man who, from the beginning, is permitted to retain his individuality, since he is the only one authorized to act. Although it enjoys no special status in the theoretical complex of Hobbes's metaphors, the head's privileged place is vindicated in the image. It at least shows in the personality of the gaze—a too-human transparency of the soul—that the destiny of the body politic, animated by the sovereign, is always entrusted to a natural body that supports its weight and enables it to move.

In short, though it may be wholly or in part a mathematically conceived machine, there is something in the state that is both human and monstrous and that remains beyond the control men have over an artificial construction. The state is thus both fragile and frightening. In this way the object that both motivates and overshadows the political order invades the figure and always inevitably returns. It covers the rational construction with the aura of myth, while divine beasts and crowned giants again conquer its image.

The new mechanical idol, although built with cold reason (to echo Nietzsche in *Thus Spake Zarathustra*), in the end resembles the coldest of all monsters. Perhaps terror dwells within technology and politics, as Sophocles seemed to intuit. This is a corporeal and monstrous terror, completely civilized and human, rather than the product of a residual animality, whose warlike blood can also pulsate within artificial and mechanical machines.

Like Antigone and Ophelia, unpolitical female bodies (which for Hobbes are maternal bodies above all, and more important in their nutritional than in their generative role) seem still to await their stories, for another history to be told, in a language by now grown modern. Especially in the shadow of this coldest of monsters and its inherent homogenizing power, this story seems ever more difficult, but ever more necessary, to tell. It must be told, if the uncanny is ever to recognize its political character and cease to project woman's image from the perspective of the male gaze. At the same time, this new story must not deny the power of myth's enigmatic residues to create new metaphorical encounters, to disturb an accepted sense of fleshly existence. In such a story, woman's body may shine in the splendor it has long awaited, the splendor it has deserved from the beginning.

# APPENDIX
# NARRATING WOMEN
# DIFFERENTLY

A THE ANTIGONE OF MARÍA ZAMBRANO
Antigone did not really commit suicide in the tomb, as
Sophocles, who made an unavoidable error, tells us" (Zambrano
1989, 17). María Zambrano's observation tears Antigone away
from the hopeless fate Sophocles reserves for her, recounting a
different story of, or maybe for, Antigone.

*La tumba de Antígona* was written in 1967 by the Spanish
philosopher María Zambrano, in the form of a brief drama preceded by an introductory essay. It is a new story that begins just
where Sophocles had interrupted Antigone's voice: in the tomb.
In Zambrano's text, the tomb is the sole scene of a conversation between Antigone, who is buried alive, and the spirits of
her family, who individually come to speak to her. This time,
Antigone not only fails to kill herself; she does not die, in the
real sense of the term. She experiences the union or the marriage between life and death, as a sort of unquenchable living
that transcends their separateness and opposition (32). In Zambrano's mystical vision, inextinguishable life—which is coterminous with being, an existence beyond the becoming of a single
living individual—emerges at the point where that being's very
individuality passes from a position of resistance to one of accep-
tance of the primeval call of being. It thus undergoes forgetfulness of self, in a flowing back into the presence of truth. The
truth is thus an enigma through which the human creature receives and becomes conscious of its own destiny, beyond and
against the arrogance of a pure and self-established reason of the
ego.

Truth is rendered, in fact, and always with trepidation, only to
one who "remains trembling and defenseless before it, 'tran-

scending all knowledge'" (Zambrano 1991, 31). Passivity of understanding is necessary for the revelation of the truth (1989, 15),
especially that passivity which consists of the sacrifice of the
innocent: where resistance to the call of light ceases (1991, 37).
Only in this circumstance can being again welcome, in full
splendor, she who offers herself to it without struggle. Like so
many other figures of virginal purity, Antigone is a heroine of
precisely this sacrifice. In Zambrano's vision, the sacrifice of the
innocent is not the customary exploitation of female passivity
for the goals of civilization. It is, rather, "the dawn of awareness"
(1989, 21), where inextinguishable life becomes transparent to a
woman, revealing all being in its only possible human expression; especially that being which, in the virginal soul alone,
depends on no ego (1991, 37).

For Zambrano, Antigone's sacrifice, even in its historical
sense, is an act of love that simultaneously embraces the three
symbolic worlds of being known already to the Greeks. These
are the sky, the earth, and the underworld. Antigone, whom
Sophocles calls the bride of Hades, is instead a sort of Per-
sephone "who was only granted one season, a spring which
cannot be repeated" (1989, 20).

But a sacrifice is necessary in order to reach the moment of
revelation. This sacrifice requires a longer period than the time
of a simple death. Sophocles denied Antigone that time, consigning her mask to the gesture of a swift suicide. Zambrano restores
this time to her within the tomb, thus granting "the time owed to
her, which coincides with the time human beings need to receive
this revelation" (1989, 36). The time Antigone needs is "an indef-
inite time, so that she can live her death" (20); so that in death
might be redeemed the sense of a life unlived if not lived in
destiny's fatal grasp. Underlining a characteristic difference between male and female, the men in Zambrano's text, especially
Antigone's brothers, have time only to kill, deluding themselves
in this way that they are "the Lords of Death" (32).

A long passion marks the stages of the chosen one toward a
dawn of awareness. This passion begins with the destiny of a race
that must be gathered together and redeemed from its unspeakable wrongs. Antigone is the bearer of a family destiny: that of

paternal incest and of the blood that becomes violent fratricide in the brothers. Though she is innocent, her heredity is binding. It is more binding on her than on her mother and father, and certainly more than on her brothers. She must accept it as guilt, according to Zambrano, so that she may complete the process of recognition in which, utterly abandoned by gods and men, her unique innocence necessarily becomes a prophetic solitude (29).

For Zambrano, the dawn of awareness, like the sacrifice that generates it, brings with it the paradox of a unique life that must be experienced in the desperate emptiness of solitude and pain, in order to save itself and come again to the transcendent source of its birth. In life, Antigone's destiny indeed overcame her, binding her to the yoke of a family history. Yet it is also something that reveals its sense beyond the inhuman fate of an unmourned death. It removes all gratuitous cruelty from her solitude and reveals her to herself as the one who, from the beginning, has been fated to the privilege of passion. Saving her from useless suffering, from the forced renunciation of her marriage to Haemon, and from the nonsense of mere fatality, this destiny also redeems Antigone's fate (29).

The Antigone María Zambrano places in her infernal scene is not Sophocles' rebellious and inflexible mask, but an unhappy maiden who alone performs the ritual "without whose lament no one may descend into the tomb" (18). Not the figure who has undergone the punishment of the law that so efficiently sets up the tragic antithesis of Sophocles' text, she is the human and female figure of a life without Eros and without marriage. So that here, where the gods have deserted and the political order grows so harsh as to allow human destiny to sink to its darkest depths, suffering is pure suffering and solitude is pure solitude. No solidarity can be invoked that would help the living being resist its grim torment.

Precisely here, from a sacrifice made in the name of a fraternity that has paradoxically produced absolute solitude (28), the second stage of the passion begins. It is now the passion of Antigone, already accustomed to the dark of the tomb. Having been buried alive, in perfect correspondence with the birth that had opened her earthly life the girl now experiences a second birth. This is a birth into the truth, a birth in which she finally recognizes herself for what she is: "A whole being, an entirely virginal girl." For this reason Antigone is worthy of sacrifice, as may be only she who is pure and she "who has not sought it" (43). Her denied wedding, along with the entire destiny of a guiltless blame, is finally explained. And the sacrifice itself becomes no longer gratuitous pain, but "vivifying, as are all those of the truth" (33).

This quasi-theatrical, performable text is composed of twelve brief "scenes." In the initial scenes, Antigone finds herself alone in the place of death, yet she feels life pulsing inside her as if the tomb were the place of her birth. Comparing the dark cavern to her mother's womb, she feels herself begin to turn around, as if to repeat the movements of her own birth. This is the mother for whom she contends with Oedipus in another scene, telling him "you always spoke of her, . . . but of my mother, mine, you never spoke. She was always yours, of her you always spoke" (50). The mother appears in the sixth scene, which, in contrast with nearly all the others, is not a dialogue, but a prayer of Antigone to the maternal shade. Here the chosen discursive logic is that of mystical discourse, which merges different beings into one.

We witness a crucial inversion of maternity, where the shade of the mother crosses the daughter's body, so that she, the young virgin, may "feel the weight of being a mother" (63). Antigone's whole speech is addressed to the maternal body as to a genealogical continuum where every mother is the mother of a daughter, but also the daughter of a mother. Genealogy, already tending toward the unitary and to fusion, may *cleanse* all individual guilt and make Life and Death, Light and Shadow appear as one thing. "The purity of the Mother is the dream of the child; and the child, by loving its obscure mystery, cleanses her" (62), Antigone says. The allusion here is not, however, to Oedipus, as we might expect, but to a maternal body that transcends Jocasta's individuality and evokes, in a series of transparent metaphors, the mythical Great Mother and the Earth. The Earth in fact is a body in which Antigone is buried, yet the very secret of maternity is mystically reachable by Antigone, as the "nameless reason of Life" (63).

This Life, with its deep secret where the opposites of birth and death are united, appears in the dream of the child. It washes all stain from the mother. The mother's stain is as dusky as the Earth and as black as her shade, since Jocasta is here the symbol of all three. But she is also the Light that shines on and purifies Antigone, reconciling mother and daughter to the now salvaged sense of their common destiny. A second birth is now possible for Antigone. It repeats the first, but also frees her from the egoistic descent into the self. This second birth permits her to dwell in the instant of a pure unfolding and to give herself up to a flood of light, yielding to its embrace.

Antigone encounters other family members, including an enamored Haemon and his brothers, who are still enemies. But in Zambrano's text, it is the prayer to the mother that signals the decisive turn of passion toward the mystical revelation of being. This is because her destiny returns to its source and delivers her, and because the union of opposites, the paradox in which the truth shines through, reveals a figure that goes back to the root of life, at once individual and impersonal. This life illuminates the dawn of the living being with transcendence and annuls her solitude.

For María Zambrano, only a pure birth changes the living being to a dawning, or *would* effect such change if the pretence of individual existence did not hinder it (1991, 24). Individual existence tears from the human being "preexisting love, the primordial waters of life, and the very nest in which its being is born" (1991, 25). Maternal flesh and transcendent embrace, the experience of being born is therefore the initial instant in which the living being, who is nonetheless forced to exist in its separate individuality, unexpectedly encounters the light. According to Zambrano, this light should be called revelation. The living being approaches it, guided by a thirst to "appear in a light that reveals, holds, and nourishes it" (1991, 32). The human being must hover in this tension between birth and existence, since existence grants it its individuality. Birth, in contrast, lifts it to the "immensity of life, without making the living being feel its own limited nature or its unlimited character" (1991, 32).

Life, in its immediacy as a presence palpitating within the flesh, is, in its immediacy, identical to being and is thus something "that exceeds the human being, as it does all other living beings" (1991, 34). Excess, dawn, a forgetfulness of self that is given to experience in shining moments of revelation, after the self has given up its resistance to the light and has fully suffered its being as guilt within redemptive solitude. We thus better understand why the fate that leads Antigone to her tomb after passion and sacrifice is for her a new birth. At the same time it is the occasion for finding herself again within the dark earth as inside the womb. Indeed, typically for mystical metaphor, light and darkness here possess the intensity of material referents. Life, and the birth from which it springs, are not mere concepts of a vocabulary weakened by abstraction, but the reality of flesh, which beats with impulses, yearnings, suffering, and beauty. Here the image of the mother is necessary only for the paradoxical fact that the mystical entrusts itself anew to the word, while the initial reawakening of the living being who experiences birth is the unrepeatable instant of the privilege not to have any image, neither of reality nor "especially of oneself" (1991, 159).

The living being is made of flesh, which is the "mediator between the skeleton and the outside covering" (1991, 162). The carnal condition always appears in a covering. This is perhaps the origin, Zambrano muses, of our images of life, and our imperious need not to take satisfaction in pure presence, simply presenting ourselves, but instead actively to give some representation of the self (162). Human beings lack the luxurious feathers, hide, or scales that cloak the animals. In animals, even the most fantastic ornament is natural immediacy, where external representation and simple presence are "assimilated to the body, which is its own cosmos" (163), while human beings must dress themselves with clothes as well as images, in a manner that is never innocent.

The true nature of flesh, on the other hand, is internal. It does not show itself and is not fit for sight. It is like something sacred kept hidden, since it is "the source and vessel of generation, both preserving the individual being and transcending it and its life, in order to produce the births of other beings, who are similar, and yet different" (1991, 161). This sacredness is located within the body, and it reconnects every being with the primeval life that beats and sustains itself within the flesh. Its undeciphered and indecipherable sense may be indicated with the Spanish *entraña* (a word in which Zambrano delights). *Entraña* can perhaps be translated with "entrails," or more literally with "bowels." It is the exact word used by Antigone in her prayer to her mother. In that impassioned speech, the girl recalls how the bowels of the Earth and those of the Mother are black and without light (1989, 62). The maternal *shade* then immediately passes through her body and brings her up again to the Light. In this mystical paradox, the profound darkness of the flesh, which here is clearly both the maternal womb and the bowels of the Earth, is the site of the germination of the truth itself, which must grow in darkness. For that which germinates the truth is not entirely visible but shows only at certain moments, when the light reveals it (1991, 33).

For Zambrano the body, as the carnal condition of human beings, is not only the source of metaphors that have faded over time; it is the very site of revelation. It is a place of trembling matter, where birth delivers each one of us to the immeasurable sea of life, and where love burns in the deep germination of the truth. It is where, faced with death, a terror of disembodiment arises that tears the flesh itself. This is, perhaps, its most insolvable mystery (1989, 155).

As Zambrano says (reversing the terms of *her* Antigone's love for the Mother), Orestes was able to spill his mother's blood only by ceasing to feel his own carnal condition. "If he had continued to feel the mediation of the flesh, between the mineral matter of the bones and the blood that gives the flesh life as it circulates, he would have fallen at Clytemnestra's feet with filial love, even though filled with anger and resentment" (1991, 156). This is precisely what Antigone, who allowed the truth to germinate within the reality of her body, knew how to do.

## INGEBORG BACHMANN'S UNDINE

Gathering within her the many-layered images of the ancient Sirens, of aquatic nymphs, of Melusine with her scaly body, and perhaps of Ophelia relinquished to the stream, Ingeborg Bachmann's Undine speaks for all of them in her monologue. The brief text written in 1961 and entitled "Undine Goes" consists of a long soliloquy, in which language flows in slippery assonances and circular waves like the ripples of the water where the inhuman creature has her home. Undine's memory is inhuman, since she is a figure in the literary sense of the term. She is an image invented by patriarchal discourse in multiple and fantastic aquatic guises. Yet she is capable of freeing herself from her own context to regain a life and language of *her own* (Bachmann 1988, 192).

In her monologue Undine speaks with harsh disdain of the women of the human species. Bachmann's writing presents the feminine in three ways. The figures of the mythical aquatic women of Western culture appear. Also present is the free and independent figure of Undine, who plays with the notion of her being and not being the icon of these figures. Finally, human women are depicted as submissive wives who lead so-called normal, flesh-and-blood lives in the world of men. The monologue's structure is complex; it weaves together the voice of Undine (who tears her own image away from the patriarchal codes of fable) and the voices of the traditional mermaids, whose words Undine echoes. The effect is a counterpoint of voices, a swift series of statements and contradictions. Much more straightforward is the representation of the human women, whom Undine categorically denounces for their servile and submissive existence.

Undine's speech, beginning with the exclamation, "You, men! You, monsters!" (185), is clearly addressed to males, who appear both en masse and as individuals but who all bear the same name: Hans. Each of them is indeed a different man who asks to be loved and in fact is loved as an individual; but each is also the banal repetition of a model that prevents the appearance of any particularity. In the duplicity of her voice, we hear that Undine not only hates these men; sometimes she also loves them, self-consciously proud of the freedom that allows her to condemn sarcastically, while still loving. She is, after all, a creature made to love by the men who dreamed her.

To them Undine says, "Don't forget that it was you who called me into the world, and you who dreamed about me: the other,

the different one, not your likeness" (189). Thus the text establishes that a *figure* is speaking, materialized in a creature who is
part of the history of the imaginary. Yet this creature is also able,
in her guise as female image invented by men, to betray the
phallocentric horizon and gain her own life, unbound from her
own textual history. The play between deconstruction and recontextualization is extremely intricate, because Undine cannot,
or perhaps does not wish to, renounce her status as *the other,* the
*difference* of which men have dreamed. At the same time, Undine
gains an alterity that is no longer imprisoned in the binary code
created by the androcentric context, as something different from
it yet always referring to it. She is a being who has decided her
own alterity, as an irreducible and originary difference that finds
its own voice.

This other, dreamed by men in the guise of an inhuman and
yet female monster, in fact serves their need to leave the confines
of a reassuring order they themselves have shaped. They dream
her so that they might occasionally taste "exile, perdition, the
incomprehensible" (189), or the delirium of death and the invasion of the instant that unsettles the time of order. This transgression takes place within a reassuring mechanism fueled by a
fascination with difference. A secret joy beckons thoughts of
escape and betrayal, where the call of what is banned from everyday life takes the form of the veil, of water, or of a thing ungraspable but possessing theriomorphic, female features (192).

"You monsters, I loved you for this, because you knew what
that call means," Undine says, thus expressing both sides of her
double image. For only a creature invented by man loves him in
return (and indeed is forced to love him ) with the love of an
accomplice. But only the figure liberated from these self-
confirming games can appreciate that kernel of truth which,
despite all, cannot be erased from the deep meaning of the call.

Water is the site of a radical otherness with respect to the
terrestrial world of men: "the wet barrier between me and myself
. . . where no one prepares a nest, builds a roof above the house
frame, or repairs under a tarpaulin" (186). Men, with their pro-
tuberant, male bodies, are totally ignorant of the wet embrace of
internal membranes known to the female body. And in their

obsession with drawing boundaries, systems, shelters, and orders (not only architectural ones), they demonstrate a nature incapable of abandoning itself to the light touch of the limitless, the free and ubiquitous liquidity of moving forms. They can only do this within the calculated inebriation of an imaginary transgression always ready to retrace its steps. So calculated is this transgression that the aquatic creature that was invented in order to experience the terror of death in a kiss (190) and to hear its sweet invitation in a note of pain resounding from the beyond (187), is then derided, as man frees himself from excessively hazardous ties with his seductive dream. "Then you knew, all of a sudden, what made you suspicious of me, the veil, the water, my ungraspable being," Undine accuses her betrayers. "Then I suddenly became a danger you had discovered just in time, and I was cursed" (192).

The figure of Undine, at least when she coincides with her traditional icons, is also a woman of the imaginary who is loved and scorned, submissive to the call and passive when the man repents during his endless shifting between transgression and safety. Because of this side of her figure, Undine can gather together within her inhuman memory all the stories of the various Sirens, Melusines, and nymphs uselessly washed by the Danube, the Rhine, the Tiber, and the Nile, "from the clear waters of the arctic seas to the inky waters of the open oceans, and those of the magic pools" (187). Uselessly because, in the legend men tell, it seems that these figures are perpetually condemned merely "to repeat the same mistake, the only one to which they are predestined" (187). Which is to run at the man's call, offering themselves calmly to his therapeutic thirst for delirium. Undine remembers everything ("I have had to think of everything again, every deception and every vile act"), since all images of the malleable creature she has been for thousands of years are deposited in her persistent memory. But now, freed from the infinite repetitions of her history, Undine has finally decided that she will never again run to answer the commands of the countless Hans-figures (186). She will never again cause them to die, as they would like, "in the absence of all order, in ecstasy and in possession of the highest reason" (192).

This Undine who is freed and animated in Bachmann's writings is now completely content in her solitude. Solitude is no longer imposed on her by men so that they might occasionally share it with her in the brief and nocturnal interlude of an antisocial intoxication. It is now a full and absolute solitude, which derives from the sovereignty of an image that no longer functions according to the logic of its inventors. Undine assures Hans (who stands for all those men): "I will never share your solitude, because mine already exists and is much more ancient and durable" (191). The sense of her solitude, in fact, is now redeemed from that solitude which was a mere characteristic given her by the men who had shaped her. These men have forced their invented Undines to think of them as "something more: knights, idols, almost a soul, worthy of the greatest royal names" (191). They covered themselves over with the stuff of fables in order to philander in the fantastic realm of literary invention with scaly and fishlike women.

Even the Hans to whom Undine speaks is shown to have a double nature. He is a figure with the realistic features of a Western man (a lord of technology, upholder of politics, philosopher of reason, but also a middle-class male with his narrow and wretched everyday existence). He is also the figure invented by that normal man and clothed as a knight to inhabit the world of the fable. A figure herself, Undine knows and rejects both of them, since one of them is the historical subject, the author who, calling her to the reality of the text, has dreamed of her for centuries, encrusting her in his secret dreams. The other, instead, is her direct companion in the text. He often called *her* in order to consummate a fantastic union with the image of the different creature dreamed by the first. The violent or meek women of the "human species" (187) who appear in the text are wives who may be either backbiting or mild, but they are always submissive toward the realistic Hans (not the figural Hans who lives in legend). They are the flesh-and-blood women—whose stereotypical behavior derives from centuries of submission to patriarchal rule—whom Hans sometimes abandons in order to frolic with the aquatic females of his dreams, so different from those human ones. In both his forms, the double, superindividual Hans knows only how to pass from one female stereotype to another. Nor is there any solidarity whatsoever between the human woman and her inhuman, figural construction. This solidarity would in any case be impossible, except on the level of the oppression that both suffer from Hans. Here Undine reweaves the web of oppression in memory, but she also tears it apart. She thus liberates an image that retains its status as literary invention, but she also reveals the kernel of unshakable otherness that the image had always possessed, buried in the text.

The water creature—which man drew from her mystery, calling her to the shore and forcing her into the net of a discourse fraught with questions and demands for explanation—is completely at home in her liquid element, which demands no explanations. "There are no questions in my life. I love the water, its dense clarity, the green of the water and the silent creatures (I too will soon be mute) and my hair among them . . . the moist barrier between me and myself" (186). Now, "the coastal air, the air of boundaries" that made Undine an amphibious creature in many senses and at many thresholds (between water and earth, human and animal, song and cry, desire and repulsion) is only an interior border in her memory. It is a limit freely passed many times in both directions, between the ancient figures and the new figure; between a voice that recalls her to the past and tells sad stories, and a voice that tells of "diving in again, reposing, moving without a waste of energy" within the primitive, uncontaminated realm of the *beyond*.

A monster of the West's phallocentric discourse, by now Undine looks at the world of men from the site of her alterity. She has escaped the binary logic of men and now looks upon *them* as monsters. The relationship between normality and monstrosity is inverted, not with a simple, reactive reversal but because of the monstrous nature of the male, who now loses his specular counterpart. With Undine's departure, he loses the potential reciprocity of the game of reversal. The male subject will in all probability continue to fashion obedient figures according to his stubborn will, dressing them in whatever ways pique his delight, but he will never again catch Undine. Indeed, as the title of the monologue discloses, Undine *goes*.

She goes to her beyond, into that beyond which has always belonged to her, and which the male imaginary has only borrowed. Having been seduced and inspired by an enigma that he never understood but merely clothed with the weariness of his nightmares, he has never been able to possess or even control it. Undine said at the beginning, "I too will soon be mute" (187), like the other silent sea creatures, and in a way her very icon is the source of this silence; but she is above all silent to the language of men. Her regained freedom from the ancient context of Western discourse seeks to speak another language now, to express itself with other signs and other gestures, in the absence of preexisting and binding codes. This, at least, is the dream, the great utopia, the inhuman desire of Undine. She withdraws forever to the greenish depths, where perhaps she sings a circular song whose echo we human women can never hear nor understand.

Undine's dream, in disheartened nights and days of exaltation, is often also *our* dream. If for us it may never come true, we may at least take comfort in the extraordinary power Ingeborg Bachmann has given to one who enjoys the privilege of ideal figural existence. Undine, light water creature, has been granted an unheard-of speech to be uttered from silent lips. And it may be that all the aquatic figures ever invented and condemned by the world's fables press about her, lingering to hear their story told in some truer version.

We would hope to find among them the pale Ophelia, free and flower-clad: she whom the mirror of the stream held suspended on its surface in the briefest coincidence with her own beautiful reflection, and who then found in the watery depths—or at least we would like the tale to go—not the claws of a muddy whirlpool, but the transparent and complicit glances of a thousand disheveled mermaids.

# NOTES

1. Cf. Hegel 1963, 7–11, as well as Hegel 1983, 177–90. As George Steiner states in *Antigones*, "the specific analyses of *Antigone* as we know them after the mid–nineteenth century derive from the debate on Hegel" (41). I am interested here in the process that brings the mature Hegel to distinguish between the modern family as marriage, from the ancient family as kinship *(Stamme),* which is more pertinent to Sophocles' tragedy, *Antigone.* Cf. Mancina 1991, 151.

2. They are all suicides: Antigone herself, then Haemon and Eurydice, son and wife, respectively, of Creon. Their common blood tie results from the fact that Creon is the brother of Jocasta, Antigone's mother. Creon thus sits on the throne and holds absolute power through his close kinship with the dead (cf. lines 173–74).

3. Both words appear significantly in line 410. As is well known, the term *soma,* which in the Homeric texts denotes only the corpse, comes later to signify the body in general, whether alive or dead.

4. Along these lines see Loraux 1981, 101ff. The reference is to the famous funeral oration that Thucydides puts into the mouth of Pericles in *The Peloponnesian War,* II.64.3.

5. In Irigaray's work Sophocles' *Antigone* receives constant critical attention and passes through various interpretive phases (on this score see Muraro 1994). In her *Speculum* essay, Irigaray examines Hegel's reading through a double hermeneutical filter that criticizes the patriarchal horizon at work in both Sophocles and in Hegel. In this context, Antigone's identification with her mother is linked to her nullification of self within a maternal desire turned prevalently toward the son.

6. It is interesting to note that, in Sophocles, it is Creon and the chorus who underscore Antigone's and her brothers' descent from Oedipus (see 193, 471, 600, 856, and 1018; in the last two, Tiresias is the speaker). The speeches assigned to Antigone, however, always allude to the maternal origins of the family (cf. 513, 862–66, 911).

7. On this score, and on the metaphor of Jocasta's body as earth twice made fecund, see the original analysis in DuBois 1990, 7–104. The legend is one of Theban autochthony. It relates that the founder of the race, Cadmus, killed a dragon and sowed the earth with its teeth, from which warriors were born, called Spartoi, that is, "sown men." These men immediately began to fight one another (concerning the complex symbolism of the legend, which appears several times in the Theban cycle elaborated by the tragedians, see DuBois 1990, 72–74).

8. Similar etymology links the Latin *natura* and the verb *nasci*. I have discussed this in relation to maternal generative power in Cavarero 1995, 57–90.

9. The literal translation of this line is, more or less, "Common, of the same sisterhood, of Ismene the head." On the numerous interpretations of the verse, see, for example, the bibliographical note of A. Sestili in his edition of *Antigone* (Editrice Dante Alighieri, "Traditio," Serie greca, vol. 68, 126–27); and Steiner 1984, 85–86.

10. Hölderlin's celebrated translation of *Antigone* condenses the two terms into the unpronounceable *Gemeinsamschwesterliches* (1952, 205).

11. I agree that Antigone's character is one of "noninstrumental relationality," as stressed in Di Nicola 1991, but I stress the corporeal quality of that relational nature. The model is loaded with obsessive carnal symbolism, which is represented as absolute. This system does not easily transfer to any other context of "values."

12. Ismene is in fact still alive, but since she has chosen to obey Creon's edict, she already belongs to the history of the polis, and no longer to the symbolic relationships that characterize Jocasta's kindred.

13. For the strong misogynistic values of the tragic horizon, see Cantarella 1981, 84ff.; and Keuls 1988.

14. For Hölderlin that intellect, however, locates the unthinkable in the chaos of natural forces to which man returns upon death. See, in this connection, Bodei, 1989. I tend to think that birth, and not death, is the backdrop for *Antigone,* thus a corporeality that harbors the natural, inscrutable, and panic-causing powers of the origin.

15. In this regard it is interesting to note that Lysias, taking up precisely the story of Polynices in the *Attic Epitaphs,* ties the custom

of burial to the civilizing role of the polis. See Epitaph 7 (Richter 1881).

16. The history of the interpretation of *deinon* is very rich: Bodeus 1984, 271–90, gives a brief bibliographical survey, linking its meaning to the Promethean myth of civilization narrated in the *Protagoras* of Plato (320c–322d), and to the positive evaluation of the *deinotes,* as technical ability theorized by Aristotle in the *Nicomachean Ethics* (1144a23–28). What seems certain is that the Sophoclean verse is among those representations that Greek culture of the fifth century devotes to the theme of human progress as a civilizing process that works through technological and political action (cf. Meier 1988, 457ff.).

17. This famous expression (in German "das noch nicht fest-gestellte Tier") derives from Nietzsche, in *Beyond Good and Evil.* It is developed, however, for anthropological philosophy in Gehlen 1983, as part of an interesting revaluation of the importance of corporeality in human evolution. For a summary of research in this field, see Bruno Accarino's excellent essay (1991, 7–63).

18. For Lacan the deep meaning of Antigone is found, however, in her incarnation of the death wish, a thesis with which I disagree.

19. For Pomeroy (1975, 106ff.), Antigone is the model of a masculine heroine. For a confutation of this theory, see Wiersma 1984, 25–55.

20. See Schmitt 1972, 111ff.; and Vernant 1981, 24–25. In addition to Plato's pages, on the conceptual horizon of the age the four terms in question belong to semantic fields that are not separated, but rather overlapping (Meier 1988, 215 n. 180). The relationship between friend and enemy characterizes, however, an archaic behavioral model within the same clan (145, 215–16). In this sense, one could hypothesize that the *echthros* in *Antigone* directly refers to the primeval female root of the clan itself.

21. I allude, of course, to *Seven against Thebes.* Cf. Vernant and Vidal-Naquet 1976–91, 2:109ff.

22. Capriglione 1990, 127, rightly points out that Antigone ascribes the time of the *aei* to uterine comembership. R. Rossanda, though not in reference to the uterine origin, underlines in *Antigone ricorrente* (57) that Antigone represents "the informality of the eternal, compared to the limited formality of the present." The essay appears as the introduction to the edition of the play I have used.

23. *Delois gar ti kalchainous'epos.* I am referring to Hölderlin's famous translation, which in German reads: "Du scheinst ein rothes Wort zu färben" (206). On this translation of *Antigone* see Treder 1992, 99–105. Hölderlin's translations of Sophocles are noted in Benjamin 1981, 52, as an example of the penetration of the original language by that of translation.

24. See Irigaray 1989, 160–69, for a complex critical reading of the *Timaeus.* For a reading of Plato as a whole, see pp. 225ff.; concerning Aristotle's interpretation of the platonic *chora,* see Irigaray 1985, 32–47. My analysis aims at a dialogue with Irigaray's interpretation, as well as with Judith Butler's discussion of it (1993). Butler orients toward the hermeneutic horizon of Foucault and Derrida and focuses on the penetrative, heterosexual paradigm within the text.

25. See Braidotti 1994 for an excellent discussion of the complexity of critical feminist epistemology as deconstruction of phallologocentric discourse and as construction of female subjectivity rooted in corporeality.

26. Throughout Western history this equality is assimilative, assuming that sexual difference is unimportant and conforming women to a male model. See Fortembaugh 1975, 1–4; Calvert 1975, 231–43; Said 1986, 142–62.

27. For the complex structure of Aristotelian embryology, see the excellent analysis in Sissa 1983, 83–145.

## CHAPTER TWO

1. A detailed history of this metaphor is found in Peil 1983, 302–488. See also Hale 1971; Struve 1978; and De Baecque 1993.

2. In 1628 William Harvey explained that the circulation of the blood by means of the heart was "comparable to what happens in machines in which, with one wheel moving another, all seems to be moving at once" (cited in Harvey 1968, 39). Harvey dedicated his treatise to Charles I as the "heart of the state" (3, 108). As we know, Hobbes employs this mechanistic notion of the body, but he defines sovereign power as the artificial soul of the body (in his introduction to *Leviathan*). I will deal with this question in the next chapter.

3. Regarding the evolution from the articulated medieval image to the image in treatises on monarchy centered on the role of the head, a comparison between the *Policraticus* of John of Salisbury

(1159) and the treatise of James I (1598) on "free monarchy" may serve as example. In the *Policraticus*—of which we will speak at length later on—an organic image is presented that is attentive to anatomical detail and the reciprocity of functions; while James's text dwells on the king who, as "head," governs a body generically identified with its subjects (1965, 64–65). Between these two extremes, various treatments of the metaphor appear, which again take up the organic emphasis of the Middle Ages in all its lavish detail, such as the famous *Dialogue between Pole and Lupset* of Thomas Starkey (1536). On this work, see Hale 1971, 61–68. It is symptomatic that the interest in anatomical detail returns within the mechanistic context of the artificial body politic of Hobbes (see, for instance, the famous introduction to *Leviathan*). Both James's and Hobbes's doctrines will be examined in detail in subsequent discussion.

4. See Machiavelli 1997, I.6, on the inevitable ruin of republics, where "all human beings are in motion and, unable to remain still, must ascend or descend." See also I.17 for the curious metaphor of a body that saves itself by "losing the head when the trunk was intact." On these passages, see the interesting reflections in Esposito 1981, 3–29, and in Zanardi 1982, 57–85.

5. This body is never the product of a pact or convention, precisely because it is a natural, and not artificial, body politic. In this connection it is interesting to note that Hobbes, in his introduction to *Leviathan*, asserts that the artificial body of the state is created by human art in imitation of that of God, who created the human body. Hobbes associates the social contract, which we will discuss in chapter 3, with the fiat God pronounced during Creation. To this too I will return later in my argument.

## CHAPTER THREE

1. See Schmitt 1983, 71–93. Concerning the concepts and the terminology in which they are couched, especially in relation to Benjamin in his *The Origin of German Tragic Drama*, see Galli 1985, 25ff.; and Esposito 1993, 93ff.

2. On James's place in political philosophy, I refer the reader to Cavarero 1980, 47–89.

3. See Ciocca 1987, 9–99. Especially significant are *Richard II,* for its theatrical narration of the doctrine of the king's two bodies (see

Kantorowicz 1957, 24–41), and *Titus Andronicus,* wherein we find a sort of reversal of Menenius Agrippa's fable that follows from the onstage mutilation and dismemberment of the Roman hero's body and the bodies of his sons.

4. I refer to the famous painting in the Tate Gallery by J. E. Millais. This canvas inspired the beautiful lines to Elizabeth Siddal, the model for the work. On that poem, see Donaldson 1981, 127–33.

5. On the influence of Lacan's analysis in the context of psycho-analytic studies in English dedicated to the character of Hamlet, see Fleming 1985, 55–71.

6. On the problems posed by the Elizabethan coding of the flowers distributed by Ophelia, see Lever 1952, 117–29.

7. See also Bronfen 1992b for an interesting discussion of this theme, with an analysis of relevant literary figures.

8. On feminist criticism of Shakespeare, see Neely 1981, 3–15; and Novy 1981, 17–27. See also Novy 1984 and Erickson 1985.

9. On the theme of mermaids, see Barina 1980; Barina et al. 1986; Lao 1985; Harflancner 1989; Clier-Colombani 1991; Calabrese 1992, 57–97; and Wandruszka 1993, 97–104.

10. I refer the reader to my book *In Spite of Plato,* in which I discuss at length the category of death and the relative concealment of that of birth, as the foundation of Western thought.

11. For a Lacanian psychoanalytic reading of Hobbes's political body, see Bergoffen 1990, 114–17.

12. Schmitt, on the other hand, understands this soul as part of the machine (1986, 56–57). See also Schmitt 1996.

13. For study of this question I refer the reader to my discussions in Cavarero 1990, 221–41, and Cavarero 1992, 32–47.

14. G. Galli (1985, 107) notes that Leviathan is female in the Bible, while Behemoth is male. According to Galli there is an echo in Hobbes (as we have seen for Plato) of a recently defeated female mystery cult.

15. On this score and on the following argument, see the intense reflections in Esposito 1993, especially in the first chapter.

16. According to K. Brown (1978, 26), the head resembles Charles I, or Oliver Cromwell, or Charles II. See also Hale 1971, 128.

# BIBLIOGRAPHY

Accarino, Bruno. 1991. "Tra libertà e decisione: Alle origini dell'antropologia filosofica." In *Ratio imaginis: Uomo e mondo nell'antropologia filosofica*. Ed. Bruno Accarino. Florence: Ponte delle Grazie.

Accattino, Paolo. 1986. *L'anatomia della città nella "Politica" di Aristotele*. Turin: Tirrenia.

Aeschylus. 1973. *Seven against Thebes*. Trans. Anthony Hecht and Helen H. Bacon. New York: Oxford University Press.

Archambault, P. 1967. "The Analogy of the *Body* in Renaissance Political Literature." *Bibliothèque d'Humanisme et Renaissance* 29.

Arendt, Hannah. 1989. *Vita Activa: La condizione umana* [The human condition]. Trans. S. Finzi. 3d ed. Milan: Bompiani. First published as *Vita Activa; oder, Vom tätigen eben* (Stuttgart: Kohlhammer, 1960).

Aristotle. 1984. *Politics*. Trans. Carnes Lord. Chicago: University of Chicago Press.

———. 1986. *Nicomachean Ethics*. Trans. Martin Ostwald. New York: Macmillan.

———. 1996. *Physics*. Trans. Robin Waterfield. Oxford: Oxford University Press.

———. 1997. *Aristotle's Poetics*. Trans. George Whalley. Montreal: McGill-Queen's University Press.

Avezzù, Elisa. 1991. "I figli di Edipo e la revoca di paternità." In *Koinon aima: Antropologia e lessico della parentela greca*. Ed. Elisa Avezzù and Oddone Longo. Bari: Adriatica.

Axton, Marie. 1977. *The Queen's Two Bodies*. London: Royal Historical Society.

Bachmann, Ingeborg. 1988. "Ondina se ne va" [Undine goes]. In *Il trentesimo anno*, trans. Magda Olivetti. Milan: Bompiani. First published as "Undine geht," in *Das dreissigste Jahr: Erzählungen* (1961; Munich: Deutscher Taschenbuch Verlag, 1994).

Bakhtin, M. M. 1979. *L'opera di Rabelais e la cultura popolare*. Turin: Einaudi. First published as *Tvorchestvo Fransua Rable i narod-*

*naia kul'tura srednevekov'ia i Renessansa* (1965; Moscow: Khu-
dozh. lit-ra, 1990).

Barina, Antonella. 1980. *La sirena nella mitologia: La negazione del
sesso femminile.* Padua: Mastrogiacomo.

Barina, Antonella, et al., eds. 1986. *Melusina: Mito e leggenda di una
donna serpente.* Rome: Utopia.

Benjamin, Walter. 1980. *Il dramma barocco tedesco.* Turin: Einaudi.
First published as *Ursprung des deutschen Trauerspiels* (1963;
Frankfurt am Main: Suhrkamp, 1982).

————. 1981. *Angelus novus: Saggi e frammenti.* Trans. Renato Solmi.
Turin: Einaudi. First published as *Angelus Novus* (vol. 1; Frankfurt am Main: Suhrkamp, 1961).

Benveniste, Emile. 1976. *Il vocabolario delle Istituzioni indo-europee.*
Trans. M. Liborio. 2 vols. Turin: Einaudi. First published as *Le
vocabulaire des institutions indo-européenes*, 2 vols. (Paris: Minuit, 1969).

Bergoffen, D. B. 1990. "The Body Politics: Democratic Metaphors,
Totalitarian Practices, Erotic Practices." *Philosophy and Social
Criticism* 16, no. 2.

Bertelli, Sergio. 1990. *Il corpo del re: Sacralità del potere nell'Europa
medievale e moderna.* Florence: Ponte delle Grazie.

Bettini, Maurizio. 1992. *Il ritratto dell'amante.* Turin: Einaudi.

Bianchi, L. 1985. "Introduzione." In *Policraticus,* by John of Salisbury. Milan: Jaca.

*The Bible.* 1987. Ed. Harold Bloom. New York: Chelsea House.

Biral, Alessandro. 1987. "Hobbes: La società senza governo." In *Il
contratto sociale nella filosofia politica moderna.* Ed. Giuseppe
Duso. Bologna: Il Mulino.

Bodei, Remo. 1989. "Hölderlin: La filosofia e il tragico." In *Sul tragico,* by F. Hölderlin. Milan: Feltrinelli.

Bodeus, R. 1984. "L'habile et le juste de l'Antigone de Sophocle au
Protagoras de Platon." *Mnemosyne* 37.

Boreau, A. 1989. "Introduzione." In *I due corpi del re,* by Ernst Kantorowicz. Turin: Einaudi.

Braidotti, Rosi. 1994. *Dissonanze: Le donne e la filosofia contem-
poranea.* Milan: La Tartaruga. First published as *Itinéraires dans
la dissonance.*

Brenot, A. M. 1991. "Les corps pour royaume. Un langage politique de la fin du XVI siècle et début du XVII siècle." *Histoire, Economie et Société* 4.

Bronfen, E. 1992a. "From Omphalos to Phallus: Cultural Representation of Femininity and Death." *Women* 3, no. 2.

———. 1992b. *Over Her Dead Body.* Manchester: Manchester University Press.

Brown, K. 1978. "The Artist of the *Leviathan* Title-page." *British Library Journal* 4.

Brown, Peter Robert Lamont. 1988. *The Body and Society: Men, Women, and Sexual Renunciation in Early Christianity.* New York: Columbia University Press.

Brunner, Otto. 1970. *Per una nuova storia costituzionale e sociale.* Trans. P. Schiera. Milan: Vita e Pensiero. First published as *Neue Wege der Sozialgeschichte* (1956; Göttingen: Vandenhoeck und Ruprecht, 1968).

Burkert, Walter. 1981. *Homo necans.* Turin: Boringhieri. First published as *Homo necans; Interpretationen altgriechischer Opferriten und Mythen* (Berlin: De Gruyter, 1972).

Butler, Judith P. 1993. *Bodies That Matter: On the Discursive Limits of "Sex."* New York: Routledge.

Cacciari, Massimo. 1990. *Dell'inizio.* Milan: Adelphi.

Calabrese, R. 1992. "Figlie dell'acqua, figlie dell'aria: Alcune variazioni sul motivo di Ondina." In *Il riso di Ondina: Immagini mitiche del femminile nella letteratura tedesca.* Ed. Rita Svandrlik. Urbino: Quattroventi.

Calvert, B. 1975. "Plato and Equality of Women." *Phoenix* 29.

Calvino, Italo. 1988. *Six Memos for the Next Millennium.* Cambridge: Harvard University Press.

Cantarella, Eva. 1981. *L'ambiguo malanno: Condizione e immagine della donna nell'antichità greca e romana.* Rome: Editori Riuniti.

Capriglione, Jolanda C. 1990. *La passione amorosa nella città "senza" donne.* Naples: Nuove Edizioni Tempi Moderni.

Cavarero, Adriana. 1980. "Giacomo I e il parlamento: Una lotta per la sovranità." In *Teorie politiche e stato nell'epoca dell'assolutismo,* by Alessandro Biral, Adriana Cavarero, and Claudio Pacchiani. Rome: Istituto dell'Enciclopedia Italiana.

———. 1986. "Il Platone di Voegelin." *Verifiche* 4.

————. 1988. "Il bene nella filosofia politica di Platone e di Aristotele." *Filosofia politica* 2.

————. 1989. "*Politica* presso i greci." *Filosofia politica* 1.

————. 1990. "Il modello democratico nell'orizzonte della differenza sessuale." *Democrazia e diritto* 2.

————. 1991. "Il moderno e le sue finzioni." In *Logiche e crisi della modernità*. Ed. Carlo Galli. Bologna: Il Mulino.

————. 1992. "Equality and Sexual Difference: Amnesia in Political Thought." In *Beyond Equality and Difference: Citizenship, Feminist Politics, and Female Subjectivity*, ed. Gisela Bock and Susan James. London: Routledge.

————. 1993. "Il corpo politico come organismo." *Filosofia politica* 7.

————. 1994a. "Figures de la corporeïtat." In *Saviesa i perversitat: Les dones a la Grècia Antiga*, ed. M. Jufresa. Barcelona: Edicions Destino.

————. 1994b. "Forme della corporeità." In *Filosofia, donne, filosofie*, ed. M. Forcina, A. Prontera, and P. Vergine. Lecce: Milella.

————. 1995. *In Spite of Plato: A Feminist Rewriting of Ancient Philosophy*. New York: Routledge.

————. 1997. *Tu che mi guardi, tu che mi racconti: Filosofia della narrazione*. Milan: Feltrinelli. Translated as *Relating Narratives: Storytelling and Selfhood* by Paul A. Kottman (London and New York: Routledge, 2000).

Centanni, M. 1992. "Antiche ferite." *Wellcome Tabloid* 4, no. 3.

Charney, M., and H. Charney. 1977. "The Language of Madwomen in Shakespeare and His Fellow Dramatists." *Signs* 3, no. 2.

Ciocca, Rossella. 1987. *Il cerchio d'oro: I re sacri nel teatro shakespeariano*. Rome: Officina Edizioni.

Clier-Colombani, Françoise. 1991. *La fée Mélusine au Moyen Age*. Paris: Le Léopard d'Or.

Cohen, I. B. 1944. "Harrington and Harvey: A Theory of the State Based on the New Physiology." *Journal of the History of Ideas* 2.

Colaiacomo, Paola. 1993. *La prova: Saggi da Shakespeare a Beckett*. Rome: Editori Riuniti.

Conti Odorisio, Ginevra. 1978. "Matriarcato e patriarcalismo nel pensiero politico di Hobbes e Locke." In *Matriarcato e potere delle donne*, ed. Ida Magli. Milan: Feltrinelli.

De Baecque, A. 1993. *Le corps de l'histoire. Métaphores et politique. 1700–1800*. Mesnil-sur-l'Estrée: Calmann-Lévy.

De Giovanni, B. 1981. "*Politica* dopo Cartesio." *Il Centauro* 1.

Descartes, René. 1994. *Discours de la méthode/Discourse on the Method.* Trans. George Heffernan. Notre Dame: University of Notre Dame Press.

Descimon, R. 1992. "Les fonctions de la métaphore du mariage politique du roi et de la république en France, XV–XVIII siècles." *Annales E.S.C.* 6.

Detienne, M. 1973. "La personne en Grèce archaique." In *Problèmes de la personne,* ed. I. Meyerson. Paris: Mouton.

Di Nicola, Giulia Paola. 1991. *Antigone: Figura femminile della trasgressione.* Pescara: Edizioni Tracce.

Diano, C. 1970. "Il problema della materia in Platone. La chora del *Timeo.*" In *Giornale critico della Filosofia Italiana* 3.

Dierauer, U. 1977. *Tier und Mensch im Denken der Antike: Studien zur Tierpsychologie, Anthropologie und Ethik.* Amsterdam: B. R. Grüner.

Dijkstra, Bram. 1986. *Idols of Perversity: Fantasies of Feminine Evil in Fin-de-siècle Culture.* Oxford: Oxford University Press.

Donaldson, S. M. 1981. "*Ophelia* in Elizabeth Siddal Rossetti's Poem 'A Year and a Day.' *Pre-Raphaelite Review* 2.

DuBois, Page. 1990. *Il corpo come metafora: Rappresentazioni della donna nella Grecia antica.* Rome: Laterza. First published as *Sowing the Body: Psychoanalysis and Ancient Representations of Women* (Chicago: University of Chicago Press, 1988).

Eliot, T. S. 1992. "Amleto e i suoi problemi." In *Opere. 1904–1939.* Milan: Bompiani. First published as "Hamlet," in *Elizabethan Essays* (New York: Haskell House, 1964).

Erickson, P. 1985. *Patriarchal Structures in Shakespeare's Drama.* Berkeley: University of California Press.

Esposito, Roberto. 1981. "Forma e scissione in Machiavelli." *Il Centauro* 1.

———. 1993. *Nove pensieri sulla politica.* Bologna: Il Mulino.

Euripides. 1995. *Suppliant Women.* Trans. Rosanna Warren and Stephen Scully. New York: Oxford University Press.

Fischer, S. K. 1990. "Hearing Ophelia: Gender and Tragic Discourse in *Hamlet.*" *Renaissance and Reformation* 26, no. 1.

Fleming, K. 1985. "Hamlet and Oedipus Today: Jones and Lacan." *Hamlet Studies* 7.

Fortembaugh, W. W. 1975. "On Plato's Feminism in *Republic* V." *Apeiron* 9.

Foucault, Michel. 1988. "Technologies of the Self." In *Technologies of the Self: A Seminar with Michel Foucault,* ed. Luther H. Martin, Huck Gutman, and Patrick H. Hutton. Amherst: University of Massachusetts Press.

————. 1991. *L'uso dei piaceri.* Vol. 2 of *Storia della sessualità,* by Foucault. Milan: Feltrinelli.

Fusini, Nadia. 1981. *La passione dell'origine: Studi sul tragico shakespeariano e il romanzesco moderno.* Bari: Dedalo.

————. 1990. *La luminosa: Genealogia di Fedra.* Milan: Feltrinelli.

Galimberti, Umberto. 1987. *Il corpo.* Milan: Feltrinelli.

Galli, Giorgio. 1985. *Manuale di storia delle dottrine politiche.* Milan: Il Saggiatore.

Gehlen, Arnold. 1983. *L'uomo. La sua natura e il suo posto nel mondo.* Milan: Feltrinelli. First published as *Der Mensch, seine Natur und seine Stellung in der Welt* (1950; Wiesbaden: Aula-Verlag, 1986).

Gilli, Gian Antonio. 1988. *Origini dell'eguaglianza: Ricerche sociologiche sull'antica Grecia.* Turin: Einaudi.

Ginzburg, Carlo. 1989. *Storia notturna: Una decifrazione del Sabba.* Turin: Einaudi.

Giorgini, Giovanni. 1993. *La città e il tiranno.* Arcana Imperii 29. Milan: Giuffrè.

Goldschmidt, Victor. 1982. *Essai sur "Cratyle": Contribution à l'histoire de la pensée de Platon.* Paris: Librairie philosophique J. Vrin.

Hale, David George. 1971. *The Body Politic: A Political Metaphor in Renaissance English Literature.* The Hague: Mouton.

Harflancner, L. 1989. *Morgana e Melusina. La nascita delle fate nel Medioevo.* Turin: Einaudi.

Harvey, William. 1968. *The Circulation of Blood and Other Writings.* London: Dent.

Havelock, Eric A. 1963. *Preface to Plato.* Oxford: Blackwell.

Hegel, Georg Wilhelm Friedrich. 1963. *Fenomenologia dello spirito.* Florence: La Nuova Italia. First published as *Phänomenologie des Geistes* (1807; Frankfurt am Main: Suhrkamp, 1970).

————. 1983. *Grundlinien der Philosophie des Rechts.* Frankfurt am Main: Suhrkamp.

Hertzbach, J. S. 1985. "Hamlet and the Integrity of Majesty." *Hamlet Studies* 7.

Hill, C. 1964. "William Harvey and the Idea of Monarchy." *Past and Present* 27.

Hobbes, Thomas. 1969. *The Elements of Law, Natural and Politic.* London: Cass.

———. 1983. *De Cive.* Ed. Howard Warrender. Oxford: Clarendon.

———. 1996. *Leviathan.* Ed. J. C. A. Gaskin. Oxford: Oxford University Press.

Hölderlin, F. 1952. *Sämtliche Werke.* Stuttgart: Kohlhammer.

———. 1989. "Note all'Antigone." In *Sul tragico.* Milan: Feltrinelli.

Homer. 1997. *The Odyssey.* Trans. Robert Fagles. New York: Penguin.

Horkheimer, Max, and Theodor W. Adorno. 1989. *Dialectic of Enlightenment.* Trans. John Cumming. New York: Continuum.

———. 1992. "Odysseus or Myth and Enlightenment." Trans. Robert Hullot-Kentor. *New German Critique* 56:109–41.

Hunt, J. 1988. "A Thing of Nothing: The Catastrophic Body in *Hamlet.*" *Shakespeare Quarterly* 39, no. 1.

Irigaray, Luce. 1985. *Etica della differenza sessuale.* Milan: Feltrinelli. Originally pubished as *Ethique de la différence sexuelle* (Paris: Minuit, 1984).

———. 1989. *Speculum: L'altra donna.* Milan: Feltrinelli. Originally published as *Speculum de l'autre femme* (Paris: Minuit, 1974).

James I. 1965. *The Trew Law of Free Monarchies.* In *The Political Works of James I.* New York: Russell and Russell.

John of Salisbury. 1985. *Policraticus.* Milan: Jaca.

Jordan, Constance. 1987. "Woman's Rule in Sixteenth Century British Political Thought." *Renaissance Quarterly* 40.

Kantorowicz, Ernst Hartwig. 1957. *The King's Two Bodies: A Study in Mediaeval Political Theology.* Princeton, N.J.: Princeton University Press.

———. 1989. *I due corpi del re* [The King's Two Bodies]. Trans., with introduction by A. Boreau. Turin: Einaudi.

Keuls, E. C. 1988. *Il regno della fallocrazia.* Trans. M. Carpi. Milan: Il Saggiatore. First published as *The Reign of the Phallus: Sexual Politics in Ancient Athens* (New York: Harper and Row, 1985).

Lacan, Jacques. 1977. "Desire and the Interpretation of Desire in *Hamlet.*" *Yale French Studies* 55–56.

———. 1986. *Le Séminaire. Livre VII: L'éthique de la psychanalyse.* Paris: Seuil.

Lanza, Diego. 1977. *Il tiranno e il suo pubblico.* Turin: Einaudi.

Lao, M. 1985. *Le sirene.* Rome: Rotundo.

Laqueur, Thomas Walter. 1990. *Making Sex: Body and Gender from the Greeks to Freud.* Cambridge: Harvard University Press.

Lever, J. W. 1952. "Three Notes on Shakespeare's Plants." *Review of English Studies* 10, no. 3.

Leverenz, D. 1978. "The Woman in *Hamlet:* An Interpersonal View." *Signs* 4, no. 2.

Livy. 1976. *Ab urbe condita. Livy in Fourteen Volumes.* Trans. B. O. Foster. Cambridge: Harvard University Press.

Locke, John. 1952. *The Second Treatise of Government.* New York: Liberal Arts Press.

Loraux, Nicole. 1981. *Invention d'Athènes.* Paris: Mouton.

———. 1988. *Come uccidere tragicamente una donna.* Rome: Laterza. First published as *Façons tragiques de tuer une femme* (Paris: Hachette, 1985).

———. 1991. *Il femminile e l'uomo greco.* Bari: Laterza. First published as *Les expériences de Tirésias: Le feminin et l'homme grec* (Paris: Gallimard, 1989).

Lyons, B. 1977. "The Iconography of Ophelia." *English Literary History* 44.

Machiavelli, N. 1997. *Discourses on Livy.* Trans. Julia Conaway Bondanella and Peter Bondanella. New York: Oxford University Press.

Mancina, Claudia. 1991. *Differenze nell'eticità: Amore, famiglia, società civile in Hegel.* Naples: Guida.

McIlwain, Charles Howard. 1956. *Costituzionalismo antico e moderno.* Venice: Neri Pozza. First published as *Constitutionalism, Ancient and Modern* (Ithaca, N.Y.: Cornell University Press, 1940).

———. 1959. *Il pensiero politico occidentale dai greci al tardo Medioevo.* Venice: Neri Pozza. First published as *The Growth of Political Thought in the West* (1932; New York: Macmillan, 1963).

Meier, C. 1988. *La nascita della categoria del politico in Grecia.* Bologna: Il Mulino. First published as *Entstehung des Politischen bei den Griechen* (Frankfurt am Main: Suhrkamp, 1983).

Muraro, L. 1994. "Female Genealogies." In *Engaging with Irigaray: Feminist Philosophy and Modern European Thought,* ed. Carolyn Burke, Naomi Schor, and Margaret Whitford. New York: Columbia University Press.

Neely, C. T. 1981. "Feminist Modes of Shakespearean Criticism: Compensatory, Justificatory, Transformational." *Women's Studies* 9.

Nestle, W. 1968. "Die Fabel des Menenius Agrippa." In *Griechischen Studien.* Aalen: Scientia.

Nietzsche, F. W. 1967. *Thus Spake Zarathustra.* Trans. Thomas Common. New York: Heritage Press.

———. 1998. *Beyond Good and Evil: Prelude to a Philosophy of the Future.* Trans. Marion Faber Oxford: Oxford University Press.

Novy, M. 1981. "Demythologizing Shakespeare." *Women's Studies* 9.

———. 1984. *Love's Argument: Gender Relations in Shakespeare.* Chapel Hill: University of North Carolina Press.

Otten, C. F. 1979. "Ophelia's *Long Purples* or *Dead Men's Fingers.*" *Shakespeare Quarterly* 30.

Peil, Dietmar. 1983. *Untersuchungen zur Staats- und Herrschaftsmetaphorik in literarischen Zeugnissen von Antike bis zur Gegenwart.* Munich: Fink.

Philip, R. 1991. "The Shattered Glass: The Story of (O)phelia." *Hamlet Studies* 13.

Plato. 1965. *Timaeus.* Trans. John Warrington. London: Dent.

———. 1991. *Protagoras.* Trans. C. C. W. Taylor. New York: Oxford University Press.

———. 1992. *Cratylus: Parmenides; Greater Hippias; Lesser Hippias* Trans. H. N. Fowler. Cambridge: Harvard University Press.

———. 1993. *Phaedo.* Trans. David Gallop. Oxford: Oxford University Press.

———. 1993. *Republic.* Trans. Robin Waterfield. Oxford: Oxford University Press.

Pomeroy, Sarah B. 1975. *Donne in Atene e Roma.* Turin: Einaudi. First published as *Goddesses, Whores, Wives, and Slaves: Women in Classical Antiquity* (New York: Schocken, 1975).

Richter, Richard. 1881. *De epitaphii qui sub Lysiae nomine fertur, genere gicendi.* Gryphiswaldiae.

Rigotti, F. 1989. *Metafore della politica.* Bologna: Il Mulino.

———. 1992. *Il potere e le sue metafore*. Milan: Feltrinelli.

Robertson, K. 1990. "The Body Natural of a Queen: Mary, James, Horestes." *Renaissance and Reformation* 26.

Rohde, Erwin. 1982. *Psyche*. Bari: Laterza. First published as *Psyche: Seelencult und Unsterblichkeitsglaube der Griechen* (Leipzig: Mohr, 1894).

Rosenzweig, Franz. 1985. *La stella della redenzione*. Casale Monferrato: Marietti. First published as *Der Stern der Erlösung* (Frankfurt am Main: J. Kauffmann, 1921).

Rossanda, Rossana. 1987. *Antigone ricorrente*. In *Antigone,* trans. Luisa Biondetti. Milan: Feltrinelli.

Rothwell, K. S. 1988. "Hamlet's *Glass of Fashion:* Power, Self, and the Reformation." In *Technologies of the Self: A Seminar with Michel Foucault,* ed. Luther H. Martin, Huck Gutman, and Patrick H. Hutton. Amherst: University of Massachusetts Press.

Said, S. 1986. "La République de Platon et la communauté des femmes." *L'antiquité classique* 55.

Sassi, M. M. 1988. *La scienza dell'uomo nella Grecia antica*. Turin: Bollati Boringhieri.

Sawday, J. 1983. "The Mint at Segovia: Digby, Hobbes, Charleton, and the Body as Machine in the Seventeenth Century." *Prose Studies* 6.

Schmitt, Carl. 1972. *Le categorie del politico*. Bologna: Il Mulino. First published as *Begriff des Politischen* (Hamburg: Hanseatische Verlagsanstalt, 1933).

———. 1983. *Amleto o Ecuba*. Bologna: Il Mulino. First published as *Hamlet oder Hekuba: Die Einbruch der Zeit in das Spiel*. ([Düsseldorf]: E. Diederichs, [1956.]).

———. 1986. *Scritti su Thomas Hobbes*. Arcana imperii 13. Milan: Giuffrè.

———. 1996. *The Leviathan in the State Theory of Thomas Hobbes: The Meaning and Failure of a Political Symbol*. Trans. George Schwab and Erna Hilfstein. Westport, Conn.: Greenwood. Originally published as *Der Leviathan in der Staatslehrer des Thomas Hobbes: Sinn und Fehlschlag eines politischen Symbols* (Hamburg: Hanseatische Verlagsanstalt, 1938).

Schnurr, R. 1979. *Individualismo e assolutismo*. Milan: Giuffrè.

Shakespeare, William. 1974. *Hamlet*. In *The Riverside Shakespeare,* ed. G. Blakemore Evans. Boston: Houghton Mifflin.

Showalter, Elaine. 1985. "Representing Ophelia: Women, Madness, and the Responsibilities of Feminist Criticism." In *Shakespeare and the Question of Theory,* ed. Patricia Parker and Geoffrey Hartman. New York: Methuen.

Sissa, Giulia. 1983. "Il corpo della donna. Lineamenti di una ginecologia filosofica." In *Madre materia,* ed. Silvia Campese. Turin: Boringhieri.

———. 1990. "Platone, Aristotele e la differenza dei sessi." In *Storia delle donne in Occidente,* ed. Georges Duby and Michelle Perrot. Rome: Laterza.

———. 1992. *La verginità in Grecia.* Rome: Laterza. First published as *Le corps virginal: La virginité féminine en Grèce ancienne* (Paris: Librairie philosophique J. Vrin, 1987).

Snell, Bruno. 1963. *La cultura greca e le origini del pensiero europeo.* Trans. Vera degli Alberti and Anna Solmi Mariotti. Turin: Einaudi. Originally published as *Die Entdeckung des Geistes: Studien zur Entstehung des europäischen Denkens bei den Greichen* (Hamburg: Claaszen and Goverts, 1946).

Sophocles. 1994. *Antigone; Oedipus the King; Electra.* Trans. H. D. F. Kitto. Oxford: Oxford University Press.

Starkey, Thomas. 1989. *A Dialogue between Pole and Lupset.* London: Royal Historical Society.

Steiner, George. 1984. *Antigones.* Oxford: Oxford University Press.

Struve, Tilman. 1978. *Die Entwicklung der organologischen Staatsauffassung im Mittelalter.* Stuttgart: Hiersemann.

Thucydides. 1998. *The Peloponnesian War.* Trans. Steven Lattimore. Indianapolis: Hackett.

Treder, U. 1992. "Antigone." In *Il riso di Ondina,* ed. Rita Svandrlik. Urbino: Quattroventi.

Vegetti, Mario. 1983. "Metafora politica e immagine del corpo." In *Tra Edipo ed Euclide: Forme del sapere antico,* ed. Mario Vegetti. Milan: Il Saggiatore.

———. 1992. "Anima e corpo." In *Il sapere degli antichi,* ed. Mario Vegetti. Turin: Bollati Boringhieri.

Vermeule, E. 1979. *Aspects of Death in Early Greek Art and Poetry.* Berkeley and Los Angeles: University of California Press.

Vernant, Jean-Pierre. 1981. *Mito e società nella Grecia antica.* Turin: Einaudi. First published as *Mythe et société en Grèce ancienne* (Paris: Maspero, 1974).

Vernant, Jean-Pierre, and Pierre Vidal-Naquet. 1976–91. *Mito e tragedia nella Grecia antica.* 2 vols. Turin: Einaudi. First published as *Mythe et tragédie en Grèce ancienne* (1972–86; Paris: Éditions La Découverte, 1995).

Voegelin, Eric. 1986. *Ordine e storia: La filosofia politica di Platone.* Bologna: Il Mulino. First published as vol. 3 of *Order and History* (5 vols.; Baton Rouge: Louisiana State University Press, 1956–87).

Wandruszka, M. L. 1993. *Orgoglio e misura.* Turin: Rosenberg e Sellier.

Webster, C. 1979. "William Harvey and the Crisis of Medicine in Jacobean England." In *William Harvey and His Age: The Professional and Social Context for the Discovery of Circulation.* Supplement to *Bulletin of History of Medicine 2.*

Wiersma, S. 1984. "Women in Sophocles." In *Mnemosyne* 37.

Wilt, J. 1981. "Comment on David Leverenz's *The Woman in 'Hamlet.'*" *Women's Studies* 9.

Yates, Frances Amelia. 1978. *Astrea.* Trans. E. Basaglia. Turin: Einaudi. First published as *Astraea: The Imperial Theme in the Sixteenth Century* (London: Routledge and Kegan Paul, 1975).

Zambrano, María. 1989. [1967]. *La tumba de Antígona.* Madrid: Mondadori Espana.

———. 1991. *Chiari del bosco.* Trans. Carlo Ferrucci. Milan: Feltrinelli. Originally published as *Claros del bosque* (Barcelona: Editorial Seix Barral, 1977).

Zanardi, M. 1982. "Il corpo rigenerato." *Il Centauro* 5.